D0267675

THE INTERNATIONAL
Guide to Drinks

REVISED AND UPDATED

THE INTERNATIONAL
Guide to
Drinks

Compiled by
The United Kingdom
Bartenders' Guild

EBURY
PRESS

DEDICATED TO PROFESSIONAL BARTENDERS THROUGHOUT THE UNITED KINGDOM
AND THEIR COLLEAGUES IN BARS ALL OVER THE WORLD

Originally published in Great Britain in 1953. This edition published by Ebury Publishing in 2006.

1 3 5 7 9 10 8 6 4 2

Text © United Kingdom Bartenders' Guild 2006
Photographs © Ian O'Leary 2006

United Kingdom Bartenders' Guild has asserted its right to be identified as the author of this work under the Copyright, Designs and Patents Act 1988.

www.randomhouse.co.uk

A CIP catalogue record for this book is available from the British Library.

Revised by Lynn Bryan,
The BookMaker, London.
Design by Mary Staples.
Photography by Ian O"Leary.
Cover photo by Amanda Hancocks

ISBN 0091912024
ISBN-13 [from January 2007]
9780091912024

Ebury Publishing
Random House,
20 Vauxhall Bridge Road,
London SW1V 2SA

Random House Australia (Pty) Limited
20 Alfred Street, Milsons Point,
Sydney, New South Wales 2061,
Australia

Random House New Zealand Limited
18 Poland Road, Glenfield,
Auckland 10, New Zealand

Random House South Africa (Pty) Limited
Isle of Houghton, Corner Boundary Road
& Carse O'Gowrie, Houghton, 2198,
South Africa

Random House Publishers India Private Limited
301 World trade Tower,
Hotel International Grand Complex,
Barakhambra Lane, New Delhi 110 001,
India

The Random House Group Limited Reg. No. 954009

Papers used by Ebury Press are natural, recyclable products made from wood grown in sustainable forests.

Printed and bound by Mackays of Chatham PLC, Chatham, Kent.

CONTENTS

PREFACE

The first edition of the UKBG's *International Guide to Drinks* was published in 1953. It was an instant hit, with subsequent editions also selling out. This was evidence of its authority and popularity, and it became a 'must-have' guide for every bartender.

I started my career in the bartending profession in 1970 at the Writers' Bar at Raffles Hotel, Singapore. As a 'greenhorn' then, I relied on cocktail books, as well as learning from my chief barman. The UKBG's *International Guide to Drinks* was presented to our bar by the General Manager at the time, who was an Englishman. This guide became known as the bar 'bible' to a few young bartenders, including me.

The fact that I have the opportunity to write this foreword to the 2006 edition is a testimony to my career advancement during the thirty years I have been involved in the hospitality industry and, in particular, in bartending. I am proud to be in this profession and have come a long way through hard work. Today, whenever I need to find some recipes, I open my copy of the *International Guide to Drinks* and refer to it.

The book has always been accepted as a reference work within the IBA fraternity since the fifth IBA president, Angelo Zola, penned the foreword for its sixth edition. Since then, many new drinks have been created and many new liquors introduced to the market. With subsequent editions these were updated.

It has been documented that the word 'cocktail' was first printed in the May 13, 1806 edition of *Balance and Columbian Repository*, a Hudson, New York publication. This year marks the 200th anniversary of that printing. It is a call for celebration. What could be more timely than the publication of this revised edition of the *International Guide to Drinks*, with recipes from past decades and the present time.

This fascinating book is not just for professional barmen but also for laymen and hobbyists who aspire to create drinks to entertain their guests. As a good host, one always tries to impress guests with fanciful decoration, food and drinks. Why not try some fanciful drinks from this guide?

Cheers!

Derrick Lee
PRESIDENT, INTERNATIONAL BARTENDERS' ASSOCIATION
MARCH 2006

FOREWORD

The first decade of the twenty-first century is an exciting time in the drinks world. Wine and spirit producers are always looking at ways to stimulate our taste buds, and are succeeding on many levels. Some fine boutique vodka and gin brands are fragrant with multi-layered flavours, and tequila and rum are also becoming more interesting to the palate. Whisky continues to fascinate and seduce those who have a yearning for the grain, and cognac (a personal passion) becomes smoother by the year. Plus, there are many new syrups and liqueurs for those with a sweet palate.

In the past decade the style of cocktails has changed dramatically. In the mid-1990s the world rediscovered the pleasure of sipping a cocktail. At first it was the classics, those that had withstood the test of time, that were being made in bars and at home. From the late 1990s the hotel bar, previously the only place in town where a cocktail *aficionado* could find a cocktail, was usurped by the style bar; an often dimly lit space serving sexy cocktails and music on demand.

There was also a surge in variations on a Martini theme; suddenly there were apple, berry, chocolate, vanilla and watermelon Martinis, with basil, ginger, spicy chilli, coriander and other Thai-influenced flavours also surfacing.

Bartenders now make and serve creative cocktails with panache, blending, muddling, shaking and stirring from dusk 'til dawn. Style bars reign on a global stage to the extent that a Flair category was added to the IBA competition.

In this book, we have standardized the way in which a recipe is presented so it can be understood in all countries. All cocktail ingredients are written in cl, with measurements for sugar and other miscellaneous ingredients written as teaspoons, tablespoons, and dashes. Fresh fruit is given as a whole, half or a quarter of a piece, and as wedges or slices in the case of a garnish. When a cherry is required, use a red maraschino cherry unless otherwise stated.

The chapters on wines, spirits and aperitifs and digestives have been written as general introductions. There are many authoritative wine books available, and these will give you much more detailed information.

Since the UKBG's *International Guide to Drinks* was first published in 1953 we have endeavoured to update the book to keep it useful and interesting to both professional and amateur bartenders, and this latest revision continues that tradition. We hope you enjoy reading the information and the recipes.

Finally, the UKBG would like to thank all its friends in the trade for their support and its fellow bartenders throughout the world for their contributions.

Salvatore Calabrese
PRESIDENT, UKBG

INTRODUCTION

In 1933 a small committee of bartenders founded the United Kingdom Bartenders' Guild which has grown into a national organization with four regions throughout the country. The UKBG is a non-political trade association for male and female cocktail bartenders and it has an active associate membership mostly drawn from kindred trades. The Executive Council is the governing body and it consists of the President, a Vice-President, the chairperson of each area and an Administrator. All officers are elected by secret ballot of bartender members and its finances are controlled by the Administrator.

The board has the power to award Honorary Life Membership to a member who has given loyal or exceptional service to the guild. Upon retiring from office, this honour is always given to Presidents.

The UKBG's primary function is the advancement of the bartending professions by promoting a high standard of workmanship, encouraging participation and maintaining a code of ethics applicable to a craft dedicated to quick, efficient service and customer satisfaction.

Education of young bartenders is recognized as being of prime importance and training courses are regularly held for members. These take the form of an intensive practical course at a catering college. Since 2005 the courses have been run in conjunction with Barconsult and Westminster Kingsway College in the heart of London. The Guild's courses are recognized by a government-approved, independent body, and attendees receive a certificate at the end of the course.

An important aspect of the Guild's activities over the decades has been to set up a channel of communication between its members and the wine and spirit trades because a thorough understanding of the products he or she is selling is a great advantage to a bartender, enabling him or her to mix drinks with confidence and to advise customers correctly. The UKBG is keen to increase public awareness of the bartender's role and regularly organizes trade exhibitions and cocktail competitions on a regional and national basis, to test the skills and creative abilities of bartenders and to increase consumer interest.

The Guild hosted the foundation meeting of the International Bartenders' Association in Torquay, England in 1951. Delegates from Denmark, Switzerland, Great Britain, Holland, Italy and Sweden met and a UKBG member, a W. J. Tarling, was appointed the first President. It was agreed that the best interests of bartending would be served by an international organization with these aims:

• to promote and maintain international relations among the member guilds; to make available the opportunity for the exchange of news, views, proposals and ideas between guilds to encourage a high standard of competence and conduct for the benefit and advancement of the profession of bartending;

- to promote a close liaison between the member guilds and the kindred industry throughout the world;

- to encourage the standardization of mixed drinks recipes;

- to organize and promote international mixed-drinks competitions;

- to provide educational facilities for the bartenders of the IBA.

Since its inauguration the IBA has expanded; by 1961 there were 17 member countries and by 1991 there were 32 member countries. This year, 2006, IBA has 51 member countries. In order to administer all these countries it has been necessary to appoint five Vice Presidents, one for each of Europe, The Far East, North America, South America, and the Southern Hemisphere. The IBA was exclusively for male bartenders until 1975 when the decision was made to admit female bartenders in accordance with the association's rules and regulations.

The IBA Training Centre was set up in 1966. Initially this annual course took place in Luxembourg, but in 1973 it went to Blackpool, England, where it came under the guidance of John Whyte, a teacher with a passion for the bar business. Upon his death, in honour of his contribution, the course was named after him. From 1977 to 1991 it was held in various European countries; in 1992, in Norway and, from 1993, in Singapore. Singapore currently runs an IBA bar training course and the European course returned to Italy where it was held until 2002. The training course is currently held in the Czech Republic.

In 1987 the Education Development Committee (EDC) was set up to ensure the various education and training courses were run to an internationally accepted format. Each country now runs a course to the format set out by the EDC.

The IBA International Cocktail Competition was held annually from 1958 until 1965, when it was held bi-annually until 1976. After 1976 it was held tri-annually, with a competition in the Pre-dinner, After-Dinner and Long Drink categories. Currently an annual competition is held in one of the three categories (chosen alternately) with one champion each year. In 1999 the Flair category was added, which is more about the skill and flair with which a bartender makes the cocktail than the composition of the cocktail.

In 1966 the Paissa Prize was initiated by Martini and Rossi as a competition for bartenders under the age of 28. In 1982 the competition took on a new name: the Martini Grand Prix. Currently it is known as the Bacardi/Martini Grand Prix. Without doubt the most honoured and desired award within the bartenders' world is the Angelo Zola Prize, awarded by the family of past IBA President Angelo Zola in his memory. It is presented periodically to the bartender who has contributed the most to the honour of the profession.

The Cocktail Bar

HISTORY OF THE COCKTAIL

It is strange that the origin of the famous and mysterious word 'cocktail' as a term for a mixed drink cannot precisely be established. Mixed drinks have been drunk since the dawn of civilization. Some claim that the first recipe for a cocktail was lemon juice and powdered adders, praised by the Emperor Commodus in the second century AD as a fine aperitif. The first 'cocktail book' might be said to be the seventeenth-century publication by the Distillers' Company of London, which describes spirituous drinks of singular complexity. These were medicinal in intention – but do we not claim therapeutic value for some of our modern mixes?

The word 'cocktail' was first defined in print as a mixture of spirits, sugar, water and bitters, in an American magazine in 1806. The term was certainly not then in common use.

In earlier years, it was common for horses of mixed stock – in Yorkshire, particularly – to have their tails docked, to distinguish them from the finer thoroughbreds; such horses were said to be 'cocktailed', and maybe mixed drinks took their name from the practice.

One popular notion is that during the American War of Independence a tavern-keeper called Betsy Flanagan, whose premises were frequented by Lafayette's as well as Washington's officers, once prepared a meal of chickens she filched from a pro-British neighbour. To celebrate this minor victory she decorated glasses used at the feast with feathers from the birds. Her French customers toasted her with cries of 'Vive le cocktail!'

Another inn story of the same period concerns a patriotic host who owned a celebrated fighting cock called Washington. One day it disappeared and he offered the hand of his daughter, Bessie, to any man finding it. The man who returned the bird was a suitor whom Bessie's father had previously spurned. However, the host held a betrothal dinner during which Bessie muddled up the drinks. In honour of the bird they named the drinks 'cock tails'.

It is said that at Campeche, on the Gulf of Mexico, visiting British sailors drank local punches called 'dracs' – possibly a corruption of Drake – which were stirred with a wooden spoon so shaped that it was known locally as 'cola de gallo' ('cock's tail'). This name was later applied to the drinks themselves.

From Mexico, another legend. After a visit to a local overlord by American naval officers, drinks were offered to the guests by the chief's daughter, X-octl. The senior American said that they would never forget her or her drinks, which in her honour they called 'cocktails' – that being the nearest they could get to pronouncing her name.

In eighteenth-century England a spirituous 'cock ale' was given to fighting cocks. Sometimes victorious birds were toasted in a mixture containing as many ingredients as the survivor had tail feathers; such drinks might easily have attracted the name of 'cocktail'.

French influence is conspicuous in the two other suggestions: first, that 'cocktail' derives from the traditional name of the mixed wine cup, 'coquetel', of the Bordeaux region; secondly, that an eccentric French physician in New Orleans served drinks in double-ended egg-cups known as '*coquetiers*', which his American friends pronounced 'cock tails'.

Far-fetched as it may sound, the final story in this list is supported by an illustration to a ballad of 1871 entitled 'An American Cock-Tale'. It appears that on old-time Mississippi river steamers, to while away the tedium, a well-heeled toper would sometimes call for a tub to be filled with every liquor on board. The glasses from which this horrible mixture was drunk were traditionally shaped roughly in the form of a cock's breast and stirred with rods approximating to a cock's tail. The implications are obvious.

In English literature both Hughes' *Tom Brown's Schooldays* and Thackeray's *The Newcomers* mentioned cocktails, in the sense of mixed drinks. The first true book of cocktails was by Jerry Thomas, who published in 1862 *The Bon Vivant's Guide, or How to Mix Drinks*. Twenty years later came Harry Johnson's *Bartenders' Manual, or How to Mix Drinks of the Present Style*. Many others followed with American influence strong, though any imbalance was corrected by the first edition of the *UKBG International Guide to Drinks* in 1953.

Cocktails as we know them first gained popularity in the United States. They were originally as much pre-mixed stimulant mixtures for taking on sporting occasions and picnics as they were bar drinks. The first American (i.e. cocktail) bar did not open in London until the first decade of the twentieth century. The great stimulus to universal interest in cocktails came with the Roaring Twenties, when Prohibition in the USA changed everyone's drinking habits. If their usual tipple was not available, people would try to put together acceptable concoctions from whatever they could find. If the initial result was unpalatable, they would seek to improve matters by means of additives – often very successfully.

Generally, the term 'cocktail' is accepted today as a generic name for all mixed drinks. The cocktail bartender, however, understands a cocktail to be a short drink of approximately 10 to 21cl, and anything larger than this he or she would call a 'mixed drink' or 'long drink'.

A renewed appreciation of 'classic' cocktails started back in the mid-1990s and, at the start of the twenty-first century, changes in consumer tastes as well as a wide selection of new products continually appearing on the market, have encouraged professional experimentation in the esoteric world of the cocktail.

Such a pity, then, that we shall never know its true origin.

BAR DESIGN

Cocktail bars are governed by certain legal requirements regarding space, storage and hygiene. Equipment may include ice makers, refrigerated cupboards, bottle skips, liquidizers, fruit squeezers, automatic cash registers and calculators, as well as a range of glasses, shakers, utensils, proprietary drinks and other obvious necessities. Bars vary widely according to their location, size and function, so not all these amenities can be regarded as standard. However, there are certain considerations affecting all bars where some standardization is desirable.

SPACE

Too much space is as undesirable as too little. The ideal distance between the back of the bar counter and the back cupboards is 100 to 125cm. The length must depend on the number of people required to work behind the counter, but preferably each should have his/her own station, that is to say his/her own ice sink, wash-up and draining area and space for glasses and equipment; he/she should also be able to reach containers of the standard drinks easily, without crossing the working areas of his/her colleagues. Each station should also incorporate an empty-bottle skip. Usually placed under the sink, this can be made of plastic or fibre glass and should be set on wheels. Crown cork bottle openers should be fixed beneath the bar counter or working surface at intervals.

THE SERVICE AREA

In addition to the requirements of each station, described above, there should be a firm horizontal surface, below the bar counter and extending from it, for preparing drinks and cutting fruit. Also, bottle racks should be sited where the most regularly needed bottles can be stored and used quickly without the bartender having to turn his/her back on the customer.

PLUMBING

In an ideal bar the wash-up area is set aside from the service area, and if there is space for this in a back room so much the better. However, if this is not possible then a plentiful supply of hot and cold water at the bar is essential. All bars now require at least two sinks. Taps should be of the swivelling kind so that they can be pushed back out of the way when not in use (many glasses have been broken on overhanging taps).

The ice sinks or wells should have drain plugs so that melting ice can drain away and also to facilitate cleaning. It also helps if the bottom of the ice sink contains a drainer tray to prevent the ice from touching the bottom, which considerably reduces the effect of condensation on the outside of the sink. All sinks should be of stainless steel. Build-up module units can be made to order.

REFRIGERATION

A refrigerator, or fan-controlled refrigerated cupboards, should be part of every bar. Cold shelves are an adequate alternative providing care is taken to ensure that they are not used just for general storage. Stock should be rotated at regular intervals so that ice does not form on the base of the bottles. Regular defrosting is essential for cold shelves. Sometimes, when the bar area adjoins a storeroom, refrigerated units have doors on both sides so that they may be filled from the rear. This makes stock rotation much easier.

STORAGE

The storeroom, containing ample reserve stock, is best sited adjacent to the bar. However, where this is not possible it is important that sufficient cupboard space is available to house the stock required for daily business. Drawers are necessary for items that require safe keeping, such as order books, documents and petty cash. Ice storage, and the question of where to site an ice maker, need careful consideration. All too often ice machines are placed in a hot kitchen with insufficient ventilation to enable them to work efficiently; the bar area itself is unsuitable, too, mainly because the machines themselves are unsightly and often noisy. A room behind the bar is the ideal place.

ELECTRICITY

As so many electric machines, such as cash registers, ice crushers and liquidizers, are now used in cocktail bars, a plentiful supply of power points is essential. Power points are best sited in the area above the working surfaces and below the bar counter, but well away from water. If they are positioned near the floor, there will be a treacherous network of cables trailing over the working area.

THE BAR COUNTER

The bar counter should be neither too high nor too wide. The recommended height is 110cm and no wider than 60cm. The surface should be of a material that is easy to clean and resistant to stains. A padded front (or one with a luxurious finish) to the counter and a foot rail contribute to the comfort of customers. A place for ladies to put their handbags (a hook is ideal) also helps to keep the counter-top clear. In most cocktail bars, the bartender also serves to the tables, and provision must be made for a flap to be incorporated in the counter. As this will remain open during service hours, it should be located so as to cause no inconvenience to customers seated at the bar counter. This area should be designated the service area and be kept separate from the customer area.

FLOORING

However careful a bartender is, it is inevitable that there will be some spillage behind the bar. The best material for the floor is one that is easily sponge-mopped dry and is as slip-resistant as possible.

EQUIPMENT

THE COCKTAIL SHAKER

This is the ideal utensil for mixing ingredients that stirring will not blend properly. To use it, add the ice and mix, secure all parts together and, using both hands, place the forefinger of one hand over the top of the shaker and the thumb of the other hand under the bottom. Grasp the shaker fully around the body, crossing little fingers to ensure the connection remains sealed. Move the wrist and forearm together. Shake sharply and briefly for a few seconds.

The Boston Shaker

Consisting of two cones, this shaker is the one favoured by professionals as it can be used quickly and strained with the aid of a Hawthorn. Some have one cone made of glass, the other of stainless steel; others consist of two cones of plated silver. One cone overlaps the other.

The Standard Shaker

This three-piece utensil is usually made of stainless steel or plated silver. It has a cone-shaped base and a dumpy top with a built-in strainer and fitted cap. This type of strainer is ideal for the home. Many bartenders who prefer to use the Standard strain the drink from the cone through a Hawthorn strainer.

THE MIXING GLASS

This is like a jug without a handle, or in some cases like a very large brandy balloon. It is used for mixing clear drinks that do not contain juices or cream.

THE STRAINER

The most popular strainer is the Hawthorn, a flat, spoon-like utensil with a spring coiled round its head. It is placed over the top of the shaker or mixing glass to hold back the ice when pouring the drink. A large-headed strainer with lugs and a short handle is available specifically for use with liquidizers.

BAR SPOON

This is a long-handled spoon with a twisted shaft and a flat muddler end. The muddler is used for crushing sugar and mint in certain drinks.

BAR LIQUIDIZER OR BLENDER

The most efficient is one designed specifically for use in the bar. The Hamilton Beach is also popular among professionals. Liquidizers are used for preparing drinks that require puréed fruit. Although most professional blenders have specially toughened blades, it is best to use crushed ice whenever possible.

DRINK MIXER

This machine is used for drinks that do not need liquidizing, especially those containing cream or ice cream. When required, use only crushed or cracked ice.

OTHER BAR UTENSILS

- 'Waiter's friend' corkscrew
- Ice buckets or trough
- Ice pick
- Ice scoop or tongs
- Fruit tongs or fork
- Plastic buckets for transporting ice
- Bottle skip or empty cases
- Broken cork extractor
- Electric drinks mixer
- Electric juice extractor or hand squeezer
- Stainless steel or plastic pourers
- Stainless steel or plastic pourers
- Spirit measures
- Stainless steel fruit knife
- Straws, stirrers and cherry sticks
- Champagne muddlers and swizzle sticks
- Champagne cooler, stopper and tongs
- Port strainer, muslin and funnel
- Crown cork bottle openers
- Bitters bottles
- Good supply of practical glassware
- Glass cloths and serviettes
- Cocktail napkins and coasters
- Plastic or glass stirrers

KITCHEN SUPPLIES

Olives	Orange flower water	Demerara sugar
Pearl onions	Angostura bitters	Eggs
Maraschino cherries	Vanilla essence	Cream
Worcestershire sauce	Beef bouillon	Mint
Ketchup	Tomato juice	Cucumber rind
Tabasco sauce	Pineapple juice	Oranges
Salt and pepper	Mango juice	Lemons
Celery salt	Cranberry juice	Limes
Cinnamon	Coffee beans	Bananas
Nutmeg	Cube sugar	Strawberries
Cloves	Caster sugar	Coconut cream

GLASSWARE

Glass has a special affinity for liquid and so enhances its appearance that the name of the substance (the constituents of which are sand, soda ash and limestone) has been adopted as the name of the utensil most commonly used to hold liquid: the glass. Choosing the right glassware is a vital element when preparing a drink if it is to be invitingly presented and give satisfaction to the consumer. Well-designed glassware combines elegance, strength and stability. Most drinks are enhanced by being served in fine-rimmed clear glass, which should be clean and well polished. Often, the style of a glass can inspire a bartender to make an extravagant and delicious cocktail. Examples of basic professional glassware may be found on pages 20-21.

1	shaker	5	strainer	9	sharp knife
2	ice scoop and bucket	6	strawberry huller	10	ice tongs
3	bitters bottle	7	zester		
4	spirit measure	8	melon ball scoop		

1. Boston shaker
2. bar spoon
3. strainer
4. mixing glass
5. blender
6. fruit squeezer
7. various stirrers
8. champagne stopper
9. waiter's friend
10. bottle opener
11. wooden mudler

BAR TOOLS 19

1 hot drinks

2 champagne flute

3 liqueur

4 cocktail/Martini

5 highball

6 old fashioned

1 tumbler

2 shot

3 Margarita

4 brandy balloon

5 red wine

6 white wine

7 sherry/port

GUIDE FOR BEGINNERS

• Always be clean and tidy.

• Treat customers in a diplomatic manner.

• Remember your hands are in constant view, so pay special attention to your fingernails.

• Smoking or drinking behind the bar is unsightly and in some countries is also illegal.

• Ice is essential for all cocktail bars. Ensure you have a plentiful supply and that it is always clean and clear.

• Always keep your glasses and equipment clean and polished. Ensure that, where necessary, glasses are chilled before serving.

• Always handle glasses by the stem or base and never put your fingers inside a glass or near to the rim.

• Remember that broken glasses kill profits.

• It is bad taste, bad for the wine and dangerous to allow a champagne cork to 'pop' on removal.

• When serving drinks or wine at a table, always serve, where practicable, from the right-hand side of each person.

• Handle a glass soda syphon by the plastic or metal part only. Glass is a poor conductor of heat and cannot stand sudden changes in temperature. The heat of the hand could cause the glass to burst – with disastrous consequences.

• You will extract considerably more juice from citrus fruit if you warm it, by soaking in hot water, before squeezing.

• Sugar of all kinds is necessary in all cocktail bars. Ensure it is dry and uncaked.

• A supply of pasteurized egg white and pasteurized egg yolk is also essential. Always break a fresh egg in a separate glass to test its freshness.

• Remember that a bartender should always carry the tools of his trade. Just as you would not think highly of a plumber who does not have a wrench, blow-lamp, etc., you will not be highly thought of as a bartender if you do not have such things as a cigarette lighter or matches, a 'waiter's friend' knife, a cigar cutter and a pen or pencil.

• Always use good-quality products. Poor-quality ones are a false economy.

• It is acceptable in a busy bar to use your own pre-mixes, i.e., a ready-seasoned tomato juice for Bloody Marys and tomato-juice cocktails, or a sour premix of lemon juice, gomme syrup and egg white.

• Never put an effervescent ingredient into your shaker, mixing glass or liquidizer.

• In a mixed order of drinks, always make the cocktails last so that they can be served fresh – 'whilst they are smiling at you'. Remember that a cocktail is a mixture and will separate if left too long.

• Do not rock your cocktail to sleep. A short, sharp, snappy action is sufficient. Shake, do not rock.

• Decoration of a cocktail or mixed drink is a matter for the individual. Normally, it will either complement the flavour of the drink, as does the twist of orange in an Adonis, or contrast with the colour; sometimes it will do both, as can be seen in the practice of many bartenders of serving a stick of celery with a Bloody Mary. This does not mean that you should make your drink into a fruit salad. Apart from being expensive, this makes it look ludicrous. Remember that when you please the eye, you invariably please the palate.

• Pour the cheapest ingredient into the mixing glass or cocktail shaker first. Then, if you make a mistake, you will have wasted only the cheapest ingredient, not the expensive spirits.

• Never fill a glass to the brim. Spillage will result in a messy counter or table and spoilt clothes.

• Try to lay out your bar so that it is both attractive to the eye and efficient to work in, and keep it that way by returning bottles to their rightful positions after use.

• Remember that a good bartender is invariably a good salesman. 'Sell' cocktails you know you make well. This will ensure that your customers return again.

DRINKS AT HOME

Served in moderation, alcohol is a useful aid to relaxation, especially in the home. A simple mixed drink can soothe tangled nerves after a hard day at the office, a cocktail with friends can enliven lagging conversation, a glass of wine can be the difference between eating and dining and a slowly sipped post-prandial drink in good company gives immense satisfaction.

However, a little organization can save a lot of panic, even in the context of serving drinks at home. Guests can be embarrassed if they hear a noisy clanging of bottles, frantic washing-up of glasses or sounds of dismay as their hosts realize there is no ice in the freezer; at least, they will get the impression that they are putting their hosts to a great deal of trouble. It is best to have stock and equipment properly stored so that drinks can be dispensed easily, and preferably without interrupting the flow of conversation.

THE HOME BAR

One of the most attractive and useful assets you can have for home entertainment is a well-equipped bar for mixing and serving drinks. Such bars can be very elaborate or very simple, and can occupy either an area set aside for the purpose or merely a small cabinet or table in a corner of the room. The type you choose will depend on the amount of space you have available and the amount of entertaining you do. Should you have sufficient time, enthusiasm and skill, you can build your own bar; otherwise bars can be bought from large department stores. There are many kinds available, but basically those sold through the shops fall into three categories.

The first of these, the mobile bar, is perhaps the most versatile and useful. The fact that it can be readily moved from place to place is its greatest asset; mounted on a trolley, for example, your equipment, glasses and bottles can be moved as a unit for the easy preparation and serving of drinks, whether it be in the living room or out on the patio.

Of the semi-permanent bars, the most familiar type is the cocktail cabinet. Here the equipment, glasses and spirits can be conveniently and attractively displayed. Take into account proximity to washing-up facilities when deciding where to position your cocktail cabinet.

Search ebay and antique and other quality second-hand stores for cocktail cabinets made in the 1950s and 1960s. These are becoming very popular among collectors and you could pick up a bargain, too.

The most ambitious of the three types, the permanent bar, forms an integral part of the interior decoration. Its design is of the greatest importance, and care must be taken that the bar, while being an eye-catching showpiece, enhances but does not overwhelm the room.

Lighting here plays a vital part; ideally it should be indirect, for this will highlight the bar in a way that is understated yet highly effective. Should you decide to make your own bar, remember that it should be of a height that is comfortable to sit at while one's drink rests on top of the bar.

EQUIPMENT

Whether it is a mobile bar, a cocktail cabinet or a separate piece of furniture, the area used for storing stock and equipment must be stable, accessible and easily cleaned. There is no need for much of the intricate equipment of a professional bar as most kitchens have many items that can be used in the preparation of drinks. These are the more useful pieces of equipment:

- Three-piece cocktail shaker with built-in strainer
- Mixing glass or large jug
- Hawthorn strainer
- Bar spoon or long-handled spoon
- Cutting board and sharp stainless steel knife

- Corkscrew and bottle opener
- Fruit squeezer
- Ice bucket or large bowl with ice tongs
- Liquidizer
- Stirrers, straws and cherry sticks
- Mineral maker

BASIC STOCK

A little imagination and thought can turn home stock into delightful drinks. The recipes in this book will provide specific instructions for mixing, but the following list is offered as a guide to home provisions.

Brandy	Crème de cacao	Grenadine syrup
Gin	Kümmel	Gomme syrup
Vodka	Advocaat	Soda water
Rum – light and dark	Crème de cassis	Tonic water
Tequila	Peppermint cordial	Dry ginger ale
Scotch whisky	Lime juice cordial	Bitter lemon
Bourbon whiskey	Limes or lemons	Cola
Vermouth — dry and sweet	Oranges	Sparkling lemonade or 7Up
Sherry	Maraschino cherries	Grated nutmeg
Tawny Port	Small cocktail olives	Tomato juice
Cointreau or triple sec	Celery salt	Pineapple juice
Crème de menthe	Coconut cream	Angostura bitters
Kahlua or Tia Maria	Cubed sugar	

GLASSWARE

The essentials of fine glassware are brilliant clarity, good balance and a fine rim. Remember when wiping glasses to use a clean dry glass cloth and rinse well to remove all traces of detergent (which flattens beer and sparkling wines, and detrimentally flavours delicate drinks). Glassware should be repolished just before use and stored out of the reach of small children. A wide variety of styles of glassware is available. The following is a guide to capacity only.

- 6cl to 9cl glass for liqueurs, schnapps and chilled vodka
- 10cl to 12cl stemmed glass for cocktails, port and sherry
- 16cl all-purpose glass, such as a goblet, for wine, spirits or mixed drinks
- 30cl to 36cl highball glass, for long drinks, cups and beers. (Glasses for mixed drinks must be large enough to contain plenty of ice plus additives.)
- Snifter glass for brandy or cognac

GIVING A PARTY

Few people are fortunate enough to have at their disposal the amount of working space and range of equipment and drinks that are available to the professional bartender. But if you throw a sizeable party, the pressure of 'business' on you is going to be almost as great, even without your other duties. One way out — unfortunately one that is all too often taken — is to cut down on the variety and quantity of what you offer. This is a shame, and sometimes means serving a single concoction, prepared long in advance, which is topped up from time to time (this can cause wild and treacherous fluctuations in its alcoholic content).

For the more ambitious, advance preparation is still the key. The following hints will, if followed, do much to guarantee an enjoyable party.

- Fruit juice should be squeezed and oranges and lemons required for garnishing sliced fairly thickly.

- When cutting peel for a twist, take only the coloured rind, not the bitter pith. Fruit cut into slices and twists will keep fresh if covered by a damp cloth or plastic wrap and stored in the refrigerator.

Make plenty of ice well in advance. A spare sink or a bath can be a good place to store it, as the ice keeps cold there and the mess caused by melting is avoided.

If you are planning drinks containing sugar, a good tip is to make up a sugar syrup in the proportions of 2 cups of sugar to 1 cup of water. Bring to the boil and simmer until the sugar is dissolved. This can be bottled and refrigerated and will keep indefinitely. Also, gomme syrup is available in most liquor retailers.

GLASSES
Have in store a good supply, ideally twice as many as the number of your guests.

NON-ALCOHOLIC DRINKS
Provide a good choice for the teetotallers at the party. See the chapter on non-alcoholic cocktails later in this book.

ADVANCE PREPARATION
Drinks made of liquor and wine may be prepared in quantity in advance, but drinks containing fruit juices and sugar will separate unless mixed just before drinking.

EQUIPMENT
Check that you have in your bar everything else you are likely to need: serving trays, water jugs, soda syphon, bar tools, knife and board for cutting and preparing fruit, oranges and lemons, cucumber, maraschino cherries, mint, toothpicks, glass cloths and sponge for mopping up.

SOME MIXED DRINKS FOR DIFFERENT OCCASIONS

Pre-dinner drinks	After-dinner drinks	Party drinks
Martini	Sidecar	Harvey Wallbanger
Champagne drinks	Frappés	Tequila Sunrise
White Lady	B & B	Cosmopolitan
Manhattan	Stinger	Moscow Mule
Old-fashioned	Golden Cadillac	Cuba Libre
Sours	Black Russian	Punches
Screwdriver	Silver Bullet	Caipirinha
Bloody Mary	Rusty Nail	Mint Julep
Negroni	Grasshopper	Pimm's No 1
Gibson	Godmother	
	Alexander	
	Irish Coffee	

Less potent drinks	Hot-weather drinks	More exotic drinks
Kir	Coolers	Mai Tai
Americano	Cups	Zombie
Spritzer	Collins	Margarita
Fruit Daiquiri	Planter's Punch	Scorpion
Pina Colada	Julep	Pousse Café
Sangria	Buck's Fizz	Blueberry Martini
	Long Island Iced Tea	Spicy Fifty

Cocktails & Mixed Drinks

EXPLANATION OF TERMS

Blend Put ingredients into electric blender, add crushed ice if required by recipe, blend until required consistency is achieved – pour unstrained into suitable glass.

Build Pour necessary ingredients directly into suitable glass without any premixing, add ice only if required by recipe. Mixed drinks made in this way are usually served with a muddler.

Mix Put ingredients into the cone of electric drink mixer, add crushed ice if specified, mix until drink reaches required consistency, then pour or strain into glass.

Shake Put ice into the cocktail shaker, pour in the necessary ingredients, shake shortly and sharply unless otherwise instructed, strain into required glass.

Stir Put ice into mixing glass, pour in the necessary ingredients, stir until cold, strain into required glass.

Stir in When topping with final ingredient use barspoon to stir as it is added.

Zest A small thin piece of citrus peel with as little pith as possible. The essential oil is squeezed on top of the drink and it is optional whether the zest is then dropped into the drink.

Twist A long zest twisted in the centre and normally dropped into the drink.

Spiral Complete peel of fruit cut in spiral fashion.

Unless otherwise stated the normal 10 to 12cl cocktail (Martini) glass should be used for these recipes.

AN A to Z of RECIPES

Following is a selection of drinks from past decades combined with creations from the start of the twenty-first century. Some of these recipes date from the 1920s and 30s; others are 60s and 80s hedonistic concoctions that we have come to love and cherish.

The accepted classics and the Martini and Martini-style cocktails are in the chapter that follows this one, listed under the heading of the type of drink of which they are representative. For instance, the original Champagne Cocktail is under Champagne and the Daiquiri and Frozen Daiquiri are under the heading Daiquiris (see page 63).

A

Abbey

2.5cl gin
1.5cl maraschino liqueur
1.5cl extra dry vermouth
2.5cl orange juice
2 dashes Angostura bitters

Shake ingredients with ice. Strain into a cocktail glass. Garnish with a cherry.

Adonis

5cl dry sherry
2.5cl sweet vermouth
dash orange bitters

Pour the dry sherry into a mixing glass. Add the vermouth and bitters. Stir. Strain into a cocktail glass. Garnish with a twist of orange.

Affinity

2.5cl Scotch
2.5cl sweet vermouth
2.5cl dry vermouth
dash Angostura bitters

Pour both vermouths into a mixing glass with ice. Add the Scotch and bitters. Stir. Strain into a cocktail glass. Add a twist of lemon.

Alaska

5cl gin
2cl yellow Chartreuse
2 dashes orange bitters

Stir the gin, Chartreuse and bitters in a mixing glass until mixed. Strain into a cocktail glass.

Alexander [Brandy]

2.5cl brandy
2.5cl white crème de cacao
2.5cl fresh double cream

Shake ingredients with ice. Strain into a cocktail glass. Sprinkle a fine layer of nutmeg on top of the drink.

Alexander [Gin]

2.5cl gin
2.5cl white crème de cacao
2.5cl fresh double cream

Shake ingredients with ice. Strain into
a cocktail glass. Sprinkle a fine layer
of nutmeg on top of the drink.

Amalfi Dream

5cl vodka
2cl limoncello
1cl fresh lemon juice
4 to 5 fresh mint leaves

Shake ingredients vigorously with ice.
Strain into a cocktail glass, letting
mint fragments slip through to create
a layer on top of the drink. Garnish
with a spiral of lemon.

American Beauty

2cl brandy
2cl extra dry vermouth
2cl fresh orange juice
1.5cl ruby port
dash white crème de menthe
dash grenadine

Shake ingredients with ice. Strain into
a wine glass.

Americano

2.5cl Campari
2.5cl sweet vermouth
soda water (optional)

Pour the sweet vermouth, then the
Campari into a highball filled with ice.
Garnish with lemon and orange twists.
Add soda water if required.

Angers Rose

2.5cl bourbon whiskey
2.5cl Cointreau
2.5cl pineapple juice
dash Campari
dash pasteurized egg white

Shake ingredients with ice. Strain into
a cocktail glass. Garnish with a cherry.

Arabian Dream

4cl honey-flavoured vodka
10cl apple juice
1.5cl fresh lemon juice
2 dashes pomegranate syrup
ground black pepper

Shake ingredients with ice. Strain into
a highball over crushed ice. Add black
pepper. Garnish with a lime wedge.

Asian Babe

1 blade lemongrass
4cl lemon vodka
4cl grapefruit juice
few stalks fresh coriander
1 teaspoon vanilla-flavoured sugar
dash orange bitters

Roll the lemongrass on the bar top,
slice off 5mm from each end. At the
thinner end of the blade, using a
stirrer, push the inner rolls through
until there is enough to pinch and
pull out. The hollow tube is the
garnish. Rinse and place to one side.
  Rinse the inners and chop into
small lengths, then place with 5 stalks
of coriander (with leaves) in a shaker.
Muddle. Add ice, then remaining
ingredients. Shake. Strain into an old-
fashioned glass filled with crushed ice.
Garnish with the stalk.

Asian Breeze

5cl Sputnik vodka
lychee juice
pomegranate juice

Pour the pomegranate juice into a
highball filled with ice. Shake the
lychee juice and vodka with ice.
Strain over the pomegranate juice.
Garnish with pomegranate seeds and a
slice of lime.

B

B & B

2.5cl brandy
2.5cl Bénédictine

Pour the brandy in a balloon glass
and float the Bénédictine over.

BP

2.5cl brandy
2.5cl ruby port

Pour the port into a port glass,
followed by the brandy. Stir.

B52

2cl Kahlua
2cl Baileys Irish Cream
2cl Grand Marnier liqueur

Pour the Kahlua into a shot glass.
Over the back of a barspoon, pour the
Baileys, then the Grand Marnier. Serve
with a stirrer on the side.

Bacardi Cocktail

5cl Bacardi white rum
2.5cl fresh lime or lemon juice
dash grenadine

Shake ingredients with ice. Strain into
a Martini glass. Garnish with a cherry
on a stick set across the glass.

Bacardi Presidente

6cl Bacardi Oro (gold) rum
2cl Martini Rosso vermouth

Shake ingredients with ice. Strain into
a Martini glass. Garnish with a cherry.

Bacardi Cuba Libre

5cl Bacardi light rum
cola
lime wedge

Pour the rum into a highball filled
with ice. Top up with cola. Squeeze
the lime wedge into the drink.

Bacardi Mojito

5cl Bacardi light rum
12 fresh mint leaves
half fresh lime
1 teaspoon caster sugar
soda water

Crush the mint leaves, sugar and lime
in a highball. Add the rum. Fill the
glass with crushed ice. Top up with
soda water. Stir. Garnish with mint.
Serve with straws and a stirrer.

Previous page
A Negroni Twist beckons those in need
of Campari served as a delicious aperitif.
It has a brilliant colour and taste.

Opposite
Martell XO cognac on the nose is first
marked by dried fruits and bees wax.
The finesse of Grande champagne is last.

Balalaika

5cl vodka
2.5cl Cointreau
2cl fresh lemon juice

Shake ingredients with ice. Strain into a cocktail glass.

Barracuda

2.5cl golden rum
2cl Galliano
2cl pineapple juice
2 dashes gomme syrup
dash fresh lime juice
champagne

Shake ingredients with ice. Strain into a flute. Fill with champagne. Decorate with a slice of lime and cherry.

Bartender

2cl gin
2cl sherry
2cl Dubonnet
2cl dry vermouth
dash Grand Marnier liqueur

Stir in a mixing glass with ice. Strain into an old-fashioned glass with ice.

Bastille

1.5cl crème de mûre
2.5cl white rum
4 blackberries
dash fresh orange juice
champagne

Shake ingredients, except champagne, with ice. Strain into a champagne flute. Fill with champagne. Garnish with a blackberry and a mint leaf on top of the drink.

Batida Morango

5cl cachaça
2.5cl fresh lime juice
4 fresh strawberries, diced
2 teaspoons caster sugar

Pour ingredients into a blender with crushed ice. Blend until smooth. Pour into a highball. Serve with a straw.

Beam Me Up Scotty

2cl coffee liqueur
2cl crème de banane
2cl Baileys Irish Cream

Pour each ingredient, in the order listed, over the back of a barspoon into a shot glass.

Bentley

5cl Dubonnet
5cl applejack brandy

Pour ingredients into a mixing glass and stir well. Strain into a cocktail glass.

Between the Sheets

2.5cl brandy
2.5cl Cointreau
2.5cl white rum
dash fresh lemon juice

Shake ingredients with ice. Strain into a cocktail glass.

Black Dream

2.5cl black sambuca
2.5cl Irish Cream liqueur

Pour the sambuca, then the Irish Cream, over the back of a barspoon into a shot glass.

Black Jack

2.5cl Scotch whisky
2.5cl Kahlua
2.5cl Cointreau
dash fresh lemon juice

Shake ingredients with ice. Strain into a cocktail glass.

Black Orchid

2.5cl Pernod
1.5cl Cointreau
1.5cl blackberry brandy
tonic water
7Up/sparkling lemonade

Pour the first three ingredients into a highball filled with ice. Stir. Add a splash of tonic water, then top up with 7Up. Stir. Garnish with a pink slipper orchid.

Black Russian

4cl vodka
2cl Kahlua

Pour the vodka into an old-fashioned glass with ice, then add the Kahlua. Stir.

Blackthorn

4cl sloe gin
2cl sweet vermouth
dash orange bitters

Pour ingredients into a mixing glass with ice. Add a twist of lemon peel.

Block & Fall

2cl brandy
2cl Cointreau
1.5cl Pernod
1.5cl calvados

Shake ingredients with ice. Strain into a cocktail glass.

Bloody Bull

2.5cl vodka
6cl beef bouillon
6cl tomato juice
1cl fresh lemon juice
2 dashes Worcestershire sauce
celery salt

Shake ingredients with ice. Strain into a highball filled with ice.

Bloody Caesar

5cl vodka
15cl clamato juice
2cl fresh lemon juice
pinch celery salt
Tabasco sauce
2 dashes Worcestershire sauce
ground black pepper

Pour the clamato and lemon juices into a highball filled with ice. Add the vodka and spices. Stir. Garnish with a wedge of lime on the rim. Serve with a stirrer.

Bloody Mary

5cl vodka
15cl tomato juice
2cl fresh lemon juice
pinch celery salt
2 dashes Worcestershire sauce
2 dashes Tabasco sauce
ground black pepper

Fill the highball with ice cubes, then pour in the tomato and lemon juices. Add the vodka. Add the spices and stir. Add a twist of black pepper. Garnish with a wedge of lime on the rim, and a stalk of celery if the customer requests it. Serve with a stirrer.

Bloody Russian

5cl Sputnik horseradish vodka
1.25cl Worcestershire sauce
1.25cl Tabasco sauce
clamato juice
pinch celery salt
twist black pepper
1 barspoon creamed horseradish
1 barspoon sweet Thai chilli sauce
1cl fresh lemon juice

Shake ingredients gently with ice. Pour into a highball filled with ice. Garnish with a fresh chilli placed on the rim of the glass.

Blue Lady

4cl gin
2cl blue curaçao
2cl fresh lemon juice
dash pasteurized egg white

Shake ingredients with ice. Strain into a cocktail glass.

Blue Lagoon

2.5cl vodka
2.5cl blue curaçao
7Up/sparkling lemonade

Pour the vodka and curaçao over ice in a highball glass. Top up with lemonade.

Blue Lychee

2.5cl vodka
1cl lychee liqueur
2cl apple juice
2 dashes blue curaçao
1cl fresh lime juice

Shake ingredients with ice. Strain into a cocktail glass.

Blue Negligée

2.5cl ouzo
2.5cl Parfait Amour
2.5cl green Chartreuse

Pour ingredients into a mixing glass with ice. Stir. Strain into a cocktail glass. Garnish with a cherry dropped in the drink.

Blushing Barmaid

2.5cl Campari
2.5cl amaretto
dash pasteurized egg white
bitter lemon

Shake ingredients, except bitter lemon, with ice. Strain into a highball filled with ice. Top up with bitter lemon and stir. Garnish with a wedge of apricot.

Bobby Burns

5cl Scotch whisky
2.5cl sweet vermouth
3 dashes Bénédictine

Shake ingredients with ice. Strain into
a old-fashioned glass with ice.

Bolton Cocktail

5cl vodka
1cl peach schnapps
2cl raspberry purée
1cl fresh lemon juice
1 teaspoon clear honey

Shake ingredients with ice. Strain into
a cocktail glass. Garnish with a few
raspberries in the middle of the drink.

Bombay

2.5cl brandy
1.5cl dry vermouth
1.5cl sweet vermouth
dash pastis
2 dashes orange curaçao

Pour ingredients into a mixing glass
with ice. Stir. Strain into a cocktail
glass.

Bosom Caresser

4cl brandy
2cl orange curaçao
dash grenadine
1 free-range egg yolk

Shake ingredients with ice. Strain into
a cocktail or small wine glass.

Bossa Nova Special

2.5cl white rum
2.5cl Galliano
dash apricot brandy
6cl pineapple juice
dash fresh lemon juice
dash pasteurized egg white

Shake ingredients with ice. Strain into
a highball filled with ice. Garnish with
a wedge of lime. Serve with a straw.

Bramble

5cl gin
4 blackberries
3cl fresh lime juice
1 teaspoon caster sugar
dash crème de mûre
soda water

Muddle the blackberries with the lime
juice and sugar in a bowl. Strain
through a cheesecloth into an old-
fashioned glass. Add the gin and
crushed ice. Top up with soda. Add
the creme de mûre. Stir. Garnish with
a slice of lime, and a blackberry. Serve
with a straw.

Brandy Cocktail

5cl brandy
2 dashes orange curaçao
2 dashes Angostura bitters

Pour ingredients into a mixing glass
with ice. Stir. Strain into a balloon.

Brave Bull

4cl tequila
2cl Kahlua

Pour ingredients into an old-fashioned
glass filled with ice. Stir.

Bronx

2.5cl gin
1.5cl dry vermouth
1.5cl sweet vermouth
2.5cl fresh orange juice

Shake ingredients with ice. Strain into
a cocktail glass. Garnish with a twist
of orange.

Bronx Terrace

5cl gin
2.5cl vermouth
2cl dash lime cordial

Pour ingredients into a mixing glass
with ice. Stir. Strain into an old-
fashioned glass with ice. Add a cherry.

Brooklyn

2.5cl rye whiskey
2.5cl sweet vermouth
dash maraschino liqueur
dash Amer Picon

Pour ingredients into a mixing glass
with ice. Stir.

Bullshot

2.5cl vodka
12cl beef bouillon or condensed
   consommé
dash fresh lemon juice
2 dashes Worcestershire sauce
celery salt
twist black pepper

Shake ingredients, except pepper, with
ice. Strain into a highball. Add a
quick twist of black pepper. Garnish
with a wedge of lime on the rim.
Serve with a stirrer.

C

Caipirinha

5cl cachaça
1 small fresh lime
2 teaspoons caster sugar

Wash the lime, slice off the top and
bottom, then cut into segments, top to
bottom. Add the lime and the sugar to
an old-fashioned glass. Crush the
lime, then muddle to dissolve the
sugar. Add ice cubes and the cachaça
then stir. Serve with a stirrer.

Caipirovska

5cl vodka
1 lime, diced
1cl fresh lime juice
2 teaspoons caster sugar

Muddle the lime and the sugar in an
old-fashioned glass. Add the vodka and
lime juice. fill the glass with crushed
ice. Stir. Garnish with a slice of lime.
Serve with a straw.

Calvados

2.5cl calvados
2.5cl orange juice
1.5cl Cointreau
dash orange bitters

Shake ingredients with ice. Strain into
a cocktail glass.

Cape Codder

5cl vodka
15cl cranberry juice

Pour the cranberry juice into a
highball filled with ice. Add the vodka.
Stir. Garnish with a wedge of lime.

Caribbean Sunset

2.5cl gin
2.5cl crème de banane
2.5cl blue curaçao
2.5cl fresh lemon juice
2.5cl fresh double cream
dash grenadine

Shake ingredients, except grenadine, with ice. Strain into a highball filled with ice. Add grenadine, which will sink to the bottom. Garnish with a cherry and a slice of orange on a cocktail stick.

Carnival

2.5cl brandy
1.5cl apricot brandy
1.5cl Lillet
dash kirsch
dash fresh orange juice

Shake ingredients with ice. Strain into an old-fashioned glass filled with ice.

Caruso

2.5cl gin
2.5cl dry vermouth
1.5cl green crème de menthe

Pour the ingredients into a mixing glass with ice. Stir with a bar spoon. Strain into a cocktail glass. Drop a cherry into the drink.

Casino

4cl gin
1.5cl maraschino liqueur
1.5cl fresh lemon juice
dash orange bitters

Shake ingredients with ice. Strain into a cocktail glass. Add a cherry.

Champs Elysée

5cl brandy
1.5cl yellow Chartreuse
1.5cl fresh lemon juice
dash Angostura bitters

Shake ingredients with ice. Strain into a cocktail glass.

Chic Elit

5cl Elit vodka
2cl frais de bois
dash fresh lemon juice
1.5cl cranberry juice
stem redcurrants

Muddle the redcurrants in a shaker. Add the remaining ingredients. Shake with ice. Strain into a cocktail glass. Garnish with a stem of redcurrants.

Chivas Cooler

5cl Chivas Regal 12-year-old whisky
ginger ale

Fill a slender highball with ice. Add the Chivas 12 and top up with ginger ale. Garnish with a wedge of lime.

Chivas 12 Number 2

Chivas Regal 12-year-old whisky

Pour a generous measure over ice in an old-fashioned glass. Swirl.

Chocolate Affair

2.5cl chocolate liqueur
1.5cl Tia Maria
1.5cl cognac
1.5cl amaretto
1.5cl fresh double cream

Shake ingredients with ice. Strain into a cocktail glass. Garnish with a thin chocolate stick.

Claridge

2.5cl gin
2.5cl dry vermouth
1.5cl Cointreau
1.5cl apricot brandy

Pour ingredients into a mixing glass with ice. Stir. Strain into a cocktail glass. Add a twist of orange.

Clover Club

5cl gin
1.5cl grenadine
1.5cl fresh lemon juice
dash pasteurized egg white

Shake ingredients with ice. Strain into a cocktail glass. Add a cherry.

Coconut Breeze

5cl dark rum
1.5cl maraschino liqueur
10cl pineapple juice
5cl coconut milk
dash orgeat syrup

Shake ingredients with ice. Strain into a highball. Garnish with a pineapple wedge and a cherry.

Cognac Mojitado

2.5cl cognac
1.5cl limoncello
1 fresh lime, diced
few fresh mint leaves
caster sugar
sparkling water

Crush the mint leaves in a highball glass with the sugar and lime pieces. Fill with crushed ice, the cognac, then the sparkling water. Stir.

Coolman Martini

5cl vodka
2cl apple juice
1.5cl Cointreau
1.5cl fresh lemon juice

Shake ingredients with ice. Strain into a cocktail glass. Garnish with an apple slice fan.

Corpse Reviver 1

2.5cl brandy
2.5cl sweet vermouth
2.5cl calvados

Pour ingredients into a mixing glass with ice. Stir. Strain into a cocktail glass.

Corpse Reviver 3

2.5cl brandy
2.5cl white crème de menthe
2.5cl Fernet Branca

Pour ingredients into a mixing glass with ice. Stir. Strain into a cocktail glass.

Cosmopolitan

5cl vodka
1cl Cointreau
1cl cranberry juice
1cl fresh lime juice

Shake ingredients with ice. Strain into
a cocktail glass. Garnish with a wedge
of lime.

Cuervo & Ginger

5cl Jose Cuervo Especiale tequila
lime wedge
ginger ale

Pour the tequila into a highball filled
with ice. Squeeze a wedge of lime into
the drink then drop it in. Top up with
ginger ale.

D

Dandy

2.5cl rye whiskey
2.5cl Dubonnet
1.5cl Cointreau
dash Angostura bitters

Pour ingredients into a mixing glass
with ice. Stir. Add a piece each of
orange peel and lemon twists.

Danielli

4cl vodka
2cl dry vermouth
2cl Campari

Build in an old-fashioned glass with
ice. Stir. Garnish with a twist of lemon.

Dark and Stormy

5cl Gossens dark rum
2cl fresh lime juice
ginger beer

Pour the rum and lime juice into a
highball with ice. Top up with ginger
beer. Stir. Garnish with a twist of lime.

Diva

4cl rye whiskey
1.5cl lychee liqueur
2.5cl fresh lemon juice
5cl cranberry juice
1cl gomme syrup
ginger ale

Shake ingredients, except ginger ale,
with ice. Strain into a highball filled
with ice. Top up with ginger ale.

Dolce Havana

4cl white rum
2cl Aperol
1.5cl Cointreau
2.5cl fresh orange juice
2cl fresh lime juice

Shake ingredients with ice. Strain into
a cocktail glass. Garnish with a Cape
Gooseberry.

Dorado

5cl tequila
2cl fresh lemon juice
2 teaspoons clear honey

Shake ingredients with ice. Strain into
a cocktail glass.

Double Vision

2.5cl lemon vodka
2.5cl blackcurrant vodka
4 dashes Angostura bitters
3cl apple juice

Shake ingredients with ice. Strain into
a cocktail glass.

Dream Cocktail

5cl brandy
2.5cl Cointreau
dash anisette liqueur

Shake ingredients with ice. Strain into
a cocktail glass.

Dubonnet

4cl gin
4cl Dubonnet

Pour ingredients into a mixing glass
with ice. Stir. Strain into an old-
fashioned glass with ice. Add a twist of
lemon peel.

E

El Cerr

2.5cl light rum
2.5cl dark rum
1.5cl orange curaçao
1.5cl Galliano
10cl pineapple juice
dash grenadine

Frost the rim of a highball glass with
sugar. Shake ingredients with ice.
Strain into the highball. Garnish with
a wedge of pineapple and a
strawberry.

Elise

4cl gin
1.5cl limoncello
1.5cl peach schnapps
7cl fresh grapefruit juice
7cl mango juice
1cl orgeat syrup

Shake ingredients with ice. Strain into
a highball filled with ice. Garnish with
a Cape Gooseberry. Serve with a
straw.

Esquire

2 kumquats, diced
4cl Irish whiskey
1.5cl mandarin liqueur
1.5cl fresh lemon juice
1 teaspoon brown sugar
ginger ale

Muddle the kumquat, lemon juice and
sugar in a highball glass. Add crushed
ice. Pour the remaining ingredients
over the top and stir. Top up with
ginger ale. Stir.

Evans

5cl rye whiskey
2.5cl apricot brandy
dash orange curaçao

Pour ingredients into a mixing glass
with ice. Stir. Strain into an old-
fashioned glass filled with ice. Add a
twist of orange.

Fallen Angel

5cl gin
1.5cl fresh lime juice
2 dashes green crème de menthe
2 dashes Angostura bitters

Shake ingredients with ice. Strain into
a cocktail glass.

Ferrari

2.5cl amaretto
5cl dry vermouth

Pour the amaretto into an old-
fashioned glass filled with ice, then
add the vermouth. Stir.

Fernet

2.5cl brandy
2.5cl Fernet Branca
dash Angostura bitters
2 dashes gomme syrup

Pour ingredients into a mixing glass
with ice. Stir. Strain into a cocktail
glass. Add a twist of lemon peel.

Femme Fatale

5cl vodka
2cl crème de framboise
1.5cl fresh lemon juice
1.5cl fresh orange juice
1 teaspoon clear honey
handful fresh raspberries

Shake ingredients with ice. Strain into
a cocktail glass. Garnish with 2
raspberries and a small sprig of mint
on a cocktail stick across the glass.

Fig Supreme

5cl Jose Cuervo aged tequila
1.5cl fresh lime juice
1.5cl Grand Marnier liqueur
dash grenadine
1 ripe, dark fig, peeled and diced

Shake ingredients with ice. Strain into
a cocktail glass, letting some ice cubes
fall into the glass. Garnish with a
wedge of fresh fig.

French Connection

5cl brandy
2.5cl amaretto

Build into ice-filled old-fashioned
glass.

French Kiss

5cl vodka
1.5cl crème de framboise
1.5cl white crème de cacao
1cl fresh double cream

Shake ingredients with ice. Strain into
a cocktail glass.

Frosty Dawn

5cl white rum
2.5cl maraschino liqueur
1.5cl falernum syrup
5cl fresh orange juice

Shake ingredients with ice. Strain into
an old-fashioned glass with ice.
Garnish with a cherry and a slice of
orange.

Fuzzy Navel

2.5cl vodka
2.5cl peach schnapps
15cl fresh orange juice

Shake ingredients with ice. Strain into a highball filled with ice. Garnish with a slice of orange and a cherry. Serve with a straw and a stirrer.

G

Garlic Affair

2.5cl cognac
1.5cl apricot brandy
1.5cl lemon juice
1 piece fresh garlic
ginger beer

Shake ingredients, except ginger beer, with ice. Strain into a highball glass filled with ice. Top up with ginger beer. Garnish with a wedge of lime.

Gimlet

5cl Plymouth gin
2cl Rose's lime cordial
soda water (optional)

Pour ingredients into an old-fashioned glass filled with ice. Stir. Add soda if required. Garnish with a wedge of lime in the drink.

Gin and It

4cl gin
4cl sweet vermouth

Build in a cocktail glass. Stir. Add a cherry and a twist of orange.

Godfather

5cl Scotch or bourbon whiskey
2.5 amaretto

Build in an old-fashioned glass filled with ice.

Godfrey

5cl cognac
1.5cl Grand Marnier liqueur
1.5cl crème de mûre
4 blackberries
1.5cl fresh lemon juice

Shake ingredients with ice. Strain into an old-fashioned glass with ice. Garnish with a blackberry and mint .

Godmother

5cl vodka
2.5cl amaretto

Build in an old-fashioned glass.

Golden Cadillac

2.5cl Galliano
2.5cl white crème de cacao
2.5cl fresh double cream

Shake ingredients with ice. Strain into a cocktail glass.

Golden Dawn

2cl gin
2cl apricot brandy
2cl calvados
2cl fresh orange juice
dash grenadine

Shake ingredients, except grenadine, with ice. Strain into a cocktail glass. Add the grenadine to create a sunrise effect.

Golden Dream

2.5cl Galliano
1.5cl Cointreau
1.5cl fresh orange juice
1.5cl fresh double cream

Shake ingredients with ice. Strain into a cocktail glass..

Golden Slipper

2.5cl yellow Chartreuse
2.5cl apricot brandy
1 egg yolk

Shake ingredients with ice. Strain into a cocktail glass.

Grasshopper

2.5cl green crème de menthe
2.5cl white crème de cacao
2.5cl fresh double cream

Shake ingredients with ice. Strain into a cocktail glass.

Green Dragon

2.5cl gin
2cl Kûmmel
2cl green crème de menthe
2cl fresh lemon juice
4 dashes peach bitters

Shake ingredients with ice. Strain into a cocktail glass.

H

Harvey Wallbanger

5cl vodka
15cl fresh orange juice
2cl Galliano

Pour the vodka and orange juice into a highball filled with ice. Stir. Float the Galliano over a barspoon. Garnish with a slice of orange. Serve with a straw and a stirrer.

Hendrick's Cucumber Collins

5cl Hendrick's gin
2cl elderflower cordial
1cl fresh lemon juice
handful diced cucumber
soda water

Muddle ingredients, except soda, in a shaker. Strain into a Collins glass filled with ice. Top up with soda. Stir. Garnish with a strip of cucumber.

Honeymoon

2.5cl applejack brandy
2.5cl Bénédictine
2.5cl fresh lemon juice
3 dashes orange curaçao

Shake ingredients with ice. Strain into a cocktail glass.

Hunter

5cl rye whiskey
2.5cl cherry brandy

Build in an old-fashioned glass with ice. Stir.

Howling Monkey

5cl Monkey Shoulder triple malt
1.5cl amaretto
dash absinthe
dash Peychaud bitters
a quarter of orange
3 fresh mint leaves
1 sugar cube

Place the mint in an old-fashioned
glass with the sugar cube. Soak with
the bitters. Squeeze the orange into
the glass. Muddle until the sugar
dissolves. Add the remaining
ingredients. Stir. Add crushed ice and
stirl. Garnish with a twist of orange.

Hurricane Marilyn

2cl Pusser rum
2cl white rum
1cl Canadian whisky
1cl Cointreau
7cl cranberry juice
7cl guava juice
2cl fresh lemon juice
2 dashes grenadine

Shake ingredients with ice. Strain into
a highball filled with ice. Garnish with
a sprig of mint set in the top of a
strawberry, and a slice of kiwifruit.

I

Incognito

4cl brandy
2cl Lillet
2cl apricot brandy
dash Angostura bitters

Pour ingredients into a mixing glass
with ice. Stir. Pour into a cocktail
glass. Garnish with a twist of orange.

Ink Street

4cl rye whiskey
2cl fresh lemon juice
2cl orange juice

Shake ingredients with ice. Strain into
a cocktail glass.

Inspiration

4cl gin
2cl dry vermouth
1.5cl calvados
1.5cl Grand Marnier liqueur

Pour ingredients into a mixing glass
with ice. Stir. Pour into a cocktail
glass. Garnish with a cherry.

Irish Nut

2.5 Irish whiskey
2.5cl Baileys Irish Cream
2.5cl Frangelico

Build in an old-fashioned glass filled
with ice.

Island Fantasy

5cl 42 Below feijoa vodka
7.5cl apple juice
2.5cl pear purée
1.5cl elderflower cordial
1.5cl fresh lime juice
few leaves fresh coriander

Shake ingredients with ice. Strain into
a highball glass filled with ice.
Garnish with a wedge of lime and
coriander leaves.

Jack-in-the-Box

4cl applejack brandy
4cl pineapple juice
dash Angostura bitters

Shake ingredients with ice. Strain into a cocktail glass.

Jack Rose

5cl applejack brandy
1cl grenadine
2cl fresh lime juice
dash gomme syrup

Frost the rim of a cocktail glass with sugar. Shake ingredients with ice. Strain into the glass.

Japanese Slipper

2.5cl Midori melon liqueur
2.5cl Cointreau
2.5cl fresh lemon juice

Shake ingredients with ice. Strain into a cocktail glass. Garnish with a small slice of melon.

Josie

dash honey-flavoured vodka
4 basil leaves
4cl Hendrick's gin
2.5cl raspberry purée
dash champagne

Add the basil into a shaker with ice. Add the remaining ingredients, except champagne. Shake. Strain into a cocktail glass. Float the champagne on top. Garnish with a leaf of basil.

Journalist

5cl gin
1cl sweet vermouth
1cl dry vermouth
dash Cointreau
dash fresh fresh lemon juice
2 drops Angostura bitters

Shake ingredients with ice. Strain into a cocktail glass. Garnish with a twist of orange.

Kamikaze

2.5cl vodka
2.5cl Cointreau
2.5cl fresh lime juice

Shake ingredients with ice. Strain into a cocktail glass. Garnish with a twist of lemon.

Kentucky Sunset

4cl bourbon whiskey
1.5cl Strega liqueur
1.5cl anisette

Pour ingredients into a mixing glass with ice. Stir. Strain into a cocktail glass. Add a twist of orange.

King Alfonse

4cl Kahlua
2cl fresh double cream

Pour Kahlua into a liqueur glass. Float the cream on top.

Kir

1.5cl crème de cassis
dry white wine (originally
  Bourgogne Aligoté)

Pour the crème de cassis into a wine
goblet. Top up with dry white wine.

Knickerbocker Special

5cl white rum
1.5cl raspberry syrup
dash fresh lemon juice
dash fresh orange juice
1.5cl orange curaçao

Shake ingredients with ice. Strain into
a highball filled with ice. Garnish with
a wedge of pineapple.

L

Liberty

4cl applejack brandy
2cl white rum
dash gomme syrup

Pour ingredients into a mixing glass
with ice. Stir. Strain into a cocktail
glass.

London Fog

2.5cl white crème de menthe
2.5cl anisette
dash Angostura bitters

Shake ingredients with ice. Strain into
a cocktail glass.

Long Island Iced Tea

1cl light rum
1cl vodka
1cl gin
1cl tequila
1cl Cointreau
2cl fresh lime juice cola, chilled

Shake ingredients, except cola, with
ice. Strain into a highball filled with
ice. Top up with cola. Garnish with a
wedge of lime. Serve with a straw and
a stirrer.

M

Maestro

4cl Stolichnaya vodka
2cl fraise liqueur
half teaspoon maple syrup
half teaspoon 8-year-old balsamic
  vinegar
dash fresh lemon juice

Shake ingredients with ice. Strain into
a cocktail glass. Garnish with half a
strawberry and a mint leaf and a drop
of balsamic vinegar placed on the rim.

Magic Trace

4cl bourbon whiskey
2cl Drambuie
1.5cl dry vermouth
1.5cl fresh orange juice
1.5cl fresh lemon juice

Shake ingredients with ice. Strain into
a cocktail glass. Garnish with a twist
of orange.

Maiden's Prayer

2.5cl gin
2.5cl Cointreau
1.5cl fresh orange juice
1.5cl fresh lemon juice

Shake ingredients with ice. Strain into
a cocktail glass. Garnish with a twist
of orange.

Mainbrace

2.5cl gin
2.5cl Cointreau
2.5cl grapefruit juice

Shake ingredients with ice. Strain into
a cocktail glass. Garnish with a twist
of grapefruit.

Mai Tai

2cl dark rum
2cl golden rum
1cl Cointreau
1cl orgeat syrup
2cl fresh lime juice
3 dashes grenadine

Shake ingredients with ice. Strain into
a goblet. Garnish with a wedge of
lime. Serve with a straw and a stirrer.

Mallorca

4cl white rum
1.5cl dry vermouth
1.5cl crème de banane
1.5cl Drambuie

Shake ingredients with ice. Strain into
a cocktail glass. Garnish with a cherry.

Manhattan

5cl Canadian Club whisky
2cl sweet vermouth
dash Angostura bitters

Pour ingredients into a mixing glass
filled with ice and stir quickly. Strain
into a chilled cocktail glass. Drop a
cherry into the drink.

Dry Manhattan

5cl Canadian Club whisky
2cl dry vermouth
dash Angostura bitters

As above. Garnish with a twist of
lemon peel.

Perfect Manhattan

5cl Canadian Club whisky
1.5cl dry vermouth
1.5cl sweet vermouth
dash Angostura bitters

As above. Garnish with a twist of
lemon and a cherry dropped in the
drink.

Maple Leaf

5cl bourbon whiskey
2cl fresh lemon juice
1 barspoon maple syrup

Shake ingredients with ice. Strain into
a cocktail glass.

Margarita

2.5cl silver tequila
2.5cl fresh lime juice
2cl Cointreau

Rub a wedge of lime around the rim of a Margarita glass. Dip it into a saucer of fine salt. Shake ingredients with ice. Strain into the glass. Garnish with a wedge of lime.

Marked Man

4cl Maker's Mark
1.5cl Campari
1.5cl limoncello
2cl fresh orange juice
4 to 6 mint leaves
2 thin slices fresh ginger

Muddle the ginger in the bottom of a shaker. Add remaining ingredients. Add ice. Shake sharply to break down the mint leaves into tiny pieces. Strain into a cocktail glass.

Martell XO & Champagne

2cl Martell XO cognac
Angostura bitters
sugar cube
champagne

Put the sugar cube in a champagne flute and soak withthe bitters. Add the cognac and fill the glass with champagne.

Mary Pickford

4cl white rum
4cl unsweetened pineapple juice
1 barspoon grenadine
dash maraschino liqueur

Shake ingredients with ice. Strain into a cocktail glass. Garnish with a cherry.

Meg's Mania

5cl vodka
1cl saké
1cl cranberry juice
1cl fresh lime juice
champagne

Shake ingredients, except champagne, with ice. Strain into a champagne flute. Fill with champagne. Stir. Add a lime spiral.

Mellow Yellow

4cl gin
2cl limoncello
2 scoops lemon sorbet
1.5cl fresh lemon juice
0.5cl coriander syrup

Place ingredients into a shaker with 3 or 4 ice cubes — enough ice to break down the sorbet mix. Shake quickly. Strain into a cocktail glass. Garnish with a fresh coriander leaf.

Melon Ball

2.5cl vodka
2.5cl Midori melon liqueur
10cl pineapple juice

Shake ingredients with ice. Strain into a highball filled with ice. Garnish with a few melon balls in the drink.

Melon Moment

2.5cl Havana rum
2cl crema de melone
2cl Aperol
dash gomme syrup

Shake ingredients with ice. Strain into a cocktail glass. Garnish with a physalis.

Millionaire No. 2

5cl rye whiskey
1.5cl Cointreau
1 teaspoon pasteurized egg white
dash pastis

Shake ingredients with ice. Strain into a cocktail glass.

Mocha Mint

2.5cl Kahlua
2.5cl white crème de menthe
2.5cl white crème de cacao

Shake ingredients with ice. Strain into an old-fashioned glass filled with ice.

Mona Lisa Smile

2.5cl fresh peach purée
2.5cl fresh raspberry purée
2cl Cointreau
champagne

Shake ingredients, except champagne, with ice. Strain into a champagne flute. Fill with champagne. Garnish with 2 raspberries and a mint leaf.

Monkey Gland

4cl gin
2.5cl orange juice
2 dashes pastis
2 dashes grenadine

Shake ingredients with ice. Strain into a cocktail glass.

Morning Glory

5cl brandy
2cl orange curaçao
2cl fresh lemon juice
8 dashes pastis
4 dashes Angostura bitters

Shake ingredients with ice. Strain into a cocktail glass. Garnish with a twist of lemon.

Moscow Mule

5cl vodka
1cl fresh lime juice
ginger beer

Pour the vodka and the lime juice into a highball filled with ice. Top up with ginger beer. Stir. Garnish with a wedge of lime. Serve with a stirrer.

Moulin Magic

2cl brandy
12cl pineapple juice
prosecco

Shake the brandy and pineapple juice with ice. Strain into a highball filled with ice. Top up with prosecco. Stir. Garnish with a stem of redcurrants.

Naked Lady

2.5cl white rum
2.5cl apricot brandy
1.5cl fresh lemon juice
dash grenadine

Shake ingredients with ice. Strain into a cocktail glass. Garnish with a cherry.

Naked New York

9cl vodka
1cl dry vermouth
few green pitted olives
slice of blue cheese

Pour ingredients, except olives and blue cheese, into a mixing glass. Stir. Strain into a cocktail glass. Stuff the olives with blue cheese and drop in.

Negroni

2.5cl Campari
2.5cl gin
2.5cl sweet vermouth
soda water (optional)

Pour ingredients into an old-fashioned glass filled with ice. Stir. Drop in a slice of orange. Serve with a stirrer.

Negroni Twist

2.5cl Campari
2.5cl Cinzano Rosso vermouth
2.5cl Martin Miller's gin
1.5cl rhubarb syrup

Build ingredients in an old-fashioned glass with ice. Garnish with a twist of orange and a twist of lemon.

Old Fashioned

5cl Bourbon whiskey
1 sugar cube
2 to 3 dashes Angostura bitters
dash soda water

Place the sugar cube in an old-fashioned glass. Soak with the bitters. Add soda water. Muddle. Add the whiskey. Garnish with a slice of orange, and a cherry. Serve with a stirrer.

Old Nick

5cl rye whiskey
1.5cl Drambuie
1.5cl fresh orange juice
dash fresh lemon juice
dash orange bitters

Shake ingredients with ice. Strain into a cocktail glass. Garnish with a cherry.

Old Pal

2.5cl rye whiskey
2.5cl dry vermouth
2.5cl Campari

Pour ingredients into a mixing glass with ice. Stir. Strain into a cocktail glass. Garnish with a twist of orange.

Orange Blossom Special

5cl gin
1.5cl Cointreau
1.5cl lychee liqueur
1cl fresh lemon juice

Shake ingredients with ice. Strain into a cocktail glass. Garnish with a fresh lychee.

Orgasm

2.5cl Cointreau
2.5cl Baileys Irish Cream

Pour ingredients into an old-fashioned glass filled with ice. Garnish with a cherry (optional).

Oriental Martini

5cl vodka
2cl sake
2cl yuzu (a Japanese lime) juice
few slices fresh ginger root

Muddle the ginger root in a shaker. Add remaining ingredients. Shake. Strain into a cocktail glass. Drop a few slices of ginger in the drink.

P

Palm Breeze

2.5cl dark rum
1.5cl yellow Chartreuse
1.5cl browncrème de cacao
dash grenadine
1.5cl fresh lime juice

Shake ingredients with ice. Strain into a cocktail glass.

Parade

5cl vodka
1.5cl fraise de bois
1.5cl Campari
1.5cl sweet vermouth

Pour ingredients into a mixing glass with ice. Stir. Strain into a cocktail glass. Garnish with a twist of orange.

Paradise

5cl golden rum
2.5cl Cointreau
dash pineapple juice
dash papaya juice
dash lime juice

Shake ingredients with ice. Strain into a cocktail glass. Add a pineapple wedge.

Perfect Lady

5cl gin
1.5cl peach schnapps
1.5cl fresh lemon juice
1 teaspoon pasteurized egg white

Shake ingredients with ice. Strain into a cocktail glass.

Petite Fleur

5cl white rum
1.5cl Cointreau
2.5cl fresh grapefruit juice

Shake ingredients with ice. Strain into a cocktail glass. Garnish with a twist of grapefruit.

Picca

2.5cl Scotch whisky
1.5cl Galliano
1.5cl Punt-e-Mes

Pour ingredients into a mixing glass with ice. Stir. Strain into an old-fashioned glass filled with ice. Decorate with a cherry.

Pimm's No. 1 Cup

5cl Pimm's No. 1 Cup
sparkling lemonade or ginger ale
few slices lemon
few slices orange
few strips cucumber peel
sprig fresh mint

Pour the Pimm's into a highball filled with ice. Top up with sparkling lemonade or ginger ale. Add the fruit, cucumber and mint. Stir. Garnish with a slice of lemon and orange, the peel of a cucumber, and a sprig of fresh mint in the glass. Serve with a straw.

Pink Gin

5cl gin
2 dashes Angostura bitters

Pour the gin and bitters into a mixing glass with ice. Stir with a barspoon. Strain into a cocktail glass.

Pink Lady

5cl Plymouth gin
2cl fresh lemon juice
1 to 2 dashes grenadine
1 teaspoon pasteurized egg white

Shake ingredients with ice. Strain into a cocktail glass. Garnish with a cherry dropped in the drink.

Pink Squirrel

2.5cl crème de Noyeau
2.5cl white crème de cacao
2.5cl fresh double cream

Frost the rim of a cocktail glass with sugar. Shake ingredients with ice. Strain into the glass. Garnish with a cherry.

Pisco Sour

5cl pisco
2cl fresh lime juice
dash pasteurized egg white
2 dashes Angostura bitters
dash gomme syrup

Shake ingredients with ice. Strain into a cocktail glass. Garnish with a wedge of lime.

Prince Charles

2.5cl cognac
2.5cl Drambuie
2.5cl fresh lemon juice

Shake ingredients with ice. Strain into a cocktail glass.

Q

Quarter Deck

5cl dark rum
1.5cl dry sherry
1.5cl lime juice cordial

Pour ingredients into a mixing glass. Stir. Strain into an old-fashioned glass with ice. Garnish with a wedge of lime.

Quiet Sunday

2.5cl vodka
1.5cl amaretto
12cl fresh orange juice
few dashes grenadine

Shake ingredients, except grenadine, with ice. Strain into a highball filled with ice. Add a few dashes grenadine.

Red Earl

5cl vodka
2 to 3 slices fresh ginger root
handful fresh raspberries
2cl limoncello

Muddle the ginger root in a shaker.
Add the raspberries, limoncello and
the vodka. Add ice cubes. Shake.
Strain into a goblet. Garnish with 2
raspberries and a sprig of mint.

Rhuby

5cl Sagatiba Pura white cachaça
2.5cl rhubarb syrup
1.5cl fresh lime juice

Frost the rim of a cocktail glass with
salt. Shake ingredients with ice. Strain
into the cocktail glass. Garnish with a
wedge of lime on the rim.

Road Runner

4cl vodka
2cl amaretto
2cl coconut milk

Shake ingredients with ice. Strain into
a cocktail glass.

Rob Roy

5cl Scotch whisky
2.5cl sweet vermouth
dash Angostura bitters

Pour ingredients into a mixing glass
with ice. Stir. Strain into a Martini
glass. Garnish with a cherry.

Roberta

2.5cl vodka
2.5cl dry vermouth
2.5cl cherry brandy
dash Campari
dash crème de banane

Shake ingredients with ice. Strain into
an old-fashioned glass filled with ice.
Garnish with a twist of orange.

Rolls-Royce

2.5cl brandy
2.5cl Cointreau
2.5cl fresh orange juice

Shake ingredients with ice. Strain into
a cocktail glass. Garnish with a cherry.

Rose

2.5cl kirsch
2.5cl dry vermouth
1 barspoon rose syrup

Pour ingredients into a mixing glass
with ice. Stir. Strain into a small
cocktail or liqueur glass. Add a cherry.

Rum Cooler

5cl white rum
2.5cl Galliano
1.5cl fresh lime juice

Shake ingredients with ice. Strain into
an old-fashioned glass with ice.
Garnish with a wedge of lime.

Russian Summer

5cl Sputnik Basil vodka
2 to 3 fresh basil leaves
6 to 8 fresh strawberries
1.25cl strawberry purée
twist black pepper
dash fresh lemon juice
dash gomme syrup

Shake ingredients with ice. Double strain into a highball filed with ice. Garnish with a strawberry coated in ground pepper and a twist of lemon.

Rusty Nail

5cl Scotch whisky
2.5cl Drambuie

Pour the whisky into an old-fashioned glass with ice. Add the Drambuie and stir. Garnish with a twist of lemon.

S

Sal's Sinner

2cl cognac
2cl green crème de menthe
2cl white crème de cacao
2cl fresh double cream
2 dashes Tabasco sauce

Pour the crème de menthe and white crème de cacao into a mixing glass with ice. Stir. Strain into the cocktail glass. Pour the cream and cognac into a shaker with ice. Shake. Float this mixture over the back of a barspoon to lay it on top of the green mixture. Add the Tabasco sauce. Garnish with a slim chocolate mint stick.

Salome

2.5cl gin
2.5cl Dubonnet
2.5cl dry vermouth

Pour ingredients into a mixing glass filled with ice. Stir. Serve in a cocktail glass. Add a twist of lemon.

Salty Dog

5cl vodka
10cl fresh grapefruit juice

Frost the rim of a highball glass with salt. Fill the glass with ice. Add ingredients. Stir.

Sapphire Cosmopolitan

5cl Bombay Sapphire gin
2.5cl triple sec/Cointreau
5cl cranberry juice
squeeze fresh lime juice

Shake ingredients with ice. Double strain into a cocktail glass. Garnish with a flaming twist of orange.

Sapphire Rose

5cl Bombay Sapphire gin
2.5cl maraschino liqueur
juice half fresh grapefruit
dash gomme syrup

Shake ingredients with ice. Double strain into a cocktail glass. Garnish with a twist of grapefruit.

Sazerac

5cl bourbon whiskey
1cl Pernod
dash Peychaud bitters
dash Angostura bitters
1 white sugar cube
dash soda water

Place a sugar cube in an old-fashioned glass and soak with the bitters. Add enough soda to cover the sugar and crush with the back of a barspoon. Add the bourbon. Stir. Float the Pernod over. Garnish with a twist of lemon.

Screaming Orgasm

2cl vodka
2cl Kahlua
2cl amaretto
2cl Baileys Irish Cream

Shake ingredients with ice. Strain into an old-fashioned glass filled with ice.

Screwdriver

5cl vodka
12cl fresh orange juice

Pour the vodka into a highball filled with ice. Add the orange juice. Stir. Garnish with a slice of orange. Serve with a stirrer.

Sea Breeze

5cl vodka
10cl cranberry juice
5cl fresh grapefruit juice

Pour the ingredients into a highball filled with ice. Stir. Garnish with a wedge of lime. Serve with a stirrer.

Serenissima

2.5cl Campari
2.5cl vodka
2.5cl fresh grapefruit juice

Shake ingredients with ice. Strain into a cocktail glass. Garnish with a twist of orange.

Sex on the Beach

2.5cl vodka
1.5cl peach schnapps
1.5cl Chambord liqueur
5cl orange juice
5cl cranberry juice

Shake ingredients with ice. Strain into a highball filled with ice. Garnish with a slice of lime.

Shamrock

2.5cl Irish whiskey
2.5cl dry vermouth
1.5cl green Chartreuse
1.5cl green crème de menthe

Pour ingredients into a mixing glass with ice. Stir. Strain into a cocktail glass.

Sidecar

2.5cl brandy
2cl Cointreau
2cl fresh lemon juice

Shake ingredients with ice. Strain into a cocktail glass. Garnish with a cherry.

Silver Bullet

5cl vodka
2.5cl Kûmmel

Build in old-fashioned glass filled
with ice. Stir.

Silver Sunset

2.5cl vodka
1.5cl apricot brandy
1.5cl Campari
9cl fresh orange juice
1.5cl fresh lemon juice
1 teaspoon pasteurized egg white

Shake ingredients with ice. Strain into
a highball with ice. Garnish with a
slice of orange and a cherry. Serve
with a straw.

Sky Dog

4cl silver tequila
1.5cl Cointreau
1.5cl fresh lime juice
1.5cl cranberry juice
1.5cl pink grapefruit juice

Frost the rim of a Margarita glass with
salt. Shake ingredients with ice. Strain
into the glass. Garnish with a wedge
of lime.

Slipstream

1.5cl brandy
1.5cl Grand Marnier liqueur
1.5cl Lillet
1.5cl orange juice
2 dashes Angostura bitters
dash pasteurized egg white

Shake ingredients with ice. Strain into
a cocktail glass.

Sloe Comfortable Screw

2.5cl vodka
1.5cl sloe gin
1.5cl Southern Comfort
12cl fresh orange juice

Shake ingredients with ice. Strain into
a highball glass filled with ice.
Garnish with a slice of orange.

Sloe Comfortable Screw Against the Wall

2.5cl vodka
1.5cl sloe gin
1.5cl Southern Comfort
12cl fresh orange juice
dash Galliano

Shake ingredients with ice. Strain into
a highball filled with ice. Garnish with
a slice of orange.

Spicy Fifty

5cl Stolychnaya vanilla vodka
1.5cl elderflower cordial
1.5cl fresh lime juice
1 teaspoon honey
2 to 3 thin slices fresh red chilli

Muddle the chilli in the bottom of a
shaker. Add ice, then the remaining
ingredients. Shake. Strain into a
cocktail glass. Garnish with a small
red chilli placed on the rim of the
glass.

Sputnik Satellite

5cl Sputnik rose petal vodka
2.5cl fresh pear purée
2.5cl clear apple juice

Shake ingredients with ice. Strain into a cocktail glass. Garnish with a thin slice of pear.

Sputnik Siberian Sling

5cl Sputnik basil vodka
1.5cl Grand Marnier liqueur
2.5cl fresh lime juice
dash gomme syrup
2 to 4 basil leaves

Shake ingredients with ice. Strain into a highball filled with ice.

Stinger

5cl brandy
2.5cl white crème de menthe

Shake ingredients with ice. Strain into a cocktail glass.

Summer Scene

4cl white rum
1cl blue curaçao
7cl mango juice
7cl pineapple juice
2cl Rose's lime cordial
1cl fresh lemon juice

Pour the pineapple, mango and lemon juices and lime cordial into a highball filled with ice. Stir until a coral color develops. In a mixing glass, pour the white rum and blue curaçao and stir. Pour this over a barspoon so it floats on the fruit juices. Garnish with a slice of star fruit on the rim. Serve with a stirrer and 2 straws.

Sweet Sue

2.5cl cognac
1.5cl Kahlua
1.5cl Frangelico
1.5cl limoncello
1.5cl fresh double cream

Pour the cognac, Kahlua, and Frangelico into a mixing glass with ice. Stir quickly. Strain into a cocktail glass. Pour the limoncello and cream into the shaker. Shake. Float this creamy mixture over a barspoon to create a layer over the cognac mixture. Using a peeler, grate shavings of semisweet or milk chocolate directly over the glass onto the creamy layer.

Sweet Yaisa

4cl cachaça
1cl Grand Marnier liqueur
7cl raspberry purée
5cl apple juice
dash passionfruit syrup

Shake ingredients with ice. Strain into a highball filled with ice. Garnish with an apple fan.

Tamarillo Martini

4cl vodka
1.5cl Cointreau
1 fresh tamarillo, diced
1.5cl cranberry juice

Shake ingredients with ice. Strain into a cocktail glass. Garnish with a thin wedge of tamarillo.

Tango

5cl vodka
1.5cl sweet vermouth
1.5cl dry vermouth
dash orange curaçao
dash orange juice

Frost the rim of a cocktail glass. Shake ingredients with ice. Strain into the glass. Add a twist of orange.

Temptation

5cl rye whiskey
1.5cl orange curaçao
dash Pernod
2.5cl Dubonnet

Shake ingredients with ice. Strain into a cocktail glass. Add a twist each of orange peel and lemon peel.

Tequila Sunrise

5cl tequila
15cl fresh orange juice
2 dashes grenadine

Pour the tequila and orange juice into a highball filled with ice. Stir. Add the grenadine slowly to trickle down through the drink. Stir just before drinking to create a sunrise effect. Garnish with a slice of orange in a spiral. Serve with a straw and a stirrer.

The Clubman

2.5cl Irish Mist
12cl orange juice
dash pasteurized egg white
dash blue curaçao

Shake ingredients with ice. Strain into a highball filled with ice. Trickle blue curaçao down inside the glass.

Three Miler

5cl brandy
2.5cl rum
dash fresh lemon juice
2 dashes grenadine

Shake ingredients with ice. Strain into a cocktail glass.

Tidal Wave

2.5cl spiced rum
5cl Grand Marnier liqueur
2.5cl Mandarine Napoléon
dash fresh lemon juice
bitter lemon

Shake ingredients, except bitter lemon, with ice. Strain into a highball filled with ice. Top up with bitter lemon. Garnish with a wedge of lemon.

Tropical Dawn

2.5cl gin
2cl Campari
5cl fresh orange juice

Shake ingredients with ice. Strain into
an old-fashioned glass filled with
crushed ice. Serve with short straws.

Tropical Spice

4cl gold rum
2cl Cointreau
4cl fresh orange juice
4cl papaya juice
2cl fresh lime juice

Shake ingredients with ice. Strain into
a goblet filled with ice. Garnish with a
slice of orange, lime and a cherry.
Serve with a straw.

V

Vampiro

5cl silver tequila
7cl tomato juice
2.5cl fresh orange juice
1 teaspoon clear honey
1cl fresh lime juice
half slice onion, finely chopped
few slices fresh red hot chilli
few drops Worcestershire sauce
salt

Pour ingredients, starting with the
juices and then the tequila, into a
shaker with ice. Shake. Strain into a
highball filled with ice. Garnish with a
wedge of lime on the rim of the glass
and a slice of chilli.

Va-Va-Voom

5cl Kremlyovska vodka
1.5cl passionfruit syrup
10cl apple juice
1.5cl fresh lime juice
1 teaspoon honey
6 fresh mint leaves

Shake ingredients with ice. Strain into
a highball filled with crushed ice.
Garnish with a wedge of apple and a
sprig of mint on the rim. Serve with a
straw.

Velvet Hammer

2.5cl Tia Maria
2.5cl Cointreau
2.5cl fresh double cream

Shake ingredients with ice. Strain into
a cocktail glass.

Venetian Sunset

5cl dry gin
1.5cl Grand Marnier liqueur
1.5cl Campari
1.5cl dry vermouth

Pour ingredients into a shaker with
ice. Strain into a cocktail glass. Add a
cherry.

Vesper

5cl gin
2.5cl vodka
1cl Lillet

Shake ingredients with ice. Strain into
a cocktail glass. Garnish with a twist
of orange.

Vodka Gimlet

5cl vodka
2cl Rose's lime cordial

Pour the vodka into an old-fashioned
glass with ice. Add the cordial. Stir.
Garnish with a wedge of lime.

Ward Eight

5cl bourbon whiskey
1.5cl fresh lemon juice
1.5cl fresh orange juice
dash grenadine
dash gomme syrup

Shake ingredients with ice. Strain into
a cocktail glass.

White Lady

2.5cl gin
2.5cl Cointreau
2.5cl fresh lemon juice

Shake ingredients with ice. Strain into
a cocktail glass.

White Russian

4cl vodka
2cl Kahlua
2cl lightly whipped cream

Pour the vodka and the Kahlua into
an old-fashioned glass filled with ice.
Stir. Float the whipped cream over the
top of the drink. Serve with a stirrer.

Yellow Bird

2.5cl light rum
1.5cl Cointreau
1.5cl Galliano
1.5cl fresh lime juice

Shake ingredients with ice. Strain into
a cocktail glass. Garnish with a spiral
of lime on the rim and a slice of
orange in the drink.

Zombie

1.5cl white rum
1.5cl golden rum
1.5cl dark rum
1cl cherry brandy
1cl apricot brandy
5cl pineapple juice
2.5cl fresh orange juice
1cl fresh lime juice
dash orgeat syrup
dash 151 proof Demerara rum

Shake ingredients, except Demerara
rum, with ice. Strain into a highball
filled with crushed ice. Float the
Demerara rum on top. Garnish with a
slice of orange, a slice of lime and a
sprig of mint. Serve with a straw and
a stirrer.

CLASSIC STYLES

The liquidizer is now standard equipment in cocktail bars, for it increases the variety of drinks the bartender can offer his or her customers and enables him or her to meet the demand for a wide range of long drinks. The actual liquidizing, or blending, time is short and, if preparation is done in advance, blended drinks can be made in multiples very quickly. Certain machines have toughened blades to cope with cubed ice, but crushed ice is preferable because it saves on wear and tear and keeps blending time to a minimum. Overblending will result in a diluted, thin-bodied drink. Presentation of blended drinks offers much scope; a variety of glassware and garnishes can be used, including novelty containers such as coconut and pineapple shells. All blended drinks should be served with thick straws.

Blue Hawaiian

2.5cl light rum
1.5cl blue curaçao
6cl pineapple juice
2.5cl coconut cream
1 scoop crushed ice

Blend. Pour into a large-bowled glass.

Caribbean Dawn

2.5cl coconut liqueur
1.5cl Jose Cuervo tequila
1 scoop strawberry ice cream
dash fraise syrup

Blend ingredients with a little crushed ice. Pour into a large wine glass. Garnish with a strawberry.

Casablanca

5cl light rum
7.5cl pineapple juice
2.5cl coconut cream
1 dash grenadine

Blend ingredients with a scoop of crushed ice. Pour into a large wine glass. Garnish with a slice of pineapple and a cherry.

Chi Chi

5cl vodka
12cl coconut cream
12cl unsweetened pineapple juice

Blend with 2 scoops of crushed ice. Serve in a large glass. Garnish with a slice of pineapple and a cherry. Serve with straws.

Chinatown

5cl gin
1.5cl kirsch
4 stoned lychees

Blend ingredients with a scoop of crushed ice. Pour into a highball filled with ice. Garnish with a lychee.

Pina Colada

5cl light rum
6cl pineapple juice
2.5cl coconut cream
2 scoops crushed ice

Blend. Pour into a large-bowled glass.
Garnish with a slice of pineapple and
a cherry. Serve with short straws.

Scorpion

5cl golden rum
2.5cl fresh orange juice
2.5cl fresh lemon juice
1.5cl brandy
2 dashes orgeat syrup

Blend with a scoop of crushed ice.
Pour into a large old-fashioned glass
filled with ice. Garnish with a slice of
orange and mint. Serve with straws.

CHAMPAGNE COCKTAILS

Alfonso

1 lump sugar
2 dashes Angostura bitters
2.5cl Dubonnet
champagne

Soak the sugar with the bitters in a
champagne flute. Add the Dubonnet.
Fill with champagne. Stir. Add a twist
of lemon.

Bellini

fresh peach juice
prosecco

Fill a champagne glass one-third full
with white peach juice. Fill with
champagne.

Black Velvet

1/2 chilled Guinness
1/2 chilled champagne

Build equal amounts of both
ingredients into a large beer glass.

Bucks Fizz

fresh orange juice
champagne

Fill a champagne glass one-third with
orange juice. Fill with champagne.

Champagne Cocktail

2cl cognac
2 dashes Angostura bitters
1 lump sugar
champagne

Place the sugar in a champagne flute,
saturate with bitters and add the
cognac. Fill with champagne. Stir.
Garnish with a slice of orange and a
cherry.

French 75

2cl gin
2cl fresh lemon juice
dash gomme syrup
champagne

Shake ingredients, except champagne,
with ice. Strain into a champagne
flute. Fill with champagne.

Kir Royale

2cl crème de cassis
champagne

Place the crème de cassis in a
champagne flute. Fill with
champagne. Stir gently.

Mimosa

6cl fresh orange juice
2 dashes Grand Marnier liqueur
champagne

Fill a champagne flute one-quarter full with orange juice. Add the Grand Marnier. Fill with champagne. Stir.

Spirit Cobblers

tequila, rum, whisky, brandy or gin
1 barspoon sugar
4 dashes orange curaçao

Fill a medium-sized wine glass with ice. Add the ingredients. Stir. Garnish with fruit. Add the sprig of mint.

COBBLERS

This drink of American origin is simple to make and attractive by virtue of its fruit and mint decoration. To make, fill a glass with ice and pour the ingredients over the top. Stir. Cobblers are usually served with straws.

Wine Cobblers

Burgundy, claret, port, Rhine wine
   or sherry
4 dashes orange curaçao
1 barspoon gomme syrup

Fill a wine glass with ice. Half-fill with the required wine. Add the curaçao and gomme syrup. Stir. Garnish with fruit. Add a sprig of fresh mint.

Previous page
Watermelon & Rosewater Martini. Made with Ketel One vodka with rose petals as a delicate decoration.
Opposite
Cuervo & Ginger. Tequila makes a long and refreshing drink when served with ginger ale over ice.

COLLINS

These are hot-weather drinks, long and refreshing, with plenty of ice. It is probable that the drinks originated in Britain. Supporting evidence is contained in Drinks of the World, published in 1892, in which John Collins, the head waiter at Limmer's, London, is immortalized in verse. The drink made by Mr Collins contained gin, soda, lemon and sugar. Among its relatives are the Gin Coolers and Gin Rickeys. Up to the late 1930s, a John C. was made with Dutch gin, and a Tom C. with 'Old Tom' gin. It is now accepted that a Tom C. is made with London Dry gin, and a John C. with whisky.

John Collins

5cl bourbon whiskey
2.5cl fresh lemon juice
1cl gomme syrup
soda water

Pour the ingredients into a highball filled with ice. Top up with soda water. Stir. Garnish with a slice of lemon. Serve with straws.

Tom Collins

AS JOHN COLLINS BUT SUBSTITUTING GIN FOR
WHISKY.

Brandy Rum or Whisky Collins

AS ABOVE, SUBSTITUTING AN ALTERNATIVE SPIRIT
FOR THE BOURBON.

COOLERS

These are almost identical to the
Collins but usually contain the
peel of the fruit cut into a spiral.

Apricot Cooler

2.5cl fresh lemon or lime juice
1 dash grenadine
5cl apricot brandy
1 dash Angostura bitters
soda water

Pour ingredients, except bitters and
soda water, into a shaker with ice.
Strain into a highball filled with ice.
Top up with soda water. Add the
bitters. Stir.

Harvard Cooler

2.5cl fresh lemon or lime juice
1cl gomme syrup
2.5cl applejack brandy
soda water

Pour ingredients, except the soda
water, into a shaker with ice. Strain
into a highball filled with ice. Top up
with soda water. Stir.

Limbo Cooler

2.5cl dark rum
1.5cl Amer Picon
2.5cl fresh lemon juice
1cl grenadine
slice of orange
7Up

Pour ingredients, except the 7Up, into
a shaker with ice and a slice of
orange. Strain into a large wine glass
filled with crushed ice. Stir in the 7Up.
Garnish with an orange slice, a cherry
and a stirrer.

Misty Cooler

2.5cl Irish Mist
2.5cl fresh lemon juice
1cl grenadine
dash pasteurized egg white
soda water

Pour ingredients, except the soda
water, into a shaker with ice. Strain
into a highball filled with ice. Top up
with soda water. Stir.

Rum Cooler

5cl dark rum
2.5cl fresh lemon or lime juice
1cl grenadine
soda water

Pour ingredients, except soda water,
into a shaker with ice. Strain into a
highball filled with ice. Top up with
soda water.

Shady Grove Cooler

5cl gin
1cl gomme syrup
2.5cl fresh lemon juice
ginger beer

Place the gomme syrup, fresh lemon juice and gin in a highball filled with ice, stirring continuously. Stir in the ginger beer.

Wine Cooler

10cl red or white wine
2.5cl grenadine
soda water

Pour the wine and grenadine into a highball filled with ice. Top up with soda water. Stir.

CRUSTAS

A crusta can be made with any spirit, the most popular being brandy. To prepare the glass, rub the rim of a large wine glass with a slice of lemon, dip the edge in powdered sugar, fit a spiral of orange into the glass and fill with cracked ice.

Brandy Crusta

1.5cl brandy
2.5cl orange curaçao
1.5cl maraschino liqueur
1.5cl fresh lemon juice

Shake or stir. Strain into the prepared glass. Add a cherry.

CUPS

Cups are of English origin, the most famous being the Stirrup Cup, served to members of a hunting party about to set off or to travellers in need of hasty refreshment. A special glass was used that had a long stem and a knob instead of a flat base, so that the contents – usually sloe gin – had to be finished before the glass could be put on the tray, upside down. The phrase 'in his cups' was a common euphemism meaning 'under the influence of alcohol'.

Today, cups are regarded as hot-weather drinks with a wine base. They are normally made in large quantities.

Champagne Cup 8-10 GLASSES

1 bottle champagne
11cl brandy
8.5cl orange curaçao
3cl maraschino liqueur

Stir ingredients together in a large jug or bowl. Add ice. Garnish with slices of fruit.

Claret Cup 14-16 GLASSES

2 bottles claret
85g sugar
14cl water
juice of 2 oranges
juice of 2 lemons
orange and lemon rind
soda water

Boil the sugar and water with the orange and lemon rind. Allow to cool. Add the fruit juices and claret. Keep refrigerated until ready to serve. Put ice in a large bowl, add the wine mixture and soda water. Float slices of cucumber, apple and orange and a sprig of mint on top.

Hock Sparkler 24-30 GLASSES

3 bottles hock
1 bottle sekt
6cl brandy
1 melon or other fresh fruit
sugar to taste

Cube the melon or slice the other fruit and place in a large bowl with the sugar and the still wine. Refrigerate for one hour, then add the sparkling wine and other ingredients just before serving. Serve slightly iced, garnished with more fruit.

Peace Cup 8-10 GLASSES

2 dozen strawberries
2 slices chopped fresh pineapple
2 tablespoons caster sugar
6cl water
6cl maraschino liqueur
1 bottle dry sparkling wine
soda water

Blend the fruit, sugar and water into a purée. Pour into a large jug with ice. Add the maraschino, wine and soda water. Stir well.

Pimm's No. 1

THE ORIGINAL AND BEST KNOWN OF THE CUPS MARKETED AS PIMM'S HAS A GIN BASE.
MAKES 1

5cl Pimm's No 1 Cup
7Up or ginger ale

Pour the Pimm's into a highball filled with ice. Top up with lemonade, ginger ale or 7Up. Garnish with slice of lemon or orange and rind of cucumber and mint.

NOTE: THERE IS ALSO A VODKA-BASED PIMM'S.

DAIQUIRIS

The origin of this drink is unknown but it was given this name early in the 1900s when American engineers were developing the Daiquiri iron mines in Cuba. As they emerged from the pits they were handed an iced drink made with rum, lime and sugar. Drink Daiquiris immediately as they separate if left to stand.

Daiquiri

5cl Bacardi light rum
2cl fresh lime juice
3 dashes gomme syrup

Shake ingredients with ice. Strain into a cocktail glass. Garnish with a wedge of lime.

Daiquiri Blossom

5cl light rum
2.5cl fresh orange juice
1 dash maraschino liqueur

Shake ingredients with ice. Strain into a cocktail glass. Garnish with a twist of orange.

Daiquiri Liberal

5cl Bacardi light rum
2.5cl sweet vermouth
1 dash Amer Picon

Pour ingredients into a mixing glass with ice. Stir. Strain into a cocktail glass.

Coconut Daiquiri

2.5cl light rum
2.5cl coconut liqueur
3cl fresh lime juice
1 dash pasteurized egg white

Shake ingredients with ice. Strain into a cocktail glass.

King's Daiquiri

5cl light rum
1.5cl Parfait Amour
1.5cl fresh lime juice
1cl gomme syrup
dash pasteurized egg white

Blend with crushed ice. Serve in a saucer-shaped glass.

FROZEN DAIQUIRIS

These blended variations of the Daiquiri cocktail are made with plenty of dry crushed ice. Made correctly, the finished drink should be of the consistency of sorbet and may be piled above the rim of a large goblet. By using fresh fruit and a complementary liqueur, a range of frozen-fruit daiquiris may be made.

Frozen Daiquiri

5cl Bacardi light rum
1.5cl maraschino liqueur
2.5cl fresh lime juice
dash gomme syrup

Blend on high speed with 2 scoops crushed ice. Pour unstrained into a large wine glass. Serve with short, thick straws.

Banana Daiquiri

5cl Bacardi light rum
2.5cl crème de banane
1.5cl fresh lime juice
half fresh banana

Prepare and serve as for Frozen
Daiquiri.

Strawberry Daiquiri

5cl Bacardi light rum
2.5cl fraise liqueur
1.5cl fresh lime juice
3 strawberries

Prepare and serve as for Frozen
Daiquiri. Garnish with a fresh
strawberry.

DAISIES

These may be made with any
spirit and are usually served in
tankards or wine glasses filled
with ice. They must be served
very cold. To reach this chilled
point requires vigorous shaking.

5cl desired spirit
2.5cl fresh lemon juice
1cl grenadine
soda water (optional)

Shake ingredients, except soda
water, with ice. Strain into the
glass. Add soda water if desired.
Garnish with sprigs of mint and
fruit.

Star Daisy

2.5cl gin
2cl calvados
1cl fresh lemon juice
1cl gomme syrup
1cl grenadine
soda water

Shake ingredients, except soda water,
with ice. Strain into the glass. Add the
soda water. Garnish with fruit.

EGG NOGGS

The traditional Christmas morning
drink, these may be made in bulk
and ladled into wine glassess at
time of serving, as long as the
proportions for individual drinks
are maintained. If you prefer a
thicker consistency, use more egg
yolk, and cream instead of milk.

Egg Nogg

1 free-range egg
1 tablespoon gomme syrup
2.5cl brandy
2.5cl dark rum
7.5cl milk

Shake ingredients, except milk, with
ice. Strain into a wine glass. Stir in
the milk. Sprinkle with nutmeg

Baltimore Egg Nogg

1 free-range egg
1cl gomme syrup
2.5cl brandy
1.5cl dark rum
2.5cl madeira
7.5cl milk

Shake ingredients, except milk, with ice. Strain into a goblet. Sprinkle with nutmeg.

Brandy Egg Nogg

5cl brandy
7.5cl milk
1cl gomme syrup
1 free-range egg yolk

Shake ingredients, except milk, with ice. Strain into a highball filled with ice. Stir in the milk. Sprinkle with nutmeg.

Breakfast Nogg

1 free-range egg
2.5cl orange curaçao
2.5cl brandy
7.5cl milk

Shake ingredients, except milk, with ice. Strain into a large wine glass. Stir in the milk. Sprinkle with nutmeg.

Rum Nogg

1 free-range egg
5cl dark rum
1cl gomme syrup
10cl milk

Shake ingredients, except milk, with ice. Strain into a wine glass. Stir in the milk. Sprinkle with nutmeg .

FIXES

A fix is a short drink made by pouring any spirit over crushed ice. It is usually garnished with fruit and served with short straws.

Brandy Fix

5cl brandy
1.5cl cherry brandy
2.5cl fresh lemon juice
1cl gomme syrup

Pour ingredients into a wine glass filled with crushed ice. Stir. Garnish with slices of lemon and orange, and a cherry. Serve with straws.

Gin Fix

5cl gin
2.5cl fresh lemon juice
dash gomme syrup

Pour ingredients into a large wine glass filled with crushed ice. Stir gently. Garnish with a slice of lemon. Serve with straws.

The Fizz is a cousin of the Collins, but is always shaken. It is served in a tall highball with ice, straws and a muddler, and should be drunk immediately.

Dubonnet Fizz

2.5cl Dubonnet
1.5cl cherry brandy
2.5cl fresh fresh lemon juice
2.5cl fresh orange juice
1 egg white
 soda water

Shake ingredients, except soda water, with ice. Strain into selected glass. Top up with soda water.

Gin Fizz

2.5cl gin
2.5cl fresh lemon juice
1 barspoon gomme syrup
soda water

Shake ingredients, except soda water, with ice. Strain into selected glass. Top up with soda water.

Morning Glory Fizz

5cl whisky
2.5cl fresh lemon juice
dash anisette
dash pasteurized egg white
1.5cl gomme syrup
soda water

Shake ingredients, except soda water, with ice. Strain into the selected glass. Top up with soda water.

New Orleans Fizz

5cl gin
1.5cl fresh lime juice
1.5cl fresh lemon juice
1.5cl gomme syrup
3 dashes orange flower water
1.5cl fresh double cream
soda water

Shake ingredients, except soda water, with ice. Strain into the selected glass. Top up with soda water.

Ramos Fizz

5cl gin
1cl fresh lime juice
1cl fresh lemon juice
3 dashes orange flower water
5cl fresh double cream
1 dash pasteurized egg white
dash gomme syrup
soda water (optional)

Shake ingredients, except soda water, with ice. Strain into the glass. Add soda water if desired. Garnish with a wedge of lime.

Royal Fizz

AS GIN FIZZ, USING A WHOLE EGG.

Silver Fizz

AS GIN FIZZ, USING EGG WHITE.

Flips belong to the same family of drinks as egg noggs. They contain the yolk of a fresh egg but never any milk. They can be made with any of the following spirits or wines: gin, whisky, brandy, rum, port, sherry or claret. Serve in a medium-sized wine glass.

Ale Flip

1 litre ale
grated rind of 1 lemon
3 free-range eggs
half barspoon ground ginger
225g brown sugar
12cl brandy

Heat the ale and lemon rind. Beat the rest of the ingredients together in separate bowl. Pour the heated ale into the egg mixture. Blend and pour back and forth from bowl to saucepan until mixture is creamy and smooth. Serve in a large wine glass with grated nutmeg on top.

Boston Flip

5cl rye whisky
5cl Madeira
1 free-range egg yolk
dash gomme syrup

Shake ingredients with ice. Strain into a wine glass. Garnish with a sprinkling of grated nutmeg.

Brandy Flip

2.5cl brandy
1 free-range egg yolk
1.5cl gomme syrup

Shake ingredients with ice. Strain into a wine glass. Sprinkle with nutmeg.

Champagne Flip

5cl fresh orange juice
2.5cl orange curaçao
dash gomme syrup
dash free-range egg yolk
champagne

Pour ingredients, except for champagne, into a shaker with ice. Shake well. Strain into a large wine glass. Top up with champagne.

Nightcap Flip

2.5cl anisette
2.5cl orange curaçao
2.5cl brandy
1 free-range egg yolk

Shake ingredients with ice. Pour into a wine glass.

Porto Flip

1.5 cl brandy
5cl port (red)
1cl pasteurized egg yolk

Pour ingredients into a shaker filled with ice. Shake. Strain into cocktail glass. Sprinkle with nutmeg.

FRAPPES

The word frappé should not be confused with 'glacé' (chilled) or 'on the rocks' (with ice cubes); it means 'served with finely crushed ice'. All frappés should be served with straws.

LIQUEUR FRAPPÉS

All kinds of liqueurs may be used for these. Fill a medium-sized stemmed glass (or large cocktail glass) with crushed ice, then pour a measure of the desired liqueur over the ice. Serve with short straws. The most commonly requested frappé is made with crème de menthe. Frappés may also be prepared with more than one ingredient, as demonstrated in two of the examples below.

Nap Frappé

2.5cl Kümmel
2.5cl green Chartreuse
2.5cl brandy

Ward's Frappé

rind of lemon in glass
2.5cl green chartreuse
2.5cl brandy

Prepare as above. Pour the brandy in last. Do not mix the ingredients.

Scotch Mist

2.5cl Scotch whisky

Shake the whisky with crushed ice. Pour unstrained into an old-fashioned glass. Add a twist of lemon.

HIGHBALLS

This very famous American contribution to the terminology of drinking is said to have originated in the nineteenth century. On some US railroads, a ball would be raised on a pole to indicate to a locoman passing through a station that he was behind schedule and should speed up. Hence the term 'high ball' became associated with a simple drink, quickly prepared.

After Dark

2.5cl Tia Maria
2.5cl cola

Add ingredients to a highball filled with ice. Stir. Garnish with a spiral of lime.

Bulldog Highball

5cl gin
5cl fresh orange juice
ginger ale

Shake ingredients, except ginger ale, with ice. Strain into a highball filled with ice. Top up with ginger ale. Stir. Serve with straws.

Cuba Libre

5cl Bacardi light rum
3cl fresh lime juice
cola

Pour the juice, then the rum into a highball filled with ice. Top up with cola. Garnish with a wedge of lime. Serve with a stirrer.

Horse's Neck

5cl brandy
dry ginger ale
dash Angostura bitters (optional)

Peel the rind of a lemon in one spiral. Place the end of the spiral over the edge of a highball filled with ice, allowing the remainder to curl inside and anchor with the ice at the bottom of the glass. Add the brandy. Fill with dry ginger ale. Add the bitters if desired.

Rye Highball

2.5cl rye whiskey
dry ginger ale or soda water

Pour the whiskey into a highball filled with ice. Top up with ginger ale or soda water. Add a twist of lemon.

Spritzer

12.5cl dry white wine
5cl soda water

Build into a large highball filled with ice. Add a twist of lemon.

HOT DRINKS

Black Stripe

5cl dark rum
1 tablespoon honey

Mix the rum with the honey in a silver tankard. Fill with boiling water. Stir. Pour into a stemmed glass. Add a twist of lemon.

Blue Blazer

5cl Scotch whisky
5cl boiling water
1 barspoon caster sugar

Use two large silver tankards with handles. Heat the whisky and put into one tankard. Put the boiling water in the other mug. Ignite whisky. While blazing, mix both ingredients by pouring them four or five times from one mug to the other. If done well, the liquid will resemble a continuous stream of liquid fire. Sweeten with the sugar. Add a twist of lemon.

Glühwein

THIS IS A GERMAN VERSION OF THE HOT TODDY.

half bottle red wine
2 cubes sugar
1 slice lemon
1 piece cinnamon

Boil ingredients in a saucepan and serve as hot as possible in a heat-proof toddy glass.

Grog

5cl dark rum
1 cube sugar
2 cloves
1cl fresh lemon juice
1 small stick cinnamon

Pour ingredients into a heat-proof glass. Fill with boiling water. Stir.

Hot Buttered Rum

5cl dark rum
1 slice butter
1 teaspoon brown sugar
pinch grated nutmeg
pinch cinnamon
4 drops vanilla extract

Mix together the butter, brown sugar, cinnamon, nutmeg and vanilla extract in a heat-proof wine glass until creamed. Add the rum. Fill with boiling water. Stir. Serve hot.

Hot Egg Nogg

2.5cl brandy
2.5cl rum
1 teaspoon caster sugar
1 free-range egg
hot milk

Pour ingredients, except milk, into a tall heat-proof glass. Top up with hot milk. Stir. Grate nutmeg on top.

Midnight Snowstorm

5cl white crème de menthe
hot chocolate
whipped cream

Pour the crème de menthe into a heat-proof glass. Fill with hot chocolate. Float the whipped cream over.

Tom and Jerry

4cl dark rum
1.5cl brandy
1 free-range egg
1 teaspoon caster sugar

Beat the egg yolk and the white separately, then combine in a heat-proof toddy glass. Add the spirits and sugar. Fill with boiling water. Grate nutmeg on top.

HOT COFFEES

Irish Coffee

2 teaspoons brown sugar
5cl Irish whiskey
10cl hot coffee
2cl whipped cream

Pour the whiskey into a heat-proof, large goblet. Add the brown sugar and stir. Add the hot coffee and stir with a teaspoon. Float the whipped cream over a barspoon to create a final layer. Do not stir. Serve while hot.

Coffee Nudge

2.5cl cognac
2.5cl Kahlua
15cl fresh hot coffee
whipped cream

Pour the cognac and the Kahlua into a heat-proof glass and stir. Top with whipped cream.

Coffee Gates

1.5cl Tia Maria
1.5cl brown crème de cacao
1.5cl Grand Marnier liqueur
15cl fresh hot coffee
whipped cream

Pour the liqueurs into a heat-proof
glass and add the coffee. Stir. Top
with whipped cream. Squeeze the zest
of an orange on top.

Coffee Juliano

2.5cl amaretto
2.5cl brown crème de cacao
15cl fresh hot coffee
whipped cream

Pour the amaretto and crème de cacao
into a heat-proof glass and add the
coffee. Top with whipped cream.

SOME LIQUEURS AND SPIRITS GO SO WELL WITH
BLACK COFFEE AND CREAM THAT SPECIAL NAMES
ARE GIVEN TO THE COMBINATIONS:

Aquavit	Scandinavian coffee
Bénédictine	Monks coffee
Calvados	Normandy coffee
Cognac	Royale coffee
Drambuie	Prince Charles coffee
Elixir d'Anvers	Belgian coffee
Genever	Dutch coffee
Kahlua	Mexican coffee
Kirsch	German coffee
Rum	Caribbean coffee
Scotch whisky	Gaelic coffee
Strega	Italian coffee
Tia Maria	Calypso coffee

MULLED WINES

A mull is hot wine with sugar and
spices added. Brandy, a liqueur or
a fortified wine can also be added
to give it extra strength. However,
do not use expensive wines: the
inexpensive ones are very good,
and economical.

Serve mulls really hot – but
never boiled, or the alcohol will
evaporate.

Apart from the ingredients, you
will need a 3 to 5 litre saucepan, a
plastic funnel and wine glasses. To
prevent the glasses from cracking,
warm them first or place a
wooden spoon in them while
pouring in the hot wine.

Christmas Cheer 30 GLASSES

4 bottles red wine
1/2 litre of water
1.5cl bottle dark rum
1 lemon
12 cloves
1/2 teaspoon ground cinnamon
nutmeg

Heat the wine, water and rum
together. Stick lemon with cloves and
bake in the oven for 15 minutes at
180°C/Gas 4. Add the cinnamon and a
little grated nutmeg to the wine
mixture. Float the hot lemon in it.
Serve hot.

Mulled Claret 8 GLASSES

1 bottle claret
1 wineglass port
14cl water
1 tablespoon sugar
rind of half lemon
12 whole cloves
pinch grated nutmeg

Put the spices into a saucepan with
the water and simmer for half an
hour. Strain. Pour the claret into a
saucepan. Add the spiced water. Add
the port and sugar and bring almost
to the boil. Serve very hot with thin
slices of lemon rind. You can use a
stick of cinnamon with the lemon.

Twelfth Night 8 GLASSES

1 bottle red wine
1 apple
cloves
hot water

Stick an apple full of cloves and float
in a bowl filled with the heated red
wine. Add hot water to dilute
according to taste.

JULEPS

Captain Marryat was the first
Englishman to write about this
American drink in 1815. There
were many varieties of juleps, he
wrote, such as those made of
claret, madeira, etc., but the one
on which he lavished the most
praise was the Mint Julep:
'Put into a tumbler about a dozen
sprigs of the tender shoots of
mint, upon them put a spoonful of
white sugar, equal proportion of
peach or common brandy so as to
fill it up to one-third or a trifle
less. Then take pounded ice and
fill up the tumbler. Epicures wet
the lip of the tumbler with a piece
of fresh pineapple and the tumbler
itself is very often encrusted with
ice. When the ice melts, you
drink.' After the Civil War,
bourbon whiskey became the
accepted spirit base.

Mint Julep

5cl bourbon whiskey
fresh mint leaves
1 teaspoon caster sugar
1 tablespoon cold water

Place 5 mint leaves in a highball.
Muddle the mint, sugar and water
together until the sugar dissolves. Add
the bourbon and fill tumbler with
crushed ice. Stir until the outside of
the glass is frosted. Garnish with a
sprig of mint. Serve with straws.

Champagne Julep

1 cube sugar
fresh mint leaves
champagne

Place the sugar in a champagne glass.
Add 2 leaves of mint and muddle
gently with a barspoon to extract the
flavour. Fill with chilled champagne.
Stir gently. Garnish with a sprig of
mint and an orange slice.

Old Georgia Julep

1 cube sugar
4 leaves mint
2.5cl peach or apricot brandy

Place the sugar in a highball glass.
Dissolve the sugar in a little water.
Add the mint. Muddle together. Add
the brandy. Fill with ice. Stir carefully.

MARTINIS

The Martini's origins are unclear.
In the 1860s a drink known as the
Matinez Cocktail contained gin,
vermouth, maraschino and bitters.
If this is the original recipe then it
was much altered by the time it
became the Martini Cocktail of
pre-World War I, when the
mixture consisted of two parts gin
to one part vermouth. After World
War II it was being served four
parts gin to one part vermouth
and became progressively drier, to
the extent that there is even a
recipe for a Naked Martini, which
is simply gin on the rocks.

Dry Martini Cocktail

10cl gin or vodka
2 dashes dry vermouth

Pour ingredients into a mixing glass
with ice. Stir. Serve straight up or on
the rocks. Add a twist of lemon or an
olive.

Gibson

10cl gin or vodka
2 dashes dry vermouth

Pour ingredients into a mixing glass
with ice. Stir. Serve straight up or on
the rocks. Add a pearl onion.

Perfect Martini

7.5cl gin
1cl dry vermouth
1cl sweet vermouth

Pour ingredients into a mixing glass
with ice. Stir. Add a twist of lemon.

VARIATIONS INCLUDE:

Sakini

7.5cl gin
2.5cl saké

Pour ingredients into a mixing glass
with ice. Stir. Serve straight up or on
the rocks. Add an olive.

Today there are a myriad of imitation Martinis, made with such fruits as apple and strawberry, and even with chocolate. These are not truly Martinis, but merely Martini-style cocktails served in a chilled Martini or cocktail glass. The most popular spirit base is vodka. If making with vodka, always keep the vodka in the freezer compartment of the refrigerator.

Apple Martini

5cl vodka
2cl apple sour liqueur
1cl Cointreau

Shake ingredients with ice. Strain into a cocktail glass. Garnish with an apple fan.

Blueberry Martini

5cl vodka
1cl blue curaçao
1cl fresh lemon juice
handful fresh blueberries, rinsed

Muddle the blueberries in the shaker. Add the remaining ingredients and ice. Shake vigorously. Strain through a sieve into the cocktail glass. Place 4 blueberries on a cocktail stick across the glass.

Breakfast Martini

5cl gin
1.5cl Cointreau
1.5cl fresh lemon juice
1 teaspoon medium-cut orange marmalade

Shake ingredients with ice. Strain into a cocktail glass. Squeeze a thin twist of orange on top. Garnish with a spiral of orange.

French Martini

4cl vodka
2.5cl pineapple juice
2cl Chambord liqueur

Shake ingredients with ice. Strain into a cocktail glass. Garnish with a twist of orange.

Sputnick Rose Martini

5cl Sputnik rose-infused vodka
2 to 3 dashes rosewater
2 dashes elderflower cordial

Shake ingredients with ice. Strain into a cocktail glass. Garnish with a rose petal.

Strawberry & Basil Martini

5cl Sputnik basil vodka
3 to 4 fresh strawberries
1 to 2 fresh basil leaves

Shake ingredients with ice. Strain into a cocktail glass. Garnish with a strawberry and a sprig of basil leaves.

Watermelon & Rosewater Martini

5cl Ketel One vodka
5 small slices watermelon, diced
0.5cl melon Schnapps
3 drops rosewater

Pour ingredients into a shaker. Shake. Strain into a martini glass. Garnish with 3 rose petals on the drink.

NON-ALCOHOLIC DRINKS

Cinderella

5cl fresh lemon juice
5cl orange juice
5cl pineapple juice

Shake ingredients with ice. Strain into a highball filled with ice.

Coconut Affair

6cl coconut milk
9cl fresh orange juice
9cl pineapple juice
6 fresh strawberries, diced

Blend ingredients until smooth. Add a scoop of crushed ice and blend again. Pour into a champagne coup.

Florida Cocktail

5cl grapefruit juice
2.5cl orange juice
dash fresh lemon juice
1.5cl gomme syrup
salt
soda water

Shake ingredients, except for soda water, with ice. Strain into a highball filled with crushed ice. Top up with soda water. Garnish with mint. Serve with straws.

Lemonade

6cl fresh lemon juice
1½ barspoons sugar

Half-fill a tumbler with cracked ice. Stir. Fill with plain water. Add a slice of lemon on top. Serve with straws.

Derby Mattoni

2cl peppermint syrup
5cl banana nectar
fresh double cream
sprig of mint
Mattoni still water

Build in a highball filled with ice. Garnish with a redcurrant, a slice of banana and some blueberries.

Dr Mattoni

2cl anise syrup
2cl fresh lime juice
2cl fresh lemon syrup
sprig fresh mint
Mattoni still water

Build in a highball filled with ice. Garnish with a sprig of mint and a lime wedge in the drink.

Pussyfoot

15cl fresh orange juice
3cl fresh lemon juice
3cl fresh lime juice
2 dashes grenadine
1 free-range egg yolk

Shake ingredients with ice. Strain into
a highball filled with ice. Garnish with
a slice of orange and a cherry on a
cocktail stick.

Shirley Temple

ginger ale
1.5cl grenadine

Pour the ginger ale into a highball
filled with ice. Add the grenadine. Stir
gently. Garnish with cherries.

Surfer's Paradise

2.5cl lime juice
3 dashes Angostura bitters
lemonade

Pour the bitters and lime juice into a
highball filled with ice. Stir in the
lemonade. Garnish with a slice of
orange.

Virgin Mary

12cl tomato juice
1.5cl fresh lemon juice
2 dashes Worcestershire sauce
2 dashes celery salt

Shake ingredients with ice. Strain into
a highball filled with ice.

PICK-ME-UPS

Bars should have a supply of
aspirin, Alka-seltzer or other such
useful aids to recovery.
Fernet Branca and Underberg are
recognized as possessing
restorative powers. However, some
digestive relief can be gained
simply by taking a few drops of
Angostura bitters or peppermint in
a glass of soda water.

Fernet Menthe

3cl Fernet Branca
1.5cl green crème de menthe

Pour into a wine glass. Stir.

Pick-me-up No. 1

2.5cl cognac
2.5cl dry vermouth
2.5cl pastis

Pour ingredients into a mixing glass.
Stir, then strain into a wine glass.

Pick-me-up No. 2

2.5cl brandy
5cl milk
dash gomme syrup
dash Angostura bitters
soda water

Shake ingredients, except soda water,
with ice. Stir. Strain into a highball
glass. Stir in the soda water.

Prairie Hen

2 dashes vinegar
2 barspoons Worcestershire sauce
1 whole free-range egg
  (do not break yolk)
2 dashes Tabasco sauce
salt and pepper to taste

Pour ingredients into a small wine
glass. Stir well to combine ingredients.
Serve and drink quickly.

Prairie Oyster

1 barspoon Worcestershire sauce
1 barspoon tomato sauce
1 free-range egg yolk
  (do not break yolk)
2 dashes vinegar
twist ground black pepper

Pour ingredients into a small wine
glass. Stir well to combine ingredients.
Add a quick twist of pepper. Serve
and drink quickly.

POUSSE CAFE

The various liqueurs in a Pousse
Café must remain strictly
separated one above the other.
What makes it possible to prepare
the drink in this way is the fact
that each liqueur has a different
specific weight or density.
Basically, syrups are heavier than
liqueurs and spirits are lighter.
Formulas differ between manufac-
turers and consequently densities
vary slightly, so it is necessary to
be certain of your recipe before
starting to prepare the drink.
  To make a Pousse Café, pour
each liqueur carefully into a small,
straight-sided glass over the back
of a spoon, held so that it touches
the inner edge of the glass. Add
the ingredients in the stated order.

Pousse Café 81

1cl grenadine
1cl crème de menthe
1cl Galliano
1cl Kümmel
1cl brandy

French Pousse Café

1.5cl green Chartreuse
1.5cl maraschino liqueur
1.5cl cherry brandy
1.5cl Kümmel

Rainbow Cocktail

1cl crème de cacao
1cl crème de violette
1cl yellow Chartreuse
1cl maraschino
1cl Bénédictine
1cl brandy

PUNCHES

Punch in its oldest and simplest form is rum and water, hot or iced, with sugar to taste and orange or fresh lemon juice (for hot punch) or fresh lime juice (for cold punch). It was in 1655, when they took Jamaica from Spain, that the English were first introduced to rum punch. In the eighteenth century this drink was 'brewed' or mixed at the table in a punchbowl by the host, with rum as one of the ingredients but including other spirits as well. Oranges and lemons in thin slices, grated nutmeg and sundry decorations and flavourings were added at the discretion of the mixer.

Brandy Punch

SERVES 6

18cl brandy
12cl orange curaçao
12cl fresh lemon juice
6cl fresh lime juice
3cl grenadine
2 teaspoons caster sugar
half orange, sliced
half lemon, slices
soda water

Pour ingredients, except for fruit and soda water, into a punch bowl. Stir. Just before guests arrive, add a block of ice, then the slices of fruit. Add the soda water. Serve in individual wine glasses.

Brandy Milk Punch

5cl brandy
6cl milk
2cl gomme syrup

Shake or mix. Strain into a double cocktail glass. Grate nutmeg on top.

Claret Punch

5cl claret
1.5cl fresh lemon juice
dash orange curaçao
dash gomme syrup
dry ginger ale

Stir together, except the ginger ale, in a large wine glass. Add ice. Garnish with a slice each of orange and lemon. Top up with dry ginger ale.

Fish House Punch

MAKES 40 DRINKS

340g sugar
2.2 litres water
1litre fresh lemon juice
2.2 litres Jamaican rum
1litre cognac
12cl peach brandy

In a large punch bowl, dissolve the sugar in the water. Stir in the remaining ingredients. Add a large block of ice. Allow to stand for two hours. Serve in punch cups.

Planter's Punch

5cl golden or dark rum
5cl fresh lemon or lime juice
dash Angostura bitters
2 barspoons grenadine
soda water

Build in a highball filled with ice, then stir in the soda water. Garnish with orange and lemon slices.

St. Charles Punch

5cl brandy
9cl port wine
4 dashes orange curaçao
2.5cl fresh lemon juice

Shake ingredients with ice. Strain into a goblet filled with crushed ice. Add fruit. Serve with straws.

RICKEYS

The Rickey is a long-drink cousin of the Collins. Whilst its origin is somewhat obscure, it seems pretty clear that the Rickey is an American drink. To quote from Jack Townsend's *The Bartenders' Book*, 'Not nearly so obscure is the origin of the Gin Rickey, a drink which can be traced not only to the city – Washington – but also to the restaurant, Shoemaker's. At this popular oasis on a dusty summer's afternoon before the turn of the century, according to the most reliable legends, a bartender squeezed limes into gin, and hosed the unsweetened result with a syphon. His first customer for the potation was "Colonel Jim" Rickey, a lobbyist whose first name was really Joe, and whose military title probably was of the honorary Kentucky variety. Shoemaker's was known as "the third house of Congress" and Congressional patrons who knew the "Cunnel" bestowed his name upon the drink.

Gin Rickey

5cl gin
juice of 1 lime
soda water

Build all but the soda water into an old-fashioned glass filled with ice. Drop in the spent lime shell. Stir in the soda water.

SANGAREES

The Sangaree is a possible relative of the Rickey. In this case, however, the drink can be made not only with the usual spirits, but also with wines and other bases. Various views exist as to its origin; it is very likely to have come from India, but other stories say it was used in the southern states of America in times of war for the wounded, and for invalids. The drink's name is supposed to be derived from 'Singari' meaning 'blood drink'.

Use an old-fashioned glass, and serve with straws.

Brandy Sangaree

1 barspoon sugar
equal parts water and brandy

Fill a glass with crushed ice. Add the sugar and brandy/water mixture to the glass. Stir. Garnish with nutmeg.

Claret Sangaree

15cl claret
2.5cl fresh lemon juice
1 barspoon sugar

Fill a glass with crushed ice. Add the claret, sugar and lemon juice to the glass. Stir, then add a slice of orange. Garnish with nutmeg.

Port Wine Sangaree

1 glass port
1 barspoon sugar

Fill a glass with crushed ice. Add the sugar and port. Stir. Grate nutmeg on top. Add a slice of lemon.

Whisky Sangaree

AS FOR BRANDY SANGAREE, SUBSTITUTING WHISKY FOR BRANDY.

SLINGS

Gin Slings are usually attributed to exotic, far-distant places with a warm climate. The origin is not too certain, however. It might well be that the story quoted in the section on the Collins also has some connection with the origin of the Sling. However, there is little doubt that the Singapore Gin Sling had as its original home the famous Raffles Hotel in Singapore, when the legendary bartender Ngiam Tom Boon created it for his illustrious clientele.

Gin Sling

5cl gin
juice of 1 lemon
2 dashes gomme syrup
soda water

Build ingredients into a highball filled with ice, then stir in the soda water.

Raffles Bar Sling

2cl gin
2cl cherry brandy
1cl Cointreau
1cl Bénédictine
1cl fresh lime juice
7cl fresh orange juice
7cl pineapple

Shake ingredients with ice. Strain into a highball filled with ice. Garnish with a slice of pineapple and a cherry. Serve with a stirrer and a straw.

Singapore Sling

4cl gin
2cl cherry brandy
2cl fresh lemon juice
soda water

Shake ingredients, except the soda water, with ice. Strain into a highball filled with ice. Stir in the soda water. Garnish with a slice of lemon and a cherry.

Straits Sling

2.5cl gin
1.5cl Bénédictine
1.5cl cherry brandy
2.5cl fresh lemon juice
soda water

Shake ingredients, except the soda water, with ice. Strain into a highball filled with ice. Stir in the soda water. Garnish with a slice of lemon.

SMASHES

A smash is a smaller version of a Julep containing sugar, mint and spirit, served with crushed ice. It can be made with any spirit and two examples follow.

Brandy Smash

5cl brandy (or other spirit)
1 teaspoon caster sugar
6 leaves fresh mint

Dissolve the sugar in a little water in an old-fashioned glass. Add mint and muddle to extract the flavour. Add the brandy. Fill the glass with crushed ice. Stir until the glass is frosted. Garnish with a lemon slice and short straws.

Mojito

5cl Bacardi golden rum
1 teaspoon caster sugar
2cl fresh lime juice
sprig fresh mint
sparkling water

Pour the lime juice and sugar into a highball. Add the mint leaves and muddle. Add the rum. Fill the glass with crushed ice. Stir until the glass frosts. Top up with sparkling water. Stir. Garnish with a sprig of fresh mint. Serve with straws and a stirrer.

SOURS

Sours must be made with fresh juices if they are to have the sharpness necessary to heighten the flavour of the drink. The most popular type is the Whisky Sour, although almost any alcoholic ingredient can be used as a base.

Scotch Sour

5cl whisky
2cl fresh fresh lemon juice
1 teaspoon pasteurized egg white
dash gomme syrup

Shake ingredients with ice. Strain into a cocktail glass. Garnish with a slice of lemon.

Fireman's Sour

2.5cl Bacardi golden rum
2.5cl fresh lime juice
1cl grenadine
dash gomme syrup
soda water

Shake ingredients, except soda water, with ice. Strain into a goblet. Add the soda water. Garnish with a slice of orange and a cherry.

Frisco Sour

3cl bourbon whiskey
1.5cl Bénédictine
1.5cl fresh lemon juice
1.5cl fresh lime juice
dash pasteurized egg white

Shake ingredients with ice. Strain into a cocktail glass. Garnish with a slice each of lemon and lime.

Mandarine Sour

5cl Mandarine Napoléon
2.5cl fresh lemon juice
dash Angostura bitters
dash pasteurized egg white

Shake ingredients with ice. Strain into a goblet. Garnish with a slice of orange.

Pisco Sour

PISCO IS A SOUTH AMERICAN BRANDY DISTILLED FROM MUSCAT GRAPES AND MATURED IN CLAY JARS. IT IS NAMED AFTER THE TOWN IN PERU.

5cl pisco
2cl fresh lime juice
dash pasteurized egg white
2 dashes Angostura bitters
dash gomme syrup

Shake ingredients with ice. Strain into a cocktail glass. Garnish with a wedge of lime.

Sourteq

5cl tequila
2.5cl fresh lemon juice
1.5cl gomme syrup
dash Angostura bitters
dash pasteurized egg white

Shake ingredients with ice. Strain into
a cocktail glass. Garnish with a slice
of lemon and a cherry.

SWIZZLES

The Swizzle takes its name from
the stick used to stir the drink,
which originated in the West
Indies. A swizzle stick was
originally the dried stem of a
tropical plant with a few smaller
branches left on the end, and was
about two feet long. The stick
would be inserted in the jug and
rubbed vigorously between the
palms of the hands – swizzling
the ice and liquor to create a frost
on the outside of the glass.

West Indies Swizzle

6 GLASSES
half bottle Jamaican rum
17cl fresh lime juice
6 barspoons sugar
6 sprigs mint

Take a glass jug and fill with ice. Add
the ingredients. Set the jug on the
floor holding it with the feet. Place
the forked end of the stick in the
mixture and roll vigorously between
the palms until the jug is frosted.

Gin Swizzle

5cl gin
2.5cl fresh lime juice
1.5cl gomme syrup
dash Angostura bitters
soda water

Add ingredients, except soda water,
into a highball filled with crushed ice.
Fill the glass with soda water. Serve
with a small swizzle stick, allowing
the consumer to do the final stirring.

TODDIES

Today, a toddy is a refresher that
may be served hot or cold. Toddies
usually contain a slice of lemon or
some lemon peel and are made
with either cinnamon, cloves or
nutmeg to spice it up.

Hot Toddy

2.5cl desired spirit
1 barspoon sugar
boiling water

Fill a medium-sized heat-proof goblet
with boiling water. Add ingredients.
Stir. Add a slice of lemon. Sprinkle
with grated nutmeg.

Hot Scotch Toddy

5cl Scotch whisky
7cl boiling water
1cl fresh lemon juice
3 dashes Angostura bitters
1 barspoon honey
3 cloves
twist of lemon

Pour the whisky, water, lemon juice
and bitters into a heat-proof toddy
glass. Stir. Spear the cloves into the
twist of lemon and add to the drink.

Toddy

2.5cl desired spirit
1 barspoon sugar

Dissolve the sugar with a little hot
water in an old-fashioned glass. Add
ice, then the spirit. Add a large twist
of lemon. Serve with a stirrer.

Countries & their Drinks

ARGENTINA

ASSOCIATION MUTUAL DE BARMEN Y AFINES
(A.M.B.A)

Gaucho

2.5cl genever gin
2.5cl Hesperidina
dash Angostura bitters

Shake ingredients with ice. Strain into
an old-fashioned glass filled with ice.
Decorate with a slice of orange.

Pampa Hot

JOSÉ LUIS MENDEZ CASTELAR

2.5cl Scotch whisky
1.5cl coconut liqueur
1.5cl Cointreau
2.5cl sweet vermouth
12cl pineapple juice

Shake ingredients with ice. Strain into
a highball filled with ice. Garnish with
a cherry and a slice of orange.

Pisco Punch

6cl pisco
3cl unsweetened pineapple juice
3cl fresh lime juice
2 dashes maraschino liqueur
2 dashes gomme syrup

Shake ingredients with ice. Strain into
a medium goblet.

Pisco Sour

5cl pisco
8cl fresh lime juice
dash gomme syrup
dash pasteurized egg white
2 dashes Angostura bitters

Shake ingredients, except bitters, with
ice. Strain into a goblet. Add the
bitters. Stir.

Sweet Love

LIONEL A. FRACHERO

2.5cl Scotch whisky
2.5cl dry vermouth
1cl peach liqueur
1cl melon liqueur
1cl Cointreau

Shake ingredients with ice. Strain into
a cocktail glass. Garnish with a cherry.

ARMENIA

ARMENIAN ASSOCIATION OF BARTENDERS (B.A.B)

Aqua Vitae

ZOHRAB BAHRIKYAN

4cl grape-flavoured Artsakh
2cl sour apple liqueur
2cl fresh lemon juice
12cl fresh apple juice

Shake ingredients with ice. Strain into
a highball filled with ice. Garnish with
an apple slice and a grape.

Calm Night

ERIC MAMIKONYAN

2.5cl gin
2.5cl vodka
2.5cl dry red wine
2.5cl fresh blackcurrant juice
1cl gomme syrup

Shake ingredients with ice. Strain into a champagne flute. Garnish with a twist of lemon, a cherry, a blackcurrant and a mint leaf.

Caprichos

ARSHAK BRUTYAN

1cl coconut syrup
2cl melon liqueur
4cl mulberry Artsakh
ginger ale

Shake ingredients, except ginger ale, with ice. Strain into a highball filled with ice. Top up with ginger ale. Garnish with a slice of melon and starfruit, a cherry and a mint leaf.

Mexican in Love

TIGRAN AVETISYAN

4cl silver tequila
2cl Parfait Amour
1.5cl orange curaçao
1cl blue curaçao
12cl fresh blackcurrant juice

Shake ingredients with ice. Strain into a hurricane glass filled with ice. Garnish with an orange slice, a cherry and a mint leaf.

AUSTRALIA

AUSTRALIAN BARTENDERS' GUILD (A.B.G)

Adam's Apple

ADAM KEANE

3cl apple liqueur
1.5cl butterscotch schnapps
1.5cl Chambord liqueur
dash cranberry juice
5 to 6 chunks of apple

Muddle the apple in the bottom of a shaker. Add ice, then the remaining ingredients. Shake. Strain into an old-fashioned glass filled with ice.

Barrier Reef

3cl gin
2.5cl Cointreau
dash Angostura bitters
1 scoop ice cream
few drops blue curaçao

Pour ingredients, except curaçao, into a mixing glass with ice. Add the curaçao. Stir well. Strain into an old-fashioned glass filled with ice. Serve with a stirrer.

Fluffy Duck

3cl gin
3cl Advocaat
1.5cl Cointreau
2.5cl fresh orange juice
soda water.

Pour ingredients, except soda water, into a highball filled with ice. Stir in the soda water. Serve with straws and a stirrer.

French Summer

ADAM KEANE

4.5cl lychee liqueur
4.5cl cranberry juice
4.5cl ruby red grapefruit juice
1.5cl lemon juice
dash melon liqueur

Shake ingredients, except melon
liqueur, with ice. Strain into a large
cocktail glass. Add the melon liqueur
so it sinks to the bottom of the glass.
Garnish with a wheel slice of lime.

Naked Passion

ADAM KEANE

4.5cl mango liqueur
1.5cl lychee liqueur
10cl combined passionfruit and
    pink grapefruit juice
4 lime chunks

Muddle the lime in a shaker. Add ice,
then remaining ingredients. Shake.
Strain into a large cocktail glass.
Garnish with a cherry.

Sinfonia

SARAH SWAYSLAND

3cl melon liqueur
3cl vanilla vodka
3cl pear purée
1cl fresh lemon juice
La Fée Absinthe to rinse

Shake first four ingredients and
double strain into a large cocktail
glass rinsed with absinthe. Garnish
with a pear fan.

South Pacific

GARY REVELL

3cl gin
1.5cl Galliano
1.5cl blue curaçao
7Up

Build the gin and Galliano into a
highball filled with cracked ice. Top
up with 7Up. Splash in the curaçao.
Garnish with a lemon slice and a
cherry. Serve with straws and a
swizzle stick.

Strawberry Night Fever

ADAM KEANE

3cl vanilla vodka
1.5cl strawberry liqueur
1.5cl vanilla de Madagascar liqueur
3cl ruby red grapefruit juice
2 to 3 strawberries
4 pineapple chunks

Muddle the fruit in the shaker. Add
ice, then remaining ingredients. Shake.
Strain into a large old-fashioned glass.
Garnish with half a strawberry.

AUSTRIA

OSTERREICHISCHE BARKEEPER UNION (O.B.U)

After One

REINHOLD HUSAR

2.5cl gin
2.5cl Galliano
2.5cl sweet vermouth
2.5cl Campari

Shake ingredients with ice. Strain into
a cocktail glass. Serve with a cocktail
cherry and a twist of orange.

Café Brazil

HANS BAND

2.5cl Kahlua
2.5cl Bacardi light rum
2 dashes gomme syrup
2.5cl kaffeeobers
dash pasteurized egg white
dash chocolate powder

Blend ingredients with ice. Strain into a cocktail glass. Garnish with a slice of banana and sprinkle chocolate powder over the top.

Green Peace

ALOIS SPANDL

2cl Stolichnaya vodka
2cl dry vermouth
2cl Pisang Ambon
1cl apricot brandy
12cl pineapple juice

Shake ingredients with ice. Strain into a highball filled with ice. Stir in the pienapple juice. Garnish with lime and orange twists, fresh mint, a strawberry and a cherry.

Sonny Boy

FRANZ STROBL

1.5cl peach brandy
1.5cl orange curaçao
2 dashes Angostura bitters
champagne

Shake ingredients, except champagne, with ice. Strain into a champagne flute. Fill with champagne.

UNION DES BARMEN DE BELGIQUE (U.B.B)

Cassandra

LUIGI SCIUSCIO

3cl Mandarine Napoleon
1.5cl amaretto
1.5cl coconut liqueur
dash fresh lemon juice
grapefruit juice

Shake ingredients with ice. Strain into a highball filled with ice. Top up with grapefruit juice. Garnish with a cherry and a sprig of mint.

Calvados Blossom

DAVID FRANÇOIS

4cl calvados
1cl Mandarine Napoléon
2cl wild strawberry liqueur
7cl pineapple juice
dash coconut syrup

Pour ingredients into a shaker with ice. Strain into a highball filled with ice. Garnish with a slice of green apple and a fresh strawberry.

Don B

OLIVIER PICHON

WINNER, 2005 BACARDI MARTINI GRAND PRIX

4cl lemon vodka
1cl cinnamon syrup
slice fresh lemon
1cl Bénédictine liqueur
8cl Bacardi Bay rum

Shake ingredients with ice. Strain into a highball filled with ice. Garnish with a strawberry, a physalis and cloves.

Josephina

DIMAH ABDEL

3cl Mandarine Napoléon
1.5cl gin
1.5cl Southern Comfort
dash grenadine
dash fresh lemon juice

Shake ingredients with ice. Strain into a cocktail glass. Garnish with a cherry, a slice of orange and mint leaves.

La Hola

GIAN PAOLO ZARDINI

2.5cl Canadian Club whisky
1.5cl Mandarine Napoléon
1.5cl Kahlua
2.5cl crème fraîche

Shake ingredients with ice. Strain into a cocktail glass. Garnish with slivers of dark chocolate.

L'île au Bosquet

JOHANA LE MEE

1cl amaretto
2.5cl VSOP cognac
2.5cl Manzanita Verde
1cl caramel syrup
2cl crème fraîche

Shake ingredients with ice. Strain into a cocktail glass. Garnish with cinnamon powder.

Opposite
Bombay Cosmopolitan (left) and Bombay Rose (right) have a gin base.
Following pages
Sputnik Rose Martini, Bloody Russian, Asian Breeze and Russian Summer are made with new flavoured vodkas.

Renaissance

RUDY BONBOIRE

2.5cl vodka
1cl coconut liqueur
1cl crème de mûre
2cl pineapple juice
2.5cl peach juice

Shake ingredients with ice. Strain into a highball filled with ice. Garnish with a pineapple slice and a cherry.

Rivoli

ROLAND ROCHAT

2.5cl gin
1.5cl Mandarine Napoléon
1.5cl amaretto
1.5cl crème de banane
fresh orange juice

Shake ingredients, except orange juice, with ice. Strain into a highball filled with ice. Top up with the orange juice. Garnish with a half-slice of lemon and a half-slice of orange.

Strawberry Night

SERGIO PEZZOLI

2cl vanilla vodka
2cl passionfruit liqueur
2cl Manzanita Verde
2cl passionfruit juice
4cl fresh strawberry juice
1cl gomme syrup

Shake ingredients with ice. Strain into a highball filled with ice. Garnish with a kumquat, a physalis, and a small vanilla pod.

Stroumf

ROCHAT ROLAND
2.5cl gin
1.5cl apricot brandy
1cl amaretto
dash fresh lemon juice
fresh orange juice

Shake ingredients, except orange juice, with ice. Strain into a highball filled with ice. Stir in the orange juice.

Yankee-Dutch

GEORGES BROUCKE
1.5cl bourbon whiskey
1.5cl vodka
1.5cl cherry brandy
1.5cl Cointreau

Shake ingredients with ice. Strain into a cocktail glass. Garnish with a twist of orange.

BRAZIL

ASSOCIACAO BRADILEIRA DE BARMEN (A.B.B)

Batida Morango

5cl cachaça
3 fresh strawberries
2 barspoons sugar

Blend ingredients with crushed ice. Serve unstrained in a medium goblet.

Batida Limo	lime
Batida Abaci	pineapple
Batida Maracuja	fruit of brazil
Batida Goiaba	guava
Batida Mango	mango
Batida Caju	cashew

Caipirinha

5cl cachaça
1 lime
caster sugar

Cut the lime into small pieces. Place in an old-fashioned glass. Sprinkle with sugar. Crush together. Fill with ice. Add the cachaça. Serve with a stirrer.

Marques Style

CARLOS FELIX
2.5cl Jack Daniel's whiskey
2.5cl St Remy
1.5cl coconut cream
3 dashes grenadine
champagne

Shake ingredients with ice. Strain into a highball glass filled with ice. Fill with champagne. Garnish with a slice of melon, fresh mint leaves, a cherry and a slice of pineapple.

Pink Deise

JOSÉ DANIEL ALEXANDRE
3cl vodka
2cl white wine
1cl peach liqueur
1cl dry vermouth

Pour ingredients into a mixing glass. Stir. Strain into a cocktail glass. Garnish with orange peel, fresh mint and a cherry.

Opposite
Rhuby cocktail, made with Sagatiba cachaça, has Latin style written all over its divine presentation.

Serrera

NELSON DIAS FILHO

3cl vodka
2cl blue curaçao
1cl fresh lemon juice
soda or lemonade

Shake ingredients, except lemonade, with ice. Strain into a highball filled with ice. Top up with soda or lemonade. Stir. Garnish with a slice of pineapple, a slice of orange and a cherry.

BULGARIA

BULGARIAN ASSOCIATION OF BARTENDERS (B.A.B)

Bartender's Blood

PENCHO PENCHEV

4cl dry gin
2cl lychee liqueur
1cl crème de cassis
2cl cassis syrup
10cl red dry wine

Shake ingredients with ice. Strain into a highball glass filled with ice. Garnish with a sprig of fresh mint.

Blue Honest Eyes

PENCHO PENCHEV

3.5cl dry gin
1.5cl Cointreau
1cl blue curacao
0.5cl peach liqueur
2cl fresh lime juice

Shake ingredients with ice. Strain into a cocktail glass filled with crushed ice. Garnish with a slice of star fruit and a cherry.

Dry Tear

VASIL KOLEV

3cl cranberry vodka
2cl chardonnay
1cl passionfruit liqueur

Pour ingredients into a mixing glass with ice. Stir. Strain into a glass. Garnish with a rose of beetroot and a few small beetroot leaves.

Golden Egg

VASIL KOLEV

2cl Advocaat
2cl watermelon liqueur
1cl butterscotch liqueur
1cl passionfruit syrup

Shake ingredients with ice. Strain into a cocktail glass. Garnish with a small ball of melon, a cherry and a slice of star fruit.

Passion for You

VASIL KOLEV

2cl currant vodka
3cl melon liqueur
1cl lychee liqueur
1cl jasmine syrup
dash fresh lemon juice

Shake ingredients with ice. Strain into a chilled cocktail glass. Garnish with a sprig of mint, a small slice of pineapple, a cherry and an apple fan.

P.P. Club

PENCHO PENCHEV

5cl grape brandy
1cl Cointreau
5cl orange juice
2.5 passionfruit juice
5cl 7Up

Shake ingredients. except 7Up, with ice. Strain into a highball glass filled with ice. Top up with 7Up. Garnish with a slice of orange and a cherry. Serve with two straws.

CANADA

BARTENDERS' ASSOCIATION OF CANADA (B.A.C)

5-Star General

JOHN TENNIER

5cl rye whisky
1.5cl amaretto
1.5cl apricot brandy
dash Angostura bitters

Pour ingredients into a mixing glass with ice. Stir. Strain into a cocktail glass. Garnish with half a slice of lemon.

Cloudy Sky

CHARLES RENDES

2cl Amaretto
1cl Cointreau
1cl Baileys Irish Cream
1cl Kahlua
5cl fresh double cream

Frost the rim of a cocktail glass with sugar. Shake ingredients with ice. Strain into a cocktail glass. Garnish with grated chocolate.

Cool Breeze

3cl cognac
1.5cl Grand Marnier liqueur
9cl fresh double cream
dash Angostura bitters
2 dashes cherry juice

Pour ingredients into a mixing glass with ice. Stir. Strain into a cocktail glass.

Golden Touch

DEAN CHRISTOFILOS

2.5cl Southern Comfort
2.5cl Galliano
dash amaretto
15cl fresh orange juice
dash peach schnapps

Shake ingredients with ice. Strain into a highball filled with ice. Garnish with a slice of orange, a slice of pineapple and a cherry.

Swan Lake

YIANNIS DARAMARAS

2cl lemon vodka
2cl peach schnapps
3cl fresh lemon juice
dash blue curaçao

Shake ingredients with ice. Strain into a cocktail glass. Garnish with a mint leaf and a yellow rose petal.

CZECH REPUBLIC

CZECH BARTENDERS' ASSOCIATION (C.B.A)

Barbados Collins

3cl Mandarine Napoléon
1.5cl mandarin syrup
1.5cl pineapple juice
1.5cl fresh lemon juice
soda water

Pour ingredients, except soda water, into a highball filled with ice. Top up with soda water. Garnish with a slice of orange.

Bohemian Rhapsody

2cl raspberry liqueur
2cl Bacardi light rum
2cl white crème de cacao
1cl grenadine
2cl fresh orange juice

Shake ingredients with ice. Strain into a cocktail glass. Garnish with a strawberry and fresh mint leaf.

Plum Cream

3cl slivovich (plum brandy)
3cl raspberry syrup
3cl fresh double cream

Shake ingredients with ice. Strain into a cocktail glass. Garnish with a cherry.

Prague Spring Rocks

5cl dry vermouth
2.5cl dry gin
1.5cl Karlovarska Becherovka liqueur

Pour ingredients into an old-fashioned glass with ice. Garnish with zest of lemon.

DENMARK

DANSK BARTENDER LAUG (D.B.L)

JR

JACK NIELSEN

2cl bourbon whiskey
2cl calvados
2cl Grand Marnier liqueur
lemonade

Shake ingredients, except lemonade, with ice. Strain into a highball filled with ice. Top up with lemonade. Garnish with a slice of orange and a cherry.

Karneval

BOB K. MATHESON

3cl melon liqueur
3cl coconut liqueur
3cl fresh double cream
1 barspoon coconut cream

Shake ingredients with ice. Strain into a cocktail glass. Garnish with a twist of orange.

Mignon

JOHN FLEMMING HANSEN

3cl gin
1.5cl banana liqueur
3cl Pisang Ambon
dash grenadine
fresh orange juice

Shake ingredients, except orange juice, with ice. Strain into a highball filled with ice. Top up with orange juice.

FINLAND

FINLAND BARTENDERS OCH SUPPORTERS KLUBB
(F.B.S.K)

Charm

JUHANI TUOMINEN

2cl Kahlua
2cl amaretto
2cl fresh double cream
2cl coconut cream

Blend ingredients with a little ice until smooth. Pour into a cocktail glass. Garnish with grated chocolate.

Dolce Donna

JUKKA ROUTALA

2cl Galliano
1cl crème de banane
1cl Kahlua
2cl strawberry syrup
4cl fresh double cream

Blend ingredients with a little ice until smooth. Pour into a cocktail glass. Garnish with a strawberry and a sprig of fresh mint leaves.

First Moment

5cl vodka
2cl Galliano
1cl Campari
dash fresh Rose's lime cordial

Pour ingredients into a mixing glass with ice. Stir. Strain into a cocktail glass. Garnish with zest of orange.

Isle

SEPPO HEINONEN

2cl bourbon
2cl Safari
4cl fresh orange juice
dash Pernod
dash grenadine

Shake ingredients with ice. Strain into a cocktail glass. Garnish with a slice of orange.

Kliffa

MATTI MAKINEN

2cl Koskenkrova Finnish liqueur
2cl crème de banane
2cl pineapple juice
1cl fresh lemon juice
2 dashes cloudberry liqueur
dash grenadine
lemonade

Shake ingredients, except lemonade, with ice. Strain into a highball filled with ice. Top up with lemonade. Garnish with a slice of pineapple and a cherry.

Sunny Afternoon

TIMO HAIMIM

2cl vodka
2cl Pisang Ambon
2cl Galliano
15cl fresh orange juice

Shake ingredients with ice. Strain into a highball filled with ice. Garnish with a slice of lime, a cherry and a sprig of mint.

FRANCE

ASSOCIATION DES BARMEN DE FRANCE (A.B.F)

Bonbon

NANDO DI VUOLO

1.5cl peach liqueur
2cl Bénédictine
1.5cl Tia Maria
1cl apricot brandy
1.5cl fresh double cream

Shake ingredients with ice. Strain into a cocktail glass. Garnish with powdered coffee.

Crazy Horse

MICHEL LE REGENT

1.5cl fraises de bois
1.5cl crème de banane
3cl whisky
champagne

Shake ingredients, except champagne, with ice. Strain into a champagne flute. Fill with champagne. Decorate with slices of lime and orange, a wild strawberry and a sprig of mint.

Eros

PHILIPPE CIAVATTA

4cl brandy
2cl fraise de bois
7cl grapefruit juice
7cl pineapple juice
dash Angostura bitters

Shake ingredients with ice. Strain into a highball filled with ice. Garnish with a slice of kiwifruit and raisin de Corinthe.

Moonlight

DANIEL PION

2cl cognac
2cl Mandarine Impériale
1cl gomme syrup
hot black coffee
fresh cream

Pour the cognac, coffee, Mandarine Impériale and the gomme syrup into a heat-proof glass. Stir. Float the cream over the top. Garnish with zest of orange and a mandarin.

Vermouth Cassis

1.5cl crème de cassis
1.5cl dry vermouth

Served chilled in a small wine goblet or on the rocks. Add a twist of lemon.

GERMANY

DEUTSCHE BARKEEPER-UNION E.V. (D.B.U)

Checkpoint

ERWIN NAGLE

5cl gin
2cl Galliano
1cl fresh lemon juice
dash gomme syrup

Shake ingredients with ice. Strain into a cocktail glass. Garnish with a slice of lemon and a cherry.

Happy End

CAMILO PARADA GONZÁLES

2.5cl maraschino liqueur
2.5cl amaretto
2.5cl fresh orange juice
1.5cl fresh double cream

Shake ingredients with ice. Strain into a cocktail glass. Garnish with two cherries.

Mandy

ALWIN PFENNLG

3cl gin
1cl red curaçao
1cl peach liqueur
12cl fresh orange juice
1cl fresh lemon juice

Blend with a little ice until smooth. Pour into a highball. Garnish with a cherry and a sprig of fresh mint.

Miss Penelope

MIRKO GARDELLIANO

2cl lemon vodka
1.5cl mandarin syrup
1cl passionfruit liqueur
1.5cl passionfruit juice
1cl fresh double cream

Shake ingredients, except cream, with ice. Strain into a cocktail glass. Float the cream. Garnish with a physalis. Sprinkle with chocolate powder in the shape of a star.

Moonwalker

ANTONIO DOMINGUEZ-RUIZ

1.5cl vodka
1.5cl peach liqueur
3cl Tia Maria
1.5cl Baileys Irish Cream
3cl fresh double cream

Blend with a little ice. Garnish with grated white and brown chocolate.

Pigas

SIGI ZEITTÄGER

3cl Bacardi light rum
1.5cl white crème de cacao
1,5cl amaretto
15cl fresh orange juice
dash dark rum
dash fresh double cream

Shake ingredients with ice. Strain into a highball filled with ice. Garnish with a cube of sugar.

Pink Heaven

UGUR DERVISOGLU

5cl Bacardi light rum
4cl Licor 43
1.5cl Batida de Coco
12cl passionfruit nectar
dash passionfruit syrup
1cl strawberry syrup
2cl fresh milk

Shake ingredients with ice. Strain into a highball filled with ice. Garnish with a strawberry and mint leaves.

UNITED KINGDOM BARTENDERS' GUILD (U.K.B.G)

Apple & Sage

LUCA CORDIGLIERI

2cl apple schnapps
5cl apple vodka
5 leaves fresh sage
4cl apple juice
dash gomme syrup
slice fresh apple
lime wedge

Dice the fresh lime and apple into tiny pieces. Muddle in a shaker or mixing glass with the gomme syrup and the sage leaves. Add the remaining ingredients. Stir. Pour into a highball filled with crushed ice. Garnish with a sage leaf.

Banarama

HUGH FRAZER

3cl Martell cognac
3cl crème de banane
3cl orange liqueur
2cl fresh lemon juice
dash pasteurized egg white

Shake ingredients with ice. Strain into a cocktail glass. Garnish with two orange cherries and a ring of banana.

Campari Nobile

SALVATORE CALABRESE

2cl vodka
2cl Campari
1cl lemoncello
10cl combined fresh orange and
    raspberry juices
bitter lemon

Shake ingredients. except bitter lemon. with ice. Strain into a highball with ice. Top up with bitter lemon. Stir. Garnish with five raspberries and a sprig of mint, and a twist of orange. Serve with a straw and a stirrer.

Guadalajara Martini

STEPHEN LOW

3.5cl Jose Cuervo gold tequila
1.5cl cherry brandy
1.5cl pineapple juice

Shake ingredients with ice. Strain into a cocktail glass.

The Gatinha

MICKAEL PERRON

WINNER, 2005 NATIONAL COCKTAIL COMPETITION

5cl Sagatiba Pura cachaça
2cl port
1cl Brasilian honey syrup
dash Angostura bitters

Shake ingredients with ice. Serve in a glass dessert coup, drizzled over lemon sorbet.

Lemon Blush

SIMON ROWE

3cl gin
3cl lemoncello
3cl fresh lime juice
12cl ginger beer
dash fraise syrup

Build all, except the fraise syrup, in a
highball filled with ice. Add the fraise
syrup. It will slowly sink to the
bottom of the glass. Garnish with a
wedge of lime, a strawberry and a
sprig of fresh mint.

Massimiliano

MASSIMILIANO ROMANO

4cl Père Magloire calvados
4cl red vermouth
3cl Cointreau
8cl pear and strawberry juice
champagne

Shake ingredients, except champagne,
with ice. Strain into a highball filled
with ice. Fill with chilled champagne.

Orchard Smash

CHRISTOPHER UNDERWOOD

4cl Père Magloire calvados
2cl apricot brandy
4cl pear juice
dash gomme syrup
fresh mint leaves

Shake ingredients with ice. Strain into
a highball filled with ice. Garnish with
a lemon twist, a sprig of mint and a
slice of apple.

Wimbledon

JULIANO MORANDINI

3cl gin
3cl lemon juice
1.5 crème de fraise
1.5 Bénédictine
dash fraise syrup
dash pasteurized egg white

Shake ingredients with ice. Strain into
a cocktail glass. Garnish with a fresh
strawberry and a sprig of mint.

GREECE

HELENIC BARMEN ASSOCIATION (H.B.A)

Eve

PETRIS IOANNIS

2cl Metaxa 5* brandy
3cl Masticha liqueur
2cl fresh double cream

Shake ingredients with ice. Strain into
cocktail glass. Garnish with a twist of
orange.

Invisible Drink

DIMITRIOS ZAPPAS

3cl ouzo
0.5cl gin
splash lemonade

Put the ouzo in a shot glass, then add
the sparkling lemonade. The drink will
become foggy. Then add the gin and
the drink will slowly become clear.

Pollen

BALLAS BASILEIOS

1cl Bombay Sapphire gin
2cl Pisang Ambon
2cl melon liqueur
1cl caramel syrup
1cl fresh double cream

Shake ingredients with ice. Strain into a cocktail glass. Garnish with a heart shape made from a piece of melon.

Porfirio Rubirosa

IOANNIS ORFANOS

4cl brandy
1cl melon liqueur
2cl sugar syrup
2cl fresh lime juice
5cl cranberry juice
1 fresh strawberry
quarter slice sour green apple

Muddle ingredients in a mixing glass, then pour into a shaker with ice. Shake. Strain into a highball filled with ice. Garnish with a lychee, a strawberry, a cranberry and a raspberry.

Sex Under the Greek Moon

ACHILLEAS KARAOULANIS

6cl vodka
2 fresh raspberries
1 fresh strawberry
1 fresh blackberry
2 tsp caster sugar

Muddle ingredients in a mixing glass. Strain into a shaker with ice. Shake and strain into a cocktail glass. Garnish with a raspberry and a blackberry.

Sparrow

DIMITRIOS ZAPPAS

2cl gin
2cl Frangelico
2cl Passoa
1.5cl fresh lime juice
1cl grenadine
tonic water

Shake ingredients with ice. Strain into a highball filled with ice. Top up with tonic water. Garnish with a sparrow made from apple, and a lime spiral.

HOLLAND

NEDERLANDSE BARTENDERS CLUB (N.B.C)

Apple Shaker

MIKAEL EKMAN

3cl sour apple liqueur
1cl crème de pêche
0.5cl melon liqueur
0.5cl cinnamon liqueur
2cl apple/peach liqueur

Shake ingredients with ice. Strain into a cocktail glass. Garnish with a cocktail apple, a slice of lime, a few bay leaves and a cinnamon stick.

Bitter Sweet Symphony

PASCALLE VAN ROON

2cl Busnel Trois Lys
2cl Licor 43
0.5cl brown crème de cacao
0.5cl Goldstrike
2cl apple juice

Shake ingredients with ice. Strain into cocktail glass. Garnish with a slice of apple, mint leaves and a vanilla pod.

Dirty Dolly

RICHARD ZIJLSTRA

1cl lemon vodka
1cl blackberry genever
2cl blueberry syrup
2cl cerise syrup
1cl Rose's lime cordial
8cl Sourcy cassis (fizzy blackcurrant)

Pour ingredients, except blackcurrant, into a mixing glass with ice. Stir. Strain into a highball filled with ice. Top up with blackcurrant. Stir. Garnish with a blackberry, a gooseberry, a slice of lemon and pineapple and fresh mint leaves.

Jungle Juice

RON BUSMAN

1.5cl gin
3cl Pisang Ambon
1.5cl Mandarine Napoléon
2cl fresh lemon juice
9cl fresh orange juice

Pour ingredients into a highball filled with ice. Decorate with a thin slice of pineapple and a cherry.

Long Island Lolita

RON BUSMAN

2cl wild strawberry syrup
1cl Mandarine Napoléon liqueur
1cl crème de pêche
2cl passionfruit juice
1cl coconut syrup
sparkling orange

Shake ingredients, except sparkling orange, with ice. Strain into a highball filled with ice. Add the sparkling orange juice and stir. Garnish with a strawberry, a blueberry, a gooseberry, a grape, a slice of orange and pineapple leaves. Spray a mist of Mandarine Napoléon over the drink.

Lord of the Drinks

CORNELL TOL

1cl three-year-old rum
2cl wild strawberry syrup
1cl blueberry syrup
2.5cl pineapple juice
dash blackcurrant syrup

Blend ingredients with a small scoop of crushed ice. Pour and garnish with a blackberry, a few redcurrants and a strawberry.

Purple Haze

PETER JANSEN

3cl lemon vodka
3cl Chablis white wine
1.5cl Parfait Amour
1.5cl fresh lemon juice
1.5cl grenadine

Shake ingredients with ice. Strain into a cocktail glass. Garnish with zest of orange, a slice of lemon and fresh red and blue cherries.

HONG KONG BARTENDERS' ASSOCIATION (H.K.B.A)

Chinois

3cl triple sec
1cl blue curaçao
7cl grapefruit juice
3cl pineapple juice
dash Pernod

Shake ingredients with ice. Strain into a champagne flute.

Hong Kong Cheong Sam

3cl gin
1cl white crème de menthe
1cl maraschino liqueur
1cl lemon juice
dash pasteurized egg white
lemonade

Shake ingredients, except lemonade, with ice. Strain into a highball filled with ice. Top up with lemonade. Garnish with fresh mint leaves and a red cherry.

Juniper Bouquet

LAU WAI WING
3cl gin
1cl crème de cassis
1cl grapefruit juice
1cl Rose's lime cordial
tonic water

Shake ingredients, except tonic water, with ice. Strain into a highball filled with ice. Top up with tonic. Garnish with mint leaves, a small slice of celery and a red grape.

Kilimanjaro

LEE CHUNG TAI
2cl gin
2cl triple sec
2cl passionfruit juice
2cl fresh orange juice
1cl fresh lemon juice

Shake ingredients with ice. Strain into a cocktail glass. Garnish with a wedge of passionfruit.

Olympic 2004

CHAN KWOK FAI
3cl gin
1cl Parfait Amour
3cl fresh orange juice
2cl fresh lemon juice
1cl grenadine

Shake ingredients with ice. Strain into a cocktail glass.

Sunflower

5cl orange juice
2cl amaretto
1cl peach liqueur
1cl coconut liqueur
2cl fresh lime juice
2cl light rum
dash pasteurized egg white
dash grenadine

Shake ingredients with ice. Strain into a large champagne saucer.

ASSOCIATION OF BARTENDERS (S.B.H)

April 27th

CHRISTIAN HOLOCSI

2cl blackcurrant vodka
1.5cl Grand Marnier liqueur
1.5cl Pisang Ambon
2cl Rose's lime cordial
pure blackcurrant juice

Shake ingredients with ice. Strain into into a highball filled with ice. Top up with blackcurrant juice. Garnish with a star fruit, a cherry and a mint leaf.

Grand Illusion

EVA JONAS

3cl Grand Marnier liqueur
1cl Eldorado rum
2cl peach syrup
1cl Rose's cranberry mix
cranberry juice

Shake ingredients, except cranberry juice, with ice. Strain into a highball filled with ice. Top up with cranberry juice. Stir. Garnish with melon, a mint leaf and a mulberry.

My Little Son

TAMAS BRODY

2cl cranberry vodka
2cl dry vermouth
1cl Cointreau
2cl pure cranberry juice
orange zest

Shake ingredients with ice. Strain into a cocktail glass. Garnish with a kumquat, a radish butterfly and a mint leaf.

One Flew Over The Cuckoo's Nest

ANTAL KISS

2cl vodka
dash blue curaçao
3cl green apple syrup
dash cinnamon syrup
1cl white chocolate liqueur

Shake ingredients with ice. Strain into a cocktail glass. Garnish with a wedge of green apple upright on the rim. Spear the cherry on top. Add two pineapple leaves and a cinnamon stick to create the look of a small bird.

Roses in the Garden

ATTILA KOTAI

4cl bourbon whiskey
2cl Cointreau
1cl Rose's lime syrup
fresh orange juice
grapefruit juice

Shake ingredients, except orange and grapefruit juices, with ice. Strain into a highball filled with ice. Top up with half orange juice and half grapefruit juice. Garnish with slices of lime and pineapple and a cherry.

Sisi

MIHALY HANDTUCH

3cl vodka
2cl Advocaat
1cl strawberry syrup
1cl coconut syrup
fresh double cream

Shake ingredients, except cream, with ice. Strain into a cocktail glass. Float the cream. Garnish with grated chocolate.

Sweet Margarete

PETER MORAFESIK

3cl Jose Cuervo silver tequila
2cl Pisang Ambon
1cl melon liqueur
1cl green apple syrup
apple juice

Shake ingredients, except apple juice, with ice. Strain into a highball filled with ice. Top up with apple juice. Garnish with a slice of lime and a mint leaf.

Zytaa

TAMAS BRODY

2.5cl cranberry vodka
0.5cl tawny port
0.5cl sour cherry syrup
2cl sour cherry juice
1.5cl fresh apple juice

Shake ingredients with ice. Strain into a cocktail glass. Garnish with fruits.

ICELAND

BARTENDERS' CLUB OF ICELAND (B.C.I)

Golden Tear

BARDUR GUDLAUGSSON

5cl lemon vodka
2cl gold liqueur
2cl dry vermouth Martini

Pour ingredients into a mixing glass with ice. Stir. Strain into a cocktail glass. Squeeze a kumquat over drink. Garnish with a kumquat, zest of lemon and orange.

Icelandair

RAGNAR PÉTURSSON

4cl Scotch whisky
1cl red vermouth
1cl fresh lemon juice
1cl amaretto

Shake ingredients with ice. Strain into a cocktail glass. Garnish with a slice of orange.

Pearl's Tear

PORKELL ERICSSON

3cl vodka
3cl pear juice
2cl Pisang Ambon
1cl crème de banane

Shake ingredients with ice. Strain into a cocktail glass. Garnish with a physalis, a blueberry and a small wedge of lime.

Pink Elephant

BJARNI ÓSKARSSON

3cl Bacardi light rum
3cl crème de banane
3cl unsweetened pineapple juice
1cl coconut cream
dash grenadine

Shake ingredients with ice. Strain into a cocktail glass. Garnish with a cherry on the side of the glass.

Viola

4cl vodka
2cl crème de banane
1cl Parfait Amour
1cl grenadine

Shake ingredients with ice. Strain into a highball glass. Top up with pineapple juice. Garnish with a slice of star fruit and a fresh strawberry.

IRELAND

BARTENDERS' ASSOCIATION OF IRELAND (B.A.I)

Bacardi Passion

GER HEALY
4.5cl Bacardi light rum
1.5cl Midori melon liqueur
1cl apple schnapps
1cl apple juice
1cl passionfruit purée

Shake ingredients with ice. Strain into a chilled cocktail glass.Garnish with half a passionfruit.

Cookies n'Nuts

DECLAN BYRNE
3.5cl Kahlua
2cl amaretto
1cl Frangelico
1cl fresh double cream

Shake ingredients with ice. Strain into a cocktail glass.

Irishman

DECLAN BYRNE
6cl Kilbeggan Irish Whiskey
6 slices cucumber
2 orange wedges
half chilli (remove seeds)
dash Angostura bitters
1cl white cranberry and grape juice
dash gomme syrup

Shake ingredients with ice. Strain through a fine strainer into a chilled cocktail glass. Garnish with slices of cucumber and orange.

Kulah Shaker

WINNER, BEST-TASTING COCKTAIL, JAPAN CUP
JAMES LANGAN
1.5cl Kahlua
1.5cl Cointreau
1.5cl crème de banane
1.5cl fresh double cream
1cl grenadine

Shake ingredients with ice. Strain into a chilled cocktail glass. Add the grenadine. Float the cream. Garnish with a sprinkle of chocolate and zest of orange.

Moonlight Serenade

DECLAN BYRNE
4cl citrus vodka
3cl passionfruit liqueur
dash of Rose's lime cordial
8cl multivitamin juice
dash grenadine

Shake ingredients, except grenadine, with ice. Strain into a highball filled with ice. Add the grenadine, which will sink, giving a beautiful visual effect. Garnish with a star fruit.

Purple Rain

PAUL LAMBERT

3.5cl Bacardi light rum
1.75cl coconut liqueur
1.75cl Cointreau
dash gomme syrup
7Up

Build in a highball filled with ice. Top up with 7Up. Garnish with a few wild berries.

Ruby Kiss

ALAN KAVANAGH

3cl vanilla vodka
2cl white crème de cacao
1cl grenadine
champagne

Shake the vanilla vodka, cacao and grenadine with ice. Strain into a highball filled with ice. Fill with champagne. Garnish with assorted berries on a cocktail stick.

Sanuk

PAUL LAMBERT

3.5cl Bacardi light rum
1.75cl Bacardi coconut
1.75cl passionfruit syrup
8cl pineapple juice
8cl cranberry juice

Shake with ice. Strain into a highball filled with ice. Garnish with a wedge of pineapple and slices of orange and lime.

Tropical Sapphire

DECLAN BYRNE

3cl Bombay Sapphire gin
3cl Cointreau
1cl Advocaat
dash fresh double cream
6cl tropical juice

Shake ingredients with ice. Strain into a highball filled with ice. Garnish with a physalis.

ISRAEL

ISRAELI GUILD OF BARTENDING & SERVICES (I.G.B.S)

Celebration

6 black grapes
2cl vodka
2cl cassis
fresh lemon juice
dash gomme syrup
champagne

Muddle the grapes in the shaker, then add the vodka, lemon juice and the cassis syrup. Shake. Strain into a chilled champagne flute. Fill with champagne.

Chiliana

4cl vodka
4cl apricot syrup
4cl peach syrup
4cl mango syrup
4cl lemon juice
ground black pepper
few coriander leaves

Shake ingredients with ice. Strain into a highball filled with ice.

Rose of Cuba

3cl Havana Club rum
1cl apricot brandy liqueur
1cl vanilla syrup
soda water
pink grapefruit juice

Add the ingredients, except soda
water, to an old-fashioned glass filled
with ice. Stir. Add soda water. Garnish
with a vanilla pod and a few fresh
rose petals.

ITALY

ASSOCIAZIONE ITALIANA BARMEN E SOSTENITORI
(A.I.B.E.S)

Green Island

ROSARIO ZAPPALA
3cl light rum
2cl vanilla syrup
1cl Midori melon liqueur
1cl white crème de menthe
few dashes fresh lemon juice

Shake ingredients with ice. Strain into
a cocktail glass. Garnish with a
strawberry, carambole, slice of yellow
melon, slice of lemon and redcurrants.

Il Geco

VANESSA VERONESE
2.5cl gin
1.5cl triple sec/Cointreau
1.5cl melon liqueur
1cl coconut liqueur
dash fresh lemon juice

Shake ingredients with ice. Strain into
a cocktail glass. Garnish with a single
blackcurrant and a sprig of mint.

Latte Piu

PAOLO FORAMITI AND CLAUDIO VIEL
2cl Drambuie
2cl Ron Papero Aniversario
0.5cl vanilla syrup
0.5cl pure ginseng
2cl fresh double cream

Shake ingredients with ice. Strain into
a cocktail glass. Garnish with a star-
anise, a slice of apple and a few
pineapple leaves.

Lena

ALBERTO CHIRICI
3cl bourbon whiskey
2cl sweet vermouth
1cl dry vermouth
1cl Campari
1cl Galliano

Shake ingredients with ice. Strain into
a cocktail glass. Garnish with a cherry.

Milan Dawn

3cl fresh orange juice
3cl gin
dash Campari

Shake the gin and orange juice with
ice. Strain into a champagne saucer.
Add the Campari on top.

My Angel

DANIELE ARCANGELI

2.5cl mandarin vodka
1cl Aperol
0.5cl amaretto
2cl pineapple purée
0.5cl strawberry syrup

Shake ingredients with ice. Strain into a cocktail glass. Garnish with a green apple and a stem of redcurrants.

One to One

LUIGI PARENTI

4cl amaretto
4cl vermouth
3 dashes Angostura bitters

Pour ingredients into a mixing glass with ice. Stir. Strain into a cocktail glass.

Pink Emotion

CLAUDIO BURALLI AND STEFANO VOLPI

8cl dark rum
5cl Cointreau
3cl strawberry syrup
12cl vanilla ice cream

Blend ingredients until smooth. Pour into a Margarita glass. Garnish with a strawberry and mint leaves.

Red Jack

5cl vodka
1.5cl dry vermouth
1cl Cointreau
1cl Campari

Pour ingredients into a mixing glass with ice. Stir. Strain into a cocktail glass. Garnish with a twist of orange.

Rheingold

4cl gin
2cl Cointreau
1cl dry vermouth
1cl Campari

Pour ingredients into a mixing glass with ice. Stir. Strain into a cocktail glass. Garnish with zest of orange.

Tiziano

3cl freshly squeezed grape juice
Spumante

Pour the grape juice into a chilled champagne flute. Fill with iced spumante.

Tramonto Sul Garda

MARIO BELLOTTI

4cl gin
1.5cl Cointreau
2.5cl grapefruit juice
dash rose syrup
champagne

Shake ingredients, except champagne, with ice. Stir. Strain into a highball. Fill with champagne.

NIPPON BARTENDERS'ASSOCIATION (N.B.A)

Bridal Cocktail

IKUO SAMAJIMA

4cl saké
2.5cl Rosse liqueur
1.5cl fresh lemon juice
dash maraschino liqueur

Shake ingredients with ice. Strain into a cocktail glass.

Carien

AKHITO SUGANUMA

2.5cl marron liqueur
1.5cl apricot brandy
1.5cl white crème de cacao
2.5cl fresh double cream

Shake ingredients with ice. Strain into a cocktail glass. Garnish with cherry, mint leaves and zest of orange.

Ma Cherie

HIRASHI KATAGIRI

3cl tequila
2.5cl sakura liqueur
1.5cl fresh lemon juice
1 teaspoon Chambord

Shake ingredients with ice. Strain into a cocktail glass.

Peace Offering

MASAHIDE MUKAI

4cl gin
2.5cl Bacardi light rum
1.5cl Irish Mist

Pour ingredients into a mixing glass with ice. Stir. Strain into a cocktail glass.

Pure Love

KAZUO UEDA

4cl gin
1.5cl framboise liqueur
1.5cl fresh lime juice
ginger ale

Shake ingredients, except ginger ale, with ice. Strain into a highball filled with ice. Stir in the ginger ale. Garnish with a slice lime.

Queen of Topaz

AKIHIRO AKASHI

4cl vodka
1.5cl amaretto
1.5cl sweet vermouth
1cl fresh lemon juice

Shake ingredients with ice. Srain into a cocktail glass.

Sourire

HIROSHI KOBAYASHI

2.5cl Martell cognac
2.5cl Grand Marnier liqueur
2.5cl red vermouth
1cl fresh lemon juice

Shake ingredients with ice. Strain into a cocktail glass.

Sunny Side

HIROSHI KOBAYASHI

3cl vodka
1.5cl framboise liqueur
1.5cl grenadine
champagne

Pour ingredients, except champagne, into a shaker with ice. Stir. Strain into a champagne flute. Top up with champagne. Garnish with lemon, a strawberry and a cherry.

KOREA

KOREAN BARTENDERS' ASSOCIATION (K.B.A)

Arirang Cocktail

HUNG GUN BONG

1.5cl vodka
2.5cl Mae Chui
1.5cl pineapple juice
2.5cl grenadine

Shake ingredients with ice. Strain into a cocktail glass. Garnish with a cherry.

Day Light

WAN SHIK BAE

5cl vodka
1.5cl Cointreau
1.5cl grapefruit juice

Shake ingredients with ice. Strain into a cocktail glass. Garnish with a slice of lemon.

Dream of Rose

HWA SIK PYO

5cl bourbon whiskey
2cl amaretto
1cl grenadine

Shake ingredients with ice. Strain into a cocktail glass. Garnish with a cherry.

88th Seoul

4cl ginseng brandy
1.5cl vodka
2.5cl fresh lemon juice
1cl orgeat syrup

Shake ingredients with ice. Strain into a cocktail glass. Garnish with a slice of lemon.

Lowe of Rose

4cl vodka
2.5cl gin
1.5cl fresh lime juice

Shake ingredients with ice. Strain into a cocktail glass.

Toad Cocktail

WON HO KIM

2cl Ginseng Ju
4cl triple sec
2cl fresh lemon juice

Shake ingredients with ice. Strain into a cocktail glass. Garnish with a slice of lemon.

ASSOCIATION LUXEMBOURG BARMEN (A.L.B)

Agma

3cl kirsch
1.5cl Cointreau
1.5cl gin
2cl fresh lemon juice

Shake ingredients with ice. Strain into a cocktail glass.

Angel Smile

2.5cl vodka
2.5cl kirsch
2.5cl Cointreau
dash grenadine

Shake ingredients with ice. Strain into a cocktail glass. Garnish with a cherry.

Carmen

CIVERCHIA FABRICE

4cl Jose Cuervo tequila
2.5cl Passoa
1.5cl Mandarine Napoléon

Pour ingredients into a mixing glass with ice. Stir. Strain into a cocktail glass. Garnish with an apple slice and a cherry.

Donarid

2.5cl whisky
2.5cl sweet vermouth
2.5cl cognac
2 dashes Cointreau

Pour ingredients into a mixing glass with ice. Stir. Strain into a cocktail glass.

Grand Ducal

PASCAL CANELLAS

3cl Bacardi light rum
2cl Pinot des Charentes
1cl Pisang Ambon
2cl Pécher Mignon

Pour ingredients into a mixing glass with ice. Stir. Strain into a cocktail glass. Garnish with orange and a cherry.

Kitty Love

2.5cl kirsch
2.5cl Carpano
2.5cl Cointreau
2 dashes fresh orange juice

Shake ingredients with ice. Strain into a cocktail glass. Garnish with a twist of orange.

Petrusse

2.5cl Mirabelle
2.5cl Prunelle
2.5cl fresh lemon juice
dash dry vermouth
dash cassis

Shake ingredients with ice. Strain into a cocktail glass.

Rosselio

PASCAL CANELLAS

3cl José Cuervo tequila
2cl Cointreau
1cl crème de banane
10cl passionfruit juice

Shake ingredients with ice. Strain into a highball filled with ice. Garnish with a wedge of lemon, a sprig of mint and a cherry.

Satin Doll

4cl Martell cognac
2cl white curaçao
2cl pineapple juice

Shake ingredients with ice. Strain into a cocktail glass.

Tendresse

RODRIGUEZ FRANCK

2cl Amanta Cream
4cl Mandarine Napoléon
1cl amaretto
1cl white crème de menthe

Shake ingredients with ice. Strain into a cocktail glass. Garnish with a sprig of mint and a slice of mandarin.

MALTA

MALTESE BARTENDERS' GUILD (M.B.G)

Bols Royal

ALFRED WILLIAMS

2cl vodka
2cl crème de banane
2cl blue curaçao
2cl fresh lemon juice

Shake ingredients with ice. Strain into a cocktail glass. Garnish with banana and a cherry.

Buccaneer

EMMANUEL ZERAFA

2.5cl Maltese liqueur
10cl passionfruit juice
1.5cl blue curaçao
1.5cl fresh lemon juice
7Up

Shake ingredients with ice. Strain into a highball filled with ice. Fill with 7Up. Garnish with a slice of lemon and cherry.

Dragon

GAETANO PSAILA

4cl brandy
1.5cl amaretto
1.5cl Punt e Mes
2 dashes peach brandy

Shake ingredients with ice. Strain into a cocktail glass. Garnish with orange and a cherry.

Gernor

NORBERT FENECH

4cl amaretto
1cl triple sec
1.5cl white rum
1.5cl coconut liqueur
dash grenadine

Shake ingredients with ice. Strain into a cocktail glass. Garnish with zest of orange and a red cherry.

Kinnie Breeze

ALFRED GAUCI

2.5cl gin
1.5cl dry vermouth
1.5cl mandarin liqueur
2.5cl blackcurrant juice
7cl pineapple juice
dash Kinnie

Pour ingredients, except the Kinnie, into a shaker with ice. Strain into a higball filled with ice. Stir in the Kinnie. Garnish with a wedge of pineapple and a sprig of mint.

Maria

ANTHONY GAUCI

3cl lemon vodka
1.5cl Campari
1.5cl dry vermouth
1cl crème de banane
1cl crème de cassis

Shake ingredients with ice. Strain into a cocktail glass. Garnish with a slice of lemon and fresh cherries.

Viva Maria

ISAAC VELLA

2cl brandy
2cl Tia Maria
2cl Galliano
2cl blackcurrant juice

Shake ingredients with ice. Strain into a cocktail glass. Garnish with a cherry.

MEXICO

ASOCIACIÒN MEXICANA DE BARMEN (A.M.B)

Bugatti '82

JOSÉ ASCENCIÒN R GRAJADA

1.5cl brown crème de cacao
1.5cl Licor de Coco
2cl Bacardi light rum
2cl Martell cognac
1.5cl black coffee

Shake ingredients with ice. Strain into a cocktail glass.

Cancun Twist

ROBERTO LEGORRETA LOPEZ

5cl Bacardi light rum
1.5cl sweet vermouth
ginger ale

Build into a highball filled with ice. Top up with ginger ale. Garnish with a red cherry and a sprig of mint.

Golden Dreams

ROBERTO LEGORRETA LOPEZ

5cl Bacardi light rum
2.5cl Cointreau
dash cream of tangerine
dash orange liqueur

Pour ingredients into a mixing glass with ice. Stir. Strain into a cocktail glass. Garnish with a slice of orange, a red cherry and a sprig of mint.

Mexico

CASTELANO TOVAR

1.5cl amaretto
2.5cl Bacardi light rum
2.5cl fresh orange juice
1.5cl sweet & sour mix

Shake ingredients with ice. Strain into a cocktail glass. Garnish with a cherry.

Midori Evergreen

ROGELIO VIDAL GONZÁLEZ

5cl melon liqueur
1.5cl aguardiente
10cl pineapple juice
1cl fresh lemon juice

Shake ingredients with ice. Strain into a highball filled with ice. Garnish with thin slices of lime and melon.

Mockingbird

5cl white tequila
7.5cl grapefruit juice
dash lime juice

Build in an old-fashioned glass filled with ice. Garnish with a cherry.

Tequador

5cl tequila
10cl pineapple juice
dash fresh lime juice
dash grenadine

Shake ingredients, except grenadine, with ice. Strain into a large goblet filled with crushed ice. Add the grenadine.

NEW ZEALAND)

NEW ZEALAND ASSOCIATION OF BARTENDERS (N.Z.B.G)

Fleur d'Orange

CRAIG WILLIAMS

2cl Cointreau
3cl cognac
dash pasteurized egg white

Shake ingredients with ice. Strain into a cocktail glass. Garnish with a cinnamon stick and a twist of orange.

Fleur's Passion

LARRY NAYLOR

3cl Bacardi light rum
3cl Cointreau
3cl Frangelico
6cl apple & orange juice

Shake ingredients with ice. Strain into a small Hurricane glass filled with ice. Garnish with an apple slice fan.

Hot Stuff

BEVIN PHILIPS

3cl whisky
3cl vodka
2cl passionfruit liqueur
1cl strawberry syrup
1cl fresh lime juice

Pour ingredients into a mixing glass filled with ice. Stir. Strain over ice into an old-fashioned glass. Garnish with a cherry and a lemon half-wheel.

Lusty Love

EDWARD HURRELL

1.5cl Bacardi light rum
1.5cl melon liqueur
0.5cl Frangelico
4.5cl apple juice
4.5cl sweet and sour mix

Pour ingredients into a blender with ice and blend. Strain into a cocktail glass.

Otto 2

SUZANNE ANDERSON

1.5cl gin
3cl melon liqueur
3cl coconut liqueur

Shake ingredients with ice. Strain into a highball filled with ice.

Red Sea Iceberg

SZILVESZTOR TOTH

3cl vodka
2cl coconut liqueur
0.5cl Cointreau
5cl pineapple juice
8cl cranberry juice

Pour ingredients into a blender with ice. Blend until smooth. Strain into a Collins glass filled with ice. Garnish with a sprig of mint.

NORSK BARTENDER FORENING (N. B. F)

Aloe Vera

HEGE SIVERTSEN

2cl lemon vodka
2cl melon liqueur
4cl sweet & sour mix
dash Rose's lime juice
7Up

Shake ingredients, except 7Up, with ice. Strain into a highball filled with ice. Top up with 7 Up. Garnish with a slice of watermelon and a twist of lime.

Boheme

KJELL FREDHEIM

4.5cl gin
1cl Bénédictine
1cl dry vermouth
0.5cl VSOP cognac

Pour ingredients into a mixing glass with ice. Stir. Strain into a cocktail glass. Garnish with a twist of orange and a physalis.

Golden Star

MARIT MORA

3cl mandarin vodka
3cl Liquor 43
3cl fresh orange juice
2cl sweet & sour mix

Shake ingredients with ice. Strain into a cocktail glass. Garnish with a physalis and an orange twist.

Little Laila

LINDA KÅRVATN

Layer 1 consists of:
3cl vodka
6cl fresh raspberry purée
1½ tablespoons fresh raspberries

Blend ingredients with crushed ice. Pour into a highball glass filled with ice.

Layer 2 consists of:
3cl sour apple liqueur
2cl green apple syrup

Blend ingredients with crushed ice. Strain over the first layer in the glass. Garnish with fresh raspberries and slices of green apple.

PERU

ASSOCIACION PERUANA DE BARMEN (A.P.B)

Campanita

2.5cl Scotch whisky
2.5cl milk
1cl gomme syrup
1cl white crème de cacao

Shake ingredients with ice. Strain into a champagne glass. Garnish with chocolate flakes.

Capitan

2.5cl sweet vermouth
5cl Pisco Puro
5 dashes Angostura bitters

Pour ingredients into a mixing glass with ice. Stir. Strain into a cocktail glass. Garnish with a red cherry.

Don't Worry Be Happy

2.5cl cream of coconut
5cl Stolichnaya vodka
10cl fresh orange juice
dash anis liqueur
dash grenadine

Shake ingredients with ice. Strain into a highball filled with ice. Garnish with a slice of lemon and a red cherry.

Pacifico

GREGORIO AYBAR ALATA

3cl vodka
2cl green crème de menthe
2cl coconut cream
pineapple juice

Shake ingredients with ice. Strain into a highball filled with ice. Top up with pineapple juice. Garnish with a cherry, a pineapple wedge and white grapes.

Puerto Escondido

3cl vodka
1.5cl gin
1.5cl white rum
1.5cl lime syrup
3 dashes Angostura bitters

Shake ingredients with ice. Strain into a cocktail glass. Garnish with a slice of lime and a cherry.

Vienna

2.5cl Scotch whisky
1.5cl amaretto
1cl anis
3cl Leche Gloria
dash grenadine

Shake ingredients with ice. Strain into a cocktail glass. Garnish with a cherry.

ASSOCIAÇÃO BARMEN DE PORTUGAL (A.B.P)

Alleluia

ANTÓNIO TEIXEIRA DE JESUS

4cl Jose Cuervo tequila
1.5cl maraschino liqueur
1.5cl blue curaçao
1.5cl fresh lemon juice
dash egg white
bitter lemon

Shake ingredients, except bitter lemon, with ice. Strain into a highball filled with ice. Stir in the bitter lemon. Garnish with a slice of lemon, zest of orange, fresh mint and two cherries.

Gabriella

GOLS DE SOUSA

5cl vodka
1.5cl Cocoribe
1.5cl blue curaçao
2 dashes Pernod
lemonade

Shake ingredients, except lemonade, with ice. Strain into a highball filled with ice. Top up with lemonade. Garnish with slices of lemon and orange, sprig of mint and green and red cherries.

Green Dream

JOSÉ GARRET CONÇALVES

2.5cl gin
2cl liqueur de prunelle
1.5cl Kilbora
1cl fresh lemon juice
dash pasteurized egg white
lemonade

Shake ingredients, except lemonade, with ice. Strain into a highball filled with ice. Stir in the lemonade. Garnish with orange and lemon slices.

Lisa

MARIE LA SALETTE RIBEIRO

2.5cl white port
1.5cl coconut liqueur
1.5cl Pisang Ambong
1.5cl fresh double cream
7Up

Shake ingredients, except 7Up, with ice. Strain into a highball filled with ice. Garnish with slices of orange and lemon, green cherries and a thin slice of apple.

Magie Negra

JOAQUIM A MATOS PEREIRA

3cl Martell cognac
1.5cl white crème de cacao
1.5cl Singeverga liqueur
1cl clear honey
1cl fresh double cream

Shake ingredients, except cream, with ice. Strain into a cocktail glass. Float the cream on top. Garnish with grated chocolate.

My Sweet

JOAQUIM F MENDES NUNES

5cl Cointreau
1cl Medronho Velho
1cl Mandarine Napoléon
1cl Natas
dash Tia Maria

Shake ingredients with ice. Strain into a cocktail glass. Garnish with a sprinkle of ground coffee.

Sweet Girl

JOSÉ JÚLIO GARRET CONÇALVES

3cl Martell cognac|
2.5cl Mandarine Napoléon
1.5cl crème de banane
1cl Batida de Coco
fresh double cream

Shake ingredients, except cream, into with ice. Strain into a cocktail glass. Float the cream. Garnish with grated chocolate.

PUERTO RICO

PUERTO RICAN BARTENDERS' ASSOCATION (P.R.B.A)

Arlene

ADALBERTO RODRIGUEZ

2.5cl cranberry juice
2.5cl passionfruit juice
2cl vodka
1cl Mandarine Napoléon liqueur

Pour ingredients into a mixing glass with ice. Stir. Strain into a cocktail glass. Garnish with zest of orange.

Racquel

JOSE MANUEL JARDIN

2.5cl Stolichnaya vodka
1.5cl Parfait Amour
1.5cl blue curaçao
1.5cl crème de cacao
1cl fresh double cream

Shake ingredients with ice. Strain into a cocktail glass. Garnish with red cherry, grated chocolate and fresh mint.

Sol Nascente

JOSÉ CRISTINO

3cl gin
1.5cl crème de banane
1cl red curaçao
1.5cl fresh lemon juice
dash pasteurized egg white
lemonade

Shake ingredients, except lemonade, with ice. Strain into a highball filled with ice. Top up with lemonade. Garnish with a slice of lemon, strip of cucumber peel, zest of orange and half a cherry.

Tropical Sex

3cl Bacardi light rum
1.5cl Galliano
7cl cranberry juice
7cl passionfruit juice

Shake ingredients with ice. Strain into a highball filled with ice. Garnish with slice of kiwifruit, zest of orange and a cherry.

BARTENDERS' ASSOCIATION OF RUSSIA (B.A.R)

Apple Grand Prix

DMITRIY SOKOLOV

2cl VSOP calvados
1cl Grand Marnier cherry
1.5cl red vermouth
2cl apple juice

Pour ingredients into a mixing glass filled with ice. Stir and strain into acocktail glass. Garnish with the peel of a red apple, a cherry and a sprig of mint.

Around the World

DMITRIY SOKOLOV

2cl honey vodka
2cl sour apple liqueur
1cl cranberry syrup
2cl orange juice
15cl fresh double cream

Shake ingredients with ice. Strain into a cocktail glass. Garnish with a cherry, mint leaves and a flower made from a fresh carrot.

In Her Eyes

DMITRIY SOKOLOV

3cl Bacardi gold rum
0.6cl pear syrup
0.6cl mandarin syrup
3cl pineapple juice
2cl cranberry juice

Shake ingredients with ice. Strain into a cocktail glass. Garnish with a kumquat and a heart made from red peach skin, and pineapple leaves.

Megachito

DMITRIY SOKOLOV

5cl Jose Cuervo tequila
2 pieces lime peel
4 sprigs mint
3cl strawberry mix
1cl peach syrup
soda water

Put the lime peel and mint into a highball glass. Muddle, then add the strawberry mix. Fill with crushed ice. Add the tequila and the syrup. Stir. Top up with soda water. Stir. Garnish with mint leaves and sugar.

New Salty Russian

DMITRIY SOKOLOV

5cl mandarin vodka
2 pieces grapefruit peel
1.5cl honey syrup
pinch salt

Muddle the two pieces of peel in an old-fashioned glass, then add crushed ice. Add the vodka, syrup and salt. Stir well.

Way of Life

DMITRIY SOKOLOV

3cl grapefruit juice
1.5cl apricot brandy
1cl blueberry liqueur
2cl red vermouth
1cl fresh lime juice

Shake ingredients with ice. Strain into a cocktail glass with mint leaves in the bottom. Garnish with a slice of apple and fresh blueberries.

SINGAPORE

ASSOCIATION OF BARTENDERS OF SINGAPORE (A.B.S)

Galaxy

HO KIAN HENG

2.5cl coconut liqueur
2.5cl crème de cacao
3cl fresh double cream

Shake ingredients with ice. Strain into a cocktail glass. Garnish with coloured chocolate chips.

Honeymoon

KEN LEE

2.5cl Scotch whisky
1.5cl melon liqueur
2.5cl starfruit juice
2.5cl pineapple juice
1.5cl fresh lime juice

Shake ingredients with ice. Strain into a large champagne flute. Garnish with a melon ball and a cherry.

Merlion City

MAC LEE HUNG HUI

2.5cl vodka
2.5cl apricot brandy
3cl guava juice
dash blue curaçao
dash fresh lemon juice

Shake ingredients with ice. Strain into a cocktail glass. Garnish with a fresh strawberry and mint leaves.

Sunriser

JACQUES KONG

2.5cl Jose Cuervo tequila
1.5cl Midori melon liqueur
5cl pineapple juice
1.5cl fresh lime juice
dash Angostura bitters

Shake ingredients with ice. Strain into a champagne flute. Garnish with an orange spiral, a red cherry and a sprig of fresh mint.

Sweetheart

ASMAH SAMAN

3cl coconut liqueur
2.5cl fresh double cream
1.5cl white crème de cacao
1cl triple sec
dash grenadine

Shake ingredients with ice. Strain into a cocktail glass. Garnish with an orange spiral.

SLOVENIA

DRUSTVO BARMANOV SLOVENIE (D.B.S)

Altona

DUSAN VRTOVEC

3cl dry vermouth
1.5cl light rum
1.5cl Galliano
1.5cl green curaçao

Pour ingredients into a mixing glass with ice. Stir. Strain into a cocktail glass. Garnish with a kumquat.

Dream of Vienna

ALES OGRIN

3cl vodka
2.5cl crème de banane
1.5cl syrup de fragola
1.5cl fresh double cream

Shake ingredients with ice. Strain into a cocktail glass. Garnish with fine powdered chocolate.

Goldstar

MIRAN SOBERL

2.5cl gin
2.5cl red vermouth
2.5cl Mandarine Napoléon
3 dashes Southern Comfort
dash amaretto

Pour ingredients into a mixing glass with ice. Stir. Strain into a cocktail glass.

SOUTH AFRICA

SOUTH AFRICAN BARTENDERS' ASSOCIATION (S.A.B.A)

Framboise Spring Punch

5cl Havana Club Añejo rum
2.5cl raspberry syrup
2.5cl Chambord liqueur
2.5cl fresh lemon juice
Russian cranberry juice

Shake first four ingredients with ice. Strain into a highball filled with ice. Top up with cranberry juice. Garnish with orange and lemon strips and a stemmed cherry. Serve with coloured straws.

Mango Mojito

5cl Havana Añejo rum
2.5cl mango syrup
2.5cl mojito syrup
8 small segments chopped limes
    and lemons
8 fresh mint leaves
soda water

Shake ingredients, except soda water, with ice. Pour directly into a highball glass. Add a splash of soda water. Garnish with a sprig of mint and a slice of dried mango.

Pear and Cranberry Martini

2.5cl vodka
2.5cl pear syrup
5cl cranberry juice

Shake ingredients with ice. Strain into a cocktail glass. Garnish with a pear slice.

Sour Banana Martini

3.75cl Stolichnaya vodka
2.5cl green banana syrup
2.5cl cloudy apple juice
1.25cl fresh lemon juice

Shake ingredients with ice. Strain twice, then pour into a cocktail glass. Garnish with a lemon twist.

ASOCIACIÓN BARMEN ESPAÑOLES (A.B.E)

Altamira

JOSÉ RAMÓN BUSTILLO IGLESIAS

5cl light rum
15cl orange Sumo
2cl Cointreau

Shake ingredients with ice. Strain into a highball filled with ice. Garnish with a slice of orange and a sprig of mint.

Heczar

ANTONIO SANCHEZ REVUELTO

3cl gin
1.5cl Cointreau
1.5cl fresh lime juice
15cl pineapple juice

Shake ingredients with ice. Strain into a highball filled with ice. Garnish with a cherry, a slice of orange and a wedge of pineapple.

Loli Ecijana

JOSÉ PARDAL RINCÓN

3cl Bacardi light rum
1.5cl Cointreau
1.5cl amaretto
1.5cl pineapple juice

Shake ingredients with ice. Strain into a cocktail glass. Garnish with a red cherry.

Sara

JESUS MARTINEZ SANTOS

4cl red vermouth
3cl Scotch whisky
1cl Cointreau

Pour ingredients into a mixing glass with ice. Stir. Strain into a cocktail glass. Garnish with red cherries and zest of orange.

Springbok

2.5cl medium dry sherry
2.5cl Lillet
2.5cl Van der Hum
2 dashes orange bitters

Pour ingredients into a mixing glass with ice. Stir. Strain into a wine goblet filled with ice.

Syllabub

SHERRY IS THE PRIME INGREDIENT OF A SYLLABUB, WHICH IS AS MUCH A DESSERT AS A COCKTAIL.

4cl sweet sherry
2cl fresh double cream
2cl milk
1 barspoon powdered sugar

Whisk well together in a mixing glass. Serve in a small wine goblet with a teaspoon.

Opposite
Chivas Cooler is an exquisite short drink made with 12-Year-Old Chivas Regal whisky and ginger ale.

Following pages
Cocktails ranging from left are Bacardi Cuba Libre, Bacardi Mojito, Bacardi On the Rocks and Bacardi Presidente.

SWEDISH BARTENDERS' GUILD (S.B.G)

Cinnamon Beach

THOMAS LIDBERG

1cl Cointreau
3cl Licor 43
4cl whipped cream flavoured with
    1 teaspoon cinnamon

Pour ingredients into a mixing glass. Stir. Strain into a cocktail glass. Float the cream. Sprinkle with ground cinnamon.

Esprio

MARTIN BERGQVIST

3cl sambuca
2cl cold espresso coffee
3cl whipped cream

Shake ingredients with ice. Strain into a cocktail glass. Sprinkle with fine chocolate powder.

Frozen Apple Bite

OSCAR HERNANDEZ

2cl Bacardi Razz rum
2cl apple sourz
0.5cl sambuca
5 basil leaves
2 red chillies

Blend ingredients without ice in a blender. Pour over crushed ice into a double cocktail glass. Garnish with a lime spiral, basil leaves and a red chilli.

Hot Shot

INVENTED IN THE MID-1980S. NOW A CULT SHOT.

2cl Galliano liqueur
3cl hot coffee
1cl whipped cream

Layer the Galliano, coffee and the cream into a shot glass.

Vanilla Starlight

SARA LUNDGREN

4cl vanilla vodka
2cl Cointreau
2cl peach syrup
10cl lemon sour
dash grenadine

Shake ingredients with ice. Strain into a highball filled with ice. Garnish with a slice of star fruit and a cherry.

SCHWEIZER BARKEEPER UNION (S.B.U)

Day and Night

BERNARD BRULLE

2.5cl eau-de-vie framboise
3cl white peach liqueur
1.5cl cherry brandy

Pour ingredients into a mixing glass with ice. Stir. Strain into a cocktail glass. Garnish with a red, stemmed cherry and a sprig of mint.

Opposite
Dr Mattoni (left) and Derby Mattoni (right) are appetizing non-alcoholic drinks made with pure Mattoni waters.

Lady Killer

PETER ROTH

3cl gin
1.5cl Cointreau
1.5cl apricot brandy
7cl passionfruit juice
7cl pineapple juice

Shake ingredients with ice. Strain into
a highball filled with ice. Garnish with
an orange spiral, sprig of mint and a
slice of green plum.

L'Aube Rouge

PHILLIPE MOUILLOT

4cl gin
1cl apricot brandy
1cl red curaçao
2cl green crème de banane

Shake ingredients with ice. Strain into
a cocktail glass. Garnish with a slice
of banana and a red cherry.

Royal Daiquiri

OLANDO FREY

2cl Bacardi light rum
1cl José Cuervo tequila
3cl crème de banane
2cl fresh lemon juice
1 barspoon sugar

Shake ingredients with ice. Strain into
a cocktail glass. Garnish with mint
and a cherry.

Sunset

PETER ROTH

3cl golden rum
1.5cl framboise liqueur
3cl passionfruit juice
10cl pineapple juice
2 dashes lemon juice

Shake ingredients with ice. Strain into
a highball filled with ice. Garnish with
an orange spiral, a sprig of mint and a
cherry.

Swiss Nostalgia

GILBERT GAILLE

4cl vodka
1.5cl amaretto
1.5cl red vermouth
1cl fresh lime juice

Shake ingredients with ice. Strain into
a cocktail glass. Garnish with zest of
lime.

URUGUAY

ASOCIACIÓN URUGUAYA DE BARMEN (A.U.D.E.B)

Mediterraneo

WALDIR DI PAOLA

5cl vodka
3cl dry vermouth
1.5cl blue curaçao
6.5cl banana syrup
dash maraschino liqueur

Shake ingredients with ice. Strain into
a highball filled with ice.

Morenita

RUBEN BASEDAS

3cl Bacardi gold rum
1cl Frangelico
4cl chocolate ice cream

Shake ingredients with ice. Strain into a cocktail glass. Garnish with grated chocolate.

Rasputin

ROBERTO PONTES

2.5cl gold rum
2.5cl whisky
4cl dry vermouth

Pour ingredients into a mixing glass with ice. Stir well. Pour into a cocktail glass. Garnish with a lemon twist and a lemon spiral.

Shaking Vegas

DANILO ORIBE

2cl Bacardi light rum
2cl strawberry liqueur
1cl peach syrup
5cl fresh orange juice
5cl fresh pineapple juice
3cl champagne

Shake ingredients, except champagne, with ice. Strain into a highball. Fill with champagne. Garnish with a slice of pineapple and a cherry.

UNITED STATES BARTENDERS' ASSOCIATION (U.S.B.A)

Añejo Highball

DALE DEGROFF

5cl Añejo rum
1.5cl orange curaçao
6cl ginger beer
1cl fresh lime juice
2 dashes Angostura bitters

Build in a highball filled with ice, then fill with ginger beer. Garnish with lime wheel and orange slice.

Note: The cocktail originally called for a dash of Wray and Nephew's Pimento Liqueur, which was imported from Jamaica, but is no longer available in the United States.

Double Down

RAY SRP

4.5cl Woodford Reserve bourbon
3cl fresh white peach purée
juice of half a lime
1cl ginger-infused sugar syrup
ginger ale

Shake the first four ingredients with ice. Strain into a double old-fashioned glass filled with ice. Top up with the ginger ale. Garnish with a mint sprig.

Mandarin Breeze

BOBBY G. GLEASON
3.5cl mandarin liqueur
2cl Irish Mist liqueur
2cl Velvet Falernum liqueur
9cl fresh sweet & sour
3cl fresh orange juice

Shake ingredients with ice. Strain into a highball filled with ice. Garnish with a lemon wheel and orange spiral. Sprinkle with grated nutmeg.

Movida

LIVIO LAURO
4.5cl citrus vodka
1cl cherry liqueur
dash Pernod
3cl fresh ruby red grapefruit juice
dash fresh lemon juice

Shake ingredients with ice. Strain into a cocktail glass. Garnish with an orange spiral.

Pan Pacific

FRANCESCO LAFRANCONI
6cl pisco
1.5cl passionfruit purée
juice of 1 lime
2 dashes of peach liqueur
1cl pasteurized egg whites
1cl rock candy syrup

Shake and strain into a cocktail glass. Garnish with a sprig of mint and freshly ground nutmeg.

Sunsplash

TONY ABOU-GANIM
4.5cl vodka
1.5cl Cointreau
4.5cl cranberry juice
3cl fresh sweet & sour

Shake ingredients with ice. Strain into a highball filled with ice. Garnish with freshly grated nutmeg and lemon and orange spirals.

VENEZUELA

ASOCIACIÓN VENEZOLANA DE BARMEN (A.V.B)

Acuario

BENITO GONZEÁLEZ
3cl rum
1.5cl triple sec
1.5cl crème de banane
10cl grapefruit juice
dash gomme syrup

Build into a highball filled with ice. Garnish with orange and a cherry.

Amor de Angel

JOSÉ ESPARTACO MOLINA
3cl vodka
1.5cl Cointreau
1.5cl Kahlua
1.5cl milk

Blend ingredients with a little ice until smooth. Garnish with a light dusting of powdered cinnamon.

Wines
of the
World

INTRODUCTION

VITICULTURE & VINIFICATION

Grapes are usually grown on flat plains because of the need for mechanical harvesting, which is essential to produce the standard of grape used for many of today's wines. Grapes grown on hillsides require an individual picker. The harvest in the Northern Hemisphere occurs between early September through to the end of October. In the Southern Hemisphere, grapes are picked between mid-February through to mid-April.

The flesh or juice of all wine grapes is almost always white, so the colour of rosé and red wines must come from the skin of the black and red grapes. The sugar contained in the juice mixes with the natural yeast on the skin or the winemaker can add yeast cultures, which produce alcohol and carbon dioxide.

Making white wine   White or black grapes are used but the juice is not left in contact with the skins. Wines are fermented at low temperatures of about 15°-20°C, stored in stainless steel, open-topped wooden or concrete vats. After fermentation, oak flavours are produced from fermentation and maturation in both new and old oak barrels. Wooden chips, oak planks or oak essence are also commonly used at this stage.

Making rosé wine   A minimum of two to three days of skin contact with the black or red grapes, which produces a light rosé colour, is required. Fermentation can last seven days.

Making red wine   Black or red grapes are left in contact with the skins for seven to 21 days, depending on the style of wine. To extract the colour the skins are punched back down into the juice or wine is pumped over the skins. Red wines are fermented at a temperature of 25°-30°C. Alcohol helps to extract the colour, tannins and flavours. After fermentation, the wine is run off into stainless steel or wooden barrels. The remaining juice is pressed from the skins and the first pressing is added in with the 'free run juice'.

WHITE GRAPE VARIETIES

Chardonnay   Chardonnay is in wines from Burgundy, Chablis, Mâcon, Pouilly Fuissé as well as the Côte D'Or and also in Vins de Pays wines. Australian, New Zealand, South African, Chilean, Argentinian and Californian wineries also make wines from the Chardonnay grape.

Sauvignon Blanc   With aromas of green fruit such as gooseberry and sometimes vegetation, this grape likes a cool climate, where it produces wines high in acid, with a light to medium body, and is dry and refreshing. It is used with Semillon to produce sweet wines from Sauternes and Barsac.

Riesling This grape produces dry wines with green apple or citrus flavours. In late harvest conditions the wines can be from medium dry through to sweet. The acidity allows the wines to age. Riesling is never blended with other grapes.

Chenin Blanc This grape produces dry through to sweet wines, with citrus flavours. In the Loire Valley it is present in *sec* (dry) *demi sec* or *doux* (sweet) styles of wine, and sparkling wine. In South Africa, where it is known as Steen, it is used for medium-bodied dry to off-dry wines.

Semillon This grape, prone to noble rot, is found in the sweet wines of Sauternes and Barsac. It is mixed with Sauvignon, which adds acidity to the Sauternes, giving the wines the ability to age for 20 years.

Gewürztraminer A highly perfumed variety, with an intense skin giving more colour, this grape produces dry, off-dry and sweet wines full in style and high in alcohol. They have floral hints of rose, orange blossom, or jasmine with lychee, peach and spicy flavours.

Other white grapes include Aligote, Marsanne, Muscadet, Muscat, Pinot Blanc, Pinot Gris, Sylvaner, Müller-Thurgau, Vernaccia, Viognier and Viura.

RED GRAPE VARIETIES

Cabernet Sauvignon In marginal areas, this grape produces under-ripe wines with herbaceous flavours; in hot areas, it produces deep-coloured, full-bodied wines with tannin and acidity, strong black fruit flavours, with hints of mint and cedar. With oak ageing, the tannins soften.

Merlot A less intense, less tannic and less acidic grape, but it has more alcohol than Cabernet Sauvignon, with fruity flavours varying from red berry and red plums to blackberry and black fruit. In some of the hotter areas, the wine has hints of fruity cake or chocolate. With oak ageing, the wines have spicy flavours.

Cabernet Franc This grape produces quality wines in damp, heavy soils in a cool climate. In the Loire Valley it is in the lighter red wines found in Chinon and Bourgueil, St Emilion, Pomerol and Merlot. It has blackcurrant-raspberry flavours with a grassy aroma.

Petit Verdot An erratic grape as far as yield is concerned, this is used in the final Bordeaux blend to give colour, and depth of flavour. It is rich and tannic.

Malbec This grape is common in Cahors wines from the south of Bordeaux. Also known as *Cot* or *Auxerrois*. In Argentina and Chile this grape variety is found in rich, high tannin wines.

Carmenere Originally from Bordeaux, this grape was taken to Chile inthe 1830s. Deep in colour, it is high in tannins, with dark spicy, fruit flavours.

Pinot Noir Grown in the Burgundy region, this thin-skinned, early ripening grape produces quality wines that will develop. It has raspberry or strawberry aromas when young, becoming scented with age, developing a fig-like smell. In other French regions it produces lighter styles. It is used to make champagne.

Syrah or Shiraz A small, thick-skinned, dark coloured grape, its wines have colour and moderate to high levels of tannin and acidity. If grown in moderate climates, the wines have a minty or eucalyptus aroma. Black fruit is the trademark taste, along with dark chocolate and spice. In hot climates there is more liquorice or cloves in the aroma. It ages well in oak, with flavours of smoke and vanilla.

Grenache This grape is found in the hot climate terroir of Southern France and in Spain (known as *Garnacha*). A thin, black-skinned grape with a large berry, it produces high sugar levels resulting in higher alcohol and low acidity. The fruit style can be strawberry/raspberry with spicy flavours such as pepper and cloves.

Tempranillo Spain's best-quality native grape is known by a number of different names in the wine regions of Spain: in Penedas, it is Ullde Llebre; in Ribera del Duero it is Tinto Fino or Tinta del Pais. In Portugal it is Tinta Roriz or Aragonas. It gives strawberry or cherry character, but it can also be spicy, with tobacco flavours. In some Rioja regions it is drunk as a young wine but it can age well, as seen in the Gran Reservas of Rioja. Plantings were made in California and Argentina.

Sangiovese This is Italy's widely planted red, but it is at its best in Tuscany, where it is used to make Chianti wines. Recent research suggests a number of different clones are available, so the styles of wine vary from pale to deep red, with cherry flavours and, sometimes, light hints of spicy undertones.

Other red grape varieties include Barbera, Carignan, Cinsault, Dolchetto, Gamay, Graciano, Mazuelo, Nebbiolo and Zinfandel.

AUSTRALIA

Vines were planted in Australia by the first English settlers in 1788. The Governor had taken cuttings with him of the 'claret' grape and the wine produced from them was encouraging enough for the settlers to ask the British government to send out someone with technical knowledge of winemaking. Two French prisoners-of-war were dispatched on the assumption that as they drank wine, they would know how to make it. Unfortunately, this was not the case.

One of the earliest pioneers of viticulture was John Macarthur, better known as the founder of Australia's merino wool industry; he took cuttings of French vines back after a trip abroad and by 1827 was selling the wine in Sydney. Another was James Busby, a young Scot who had been sent to Australia to take charge of an orphanage; he was also required to tend the school's small vineyard. Busby persuaded growers such as Macarthur to distribute their surplus cuttings to other settlers and when he later toured Europe he bought cuttings which were sent back to Sydney and Adelaide.

Vineyards were also planted around the settlement of Port Phillip (now Melbourne) and in the 1850s a group of German Lutheran immigrants settled in the Barossa Valley just north of Adelaide. They had been winemakers in Germany and chose the valley as the best place to establish their new vineyards. From these beginnings viticulture spread to other parts of the country.

Britain's entry into the European Union terminated existing preferential trading terms, but the UK remains the main export for Australia wines. In 2005 sales to the USA reaped the Australian producers $AU933 million, only $AU6 million below the figures for Britain. Together, the US and Britain comprise two-thirds of the export market. Australia produces 4 percent of the world's wine.

The main wine-growing regions are in the south, and cover the three states of New South Wales, Victoria and South Australia in the east and Western Australia. Tasmania is the newcomer. Some of the large companies have vineyards in a number of regions and may blend the wines to market under brand names, but quality wine is sold under a regional label. Each region has its own style and this is more evident in the wines of the smaller family concerns.

The main red grape varieties are:
Shiraz
Cabernet Sauvignon
Merlot
Grenache
Pinot Noir
Ruby Cabernet (Cabernet
  Sauvignon x Carignan).

The white varieties are:
Chardonnay
Semillon
Rhine Riesling
Colombard
Chenin Blanc

NEW SOUTH WALES

Hunter Valley This rural area, two hours' drive north of Sydney, is noted for high quality table wine. It is split into two main regions –The Lower and Upper Hunter valleys, which are 104km apart. The area has become known for sweet Semillon wines. Wineries include: Brokenwood, Tyrell's, Rothbury, Lindeman's.

The Lower Hunter Valley Vineyards are in the districts of Pokolbin and Rothbury. The climate is hot, but, hailstones and rain can cause problems at harvest time. Grapes planted include Shiraz, Cabernet Sauvignon and Pinot Noir and Semillon and Chardonnay for whites. The Upper Hunter Valley is a hot region and dry. Mainly a white wine area, the Semillon grapes do well.

Mudgee This area is on the same latitude as the Hunter Valley, but 130km further west and 600m above sea level. The location and its ideal soil attract winegrowers. Wines are noted for their rich fruit and longevity. Wineries include: Craigmoor.

Riverina Around 10 percent of the everyday drinking wine of New South Wales comes from here and quality is good as growers have concentrated on planting premium grape varieties. This is an area of small farmers who contract their harvest to the big companies such as De Bortoli and McWilliams. Many of the farmers make their own wine, which can be bought at the winery.

VICTORIA

Victoria has long, hot dry summers and cold winters with frequent frosts. Modern winemaking skills have changed the wines produced here from big and dark to styles that are more acceptable to the modern palate and wines from this State are now highly regarded. Phylloxera is still a problem.

North East Vines were planted in the 1850s and fortified wine was produced. The area is still known for this type of wine.

Rutherglen This region lies 200km north-east of Melbourne and produces some of the best liqueur and dessert wines in Australia made from Muscat and Muscadelle grape varieties.

Milawa The foothills of the Australian Alps is home to the Brown Brothers estate (established in 1889), one of the few estates to replant after phylloxera. Many different grape varieties flourish in the micro-climate and these are used to produce a range of wines. The King Valley is another region where the Brown family select Chardonnay and Pinot Noir to produce sparkling wines.

Central Victoria, Goulburn Valley Quality red and white wines from favourite, and less favourite, varieties are also produced here. Wineries include: Chateau Tahbilk and Mitchelton.

Great Western/Grampians Spring frosts require growers to be careful about site selection. Poor soils and a hilly terrain create harsher conditions. Great

Western is home to some sparkling wines. Both traditional and transfer methods are used to retain the bubble in the bottle. Wineries include: Seppelt, which brings in grapes from other regions.

The Sunraysia is a vast area straddling the two states of Victoria and New South Wales. The Murray River provides the irrigation for this hot region. The area produces average quality wines. Wineries include: Lindemans at Karadoc (Southcorp) and Mildara wines (Beringer Blass).

Yarra Valley Vineyards were established in the 1970s. Due to a mixture of generally cool climate and soil variations, a range of grape varieties were planted. Wineries include: Green Point Vineyard (Domaine Chandon), Coldstream Hills, Yarra Ridge, Yarra Yering.

Other districts to look out for are:
Gippsland, Mornington Peninsula, Geelong and the **Bendigo Macedon Ranges.**

SOUTH AUSTRALIA

This is Australia's biggest grape-growing state. About two-thirds of the country's annual wine production comes from here and most of the vines are planted within a 200km radius of Adelaide, the capital city.

Adelaide Hills Mount Lofty and Picadilly valleys lie just a 25-minute drive from the centre of Adelaide. There, the climate is that bit cooler. Wineries include: Hensche, Mountadam, Petaluma, Shaw and Smith, and the famous Penfolds Magill Estate.

Adelaide Plains is a much hotter region and needs irrigation. This region is known for its low-cost wines produced from high-yielding vineyards.

Barossa Valley This region is known to wine drinkers as Australia's top wine region. The Germanic influence has played its part in the drive for quality wine. The Germanic influence has played its part in the drive for quality wine. Climatically similar to Portugal, this fertile valley produces great quantities of table wine, sparkling wine and brandy. The vines are ungrafted, as phylloxera never hit the valley, and it has become a source of historic wineries and some old vine plantings. The climate is being compared to the ripening temperatures found in Bordeaux and Western Australia. Cabernet and Merlot do well, as does Shiraz. Wineries include: Peter Lehmann, Wolf Blass and Yalumba, Penfolds, Seppelt, Bethany, Grant Burge and Chateau Yaldara.

Clare Valley This hot, dry region is further north of Adelaide and is becoming known for quality Riesling wine. Wineries include: Jim Barry, Tim Knappstein, Leasingham and Taylors.

Coonawarra The region is recognised as one of Australia's great wine regions, and is located 350km south-east of Adelaide. With a low degree of sunshine, the grapes ripen slowly. The vintage can be as late as April and May. It is famous for its subsoil, known as terra rossa (limestone). Wineries include: Wynns, Lindemans, Hollicks and Penfolds.

Eden Valley is situated to the east of the Barossa Valley and its history of winemaking is as long as that of the Barossa Valley, with planting records that date back to 1847. It has a reputation for Riesling wines. Wineries include Pewsley Vale, Henschke's Hill of Grace and Mountadam.

Langhorne Creek Forty kilometres east of Adelaide, this is source of commercial wines. Wineries include: Seppelt, Penfolds, Wolf Blass, Jacob's Creek.

McLaren Vale South of Adelaide, this is where John Reynell planted vines in 1838, employing a young man called Thomas Hardy. These young men helped develop this wine region. With low summer rain, the need to irrigate is essential. With different microclimates throughout the McLaren Vale, many grape varieties are planted. Wineries include: Chapel Hill, D'Arenberg, Seaview, Hardy's, Maglieri, Chateau Reynella.

Padthaway Situated 64 km north of Coonawarra, the soil structure and climate here are similar to Coonawarra's. White wines are made from Chardonnay and Riesling varieties; reds are made from Cabernet Sauvignon and Shiraz. Wineries include: Seppelts, Lindemans and Wynns.

Riverland The longest river in Australia, the Murray River, helps to irrigate the land around the South Australia and Victoria border. Vast quantities of commercial wine and brandy come from around Renmark.

WESTERN AUSTRALIA

The vineyards are located in the south-west corner of the state, in the Perth Hills, 22km from the city of Perth.

Swan Valley More than 50 vineyards lie scattered over the fertile alluvial flats west of the Darling Range escarpment, many still owned by descendants of the Yugoslav and Italian emigrés who made the Swan Valley their home after World War II. Grapes were planted in this region as far back as 1829 and for 150 years this was the only wine region in Western Australia. Originally a producer of table wine, in the 1930s the region became the state's major producer of fortified styles.

The hot climate allows grapes such as Chenin Blanc and Verdelho to grow alongside Chardonnay. The valley produces some of the finest fortified wines in Australia, along with the state's biggest range of ports, Tokays, Muscats and rich, liqueured wines. Watch out for liqueur Verdelho and liqueur Shiraz – both are rarely made outside the Swan Valley.

In recent years, winemakers have added finesse to the table wines. Nestled among international players are many smaller wineries. Many winemakers avoid chain-store discounting and only sell direct to their customers. Wineries include: Sandalford, Houghton (BRL Hardy, home to Australia's most famous white Burgundy).

Margaret River The climate is maritime, with an even accumulation of warmth, compared to St Emilion and Pomerol in a dry vintage. Merlot and Cabernet Sauvignon are favoured, as are Sauvignon and Semillon. Chardonnay does very well in this region, too, with some outstanding wines coming from the Leeuwin Estate. Wineries include: Cape Mentelle, Vasse Felix, Evans and Tate.

Other WA regions to look out for include:
Pemberton and **Great Southern Region.**

TASMANIA

Tasmania is recognised as the pre-eminent Australian region for Pinot Noir production. Sparkling wine will develop further as the local wine-growing associations aim to be recognised as the best sparkling wine in the world outside Champagne. The dominant fruit variety is Pinot Noir followed by Chardonnay, while Riesling, Sauvignon Blanc, Pinot Gris and Cabernet Sauvignon round off the high quality wines. Tasmania produces only approximately 0.2 percent of the total Australian Wine Crush but over 10 percent of the premium and ultra premium bottled market.

One of the most climatically extreme wine-growing regions, Tasmania is 'The Cool Climate' wine growing state in Australia. Tasmanian sparkling wines are gaining acclaim worldwide; Rieslings and other aromatics are catching the attention of many for their elegance, persistence and incredible longevity. The better-known regions include the Pipers River, Tamar Valley and South Tasmania. Wineries include: Pipers Brook (for Pinot Noir), Stefano Lubiana Wines, Domaine A/Stoney Vineyard, Moorilla Estate.

AUSTRIA

There is a system of grading wines according to sweetness from *kabinett* through to *trockenbeerenauslese*, similar to that of Germany. A major contribution to viticulture was made by Lenz Moser, who developed a method of planting and training vines so that they could be harvested by tractors, even on steep slopes, so reducing labour costs. The standards of quality are high and strict controls are maintained over all aspects of production. Once a wine has passed a chemical analysis and tasting test, it is officially declared quality wine and awarded the '*Weingutesiege 1*' – a red and white goblet on a gold background.

In Austria, as a rule of thumb, hot and dry years favour red wines, while cool and humid years are better for whites. Fortunately, there are also years that offer ideal conditions for white and red: such years were 1999, 1997 and 1993. After the controversial vintage of 2004 a different phenomenon was observed: cool and changeable weather resulted in top qualities for some of the red wine types such as Zweigelt, St Laurent and Pinot Noir, which were harvested before the great rains around Lake Neusiedl, but also in the Lower Austrian red wine islands of Thermenregion and Carnuntum. These are attractive wines with beautiful colours, power, and great length. For the 2003 vintage look for red wines full of body and generosity, especially Blaufränkisch and Cabernet Sauvignon, which presented a sensational fruit in this year.

The four wine regions are defined as:

Lower Austria Consists of Weinviertel, Wachau, Kremstal, Kamptal, Traisental, Donauland, Carnuntum and Thermenregion. Gruner Veltliner is the most widely planted grape, producing peppery spice, fruity and usually dry white wines. With a share of a third of the total viticultural area, this is the most important variety grown. The quality spectrum of the Grüner Veltliner is sweeping, extending from light, effervescent wines that are best drunk young – as 'Heuriger' – to spätlese wines that are rich in extracts and alcohol and age particularly well. The wine towns are Retz, Krems and Langenlois.

Burgenland A tiny province located near the Hungarian border planted with Reisling and Müller-Thurgau grapes that flourish in the sandy soil. The mists from Lake Neusiedl play a part in the development of noble rot botrytis, which shrivels grapes and concentrates the sugar. The town of Rust is the centre for Austria's quality sweet wines, the best known being Ruster Ausbruch.

Styria Located along the border of Slovenia, this area has volcanic soil, which suits the Traminer grape, producing spicy aromatic wine. Fruit-driven wines come from the WelschRiesling, Muskateller, Pinot Blanc and Sauvignon grapes grown here.

Vienna (Wien) The vineyards are within the city limits and in the famous Vienna Woods, the best-known wine suburb being Grinzig.

CENTRAL EUROPE

BULGARIA

Bulgaria has a moderate climate with a warm summer and a relatively cold winter. The soils are diverse, varied and favourable for vine growing, the proper ripening of grapes and the production of quality white and red wines. Unfortunately, the wine industry of Bulgaria has been affected by the political changes of the late 1980s. A shortage of grapes and the high price demanded for them has meant that Bulgarian wines are not as competitive as they once were. From sales of four million cases per year into the UK prior to upheavals, this figure has dropped to less than half a million cases. Bulgaria has five major vine and wine regions, which have been defined according to the soil and the climatic conditions, as well as the grape varieties produced: the Danube Plains (Northern Bulgaria), the Black Sea (Eastern Bulgaria), the Rose Valley, the Thracian Lowlands (Southern Bulgaria) and the Strouma Valley (South-western Bulgaria). The wide flat plains of the Danube and Meritza valleys are easily cultivated mechanically.

The Balkan Mountains run east to west, and the local red grapes Mavrud, Pamid and Gamza are planted north of the range, along the Danube, to produce everyday drinking wine. The valley to the south of the mountains produces sweet wines as well as a dry Miskat. Eastern Bulgaria supplies good dry whites from the local Dimiat grape. The preference to plant international grape varieties has seen Cabernet Sauvignon, Merlot and Pinot Noir being planted to produce red wines and Rhine Riesling, WelschRiesling Chardonnay and Sauvignon Blanc to produce white options.

GREECE

Considering the long historical association between Greece and wine, the country's wine production is small. One custom that has survived thousands of years is that of adding pine resin to the must (the material left after the initial grape pressing) during fermentation. The white wine that results from this process is known as Retsina. Entry into the EU has provided funding to assist with the purchase of stainless steel vats and new oak barrels, which has had a positive effect on the quality of the wine produced in Greece. Small farmers sell their grapes to a local co-operative or to one of the leading companies, such as Achaia Clauss, Boutari or Tsantalis. Native grapes are still used primarily, but some producers are also experimenting with the international varieties. Monemvasia on the Peloponnesian peninsula is the original home of the Malvasia grape, which is now used in other parts of the world. Mavrodaphne, a sweet red wine fortified with brandy, is still popular. The wine laws have been absorbed into the EU wine regime. The vast amount of Greek wine is table wine. *Vin de pays* is produced in a number of regions, of which the Peleponnese and Crete produce the most popular. Quality wines produced in a specific region are graded as *Appellation d'Origine* and *Appellation d'Origine de Qualité Supérieure*. Wine is produced on the mainland and on many of the islands. The overall quality of Greek wine is improving, but the main challenge for producers is to increase the awareness of the regions and unfamiliar grape varieties among the wine-buying public.

HUNGARY

Although surrounded by mountains, most of Hungary is a vast flat plain dominated by the largest lake in Europe, Lake Balaton. Recent historical developments and political changes in central and Eastern Europe have had a major effect on the export markets. In addition, Hungarian winemakers have had to learn to improve their standards to suit the more demanding western wine buyers. Privatization of the vineyards and wine production is still taking place and we are beginning to see more private companies and growers' co-operatives leading the fight to regain market share.

The phrase *minöségi bor* is recognised by the EU as indicating a quality wine and is equivalent to *Appellation Contrôlée*. The top wines carry the label *Különleges Minöségi Bor* (Special Quality Wine). These special wines fall into four groups: wines made from late-harvested grapes (spätlese); wines made from selected grapes (auslese); wines made from shriveled (botrytized) grapes (beerenauslese or trockenbeerenauslese) and aszu (dessert) wines.

The main wine-growing regions are Tokaj-Hegyalja, Northern Massive, Eger, Etyek, North and South Balaton and Villany-Siklos. Local grape varieties include the Irsai Olivér, Furmint, Hárslevelü, Muscat Lunel and Kardarka.

Tokay This is a small village in the north-east of Hungary near the Slovakia and Ukraine borders. The volcanic soil, river mist and long, dry, warm autumns create excellent conditions for ripening the furmint and hárslevelü grapes to full maturity. The noble rot botrytis settles on the fruit, absorbs its water content and leaves the shrivelled berry full of concentrated sugar. The most shrivelled of all are known as Aszú grapes and these go into a wooden tub called a puttonyos. It is mixed in with the base wine and allowed to ferment. The level of sugar left in the wine determines the Puttonyos's grade. Tokay Furmint, a dry to medium-dry wine, is made with grapes not affected with botrytis. Foreign investment by other wine and spirit companies has seen a considerable change to the quality of the wines from this region.

ROMANIA

Romania has long been an important wine-producing country in Central Europe, but it has yet to prove itself a provider of quality wine. The country does have the potential to produce better-quality wines and with continued investment in the vineyards and more funding in the wineries this improvement is taking place. Contributing to this process may be an outbreak of phylloxera, which prompted Romanian producers to turn to France for help in re-establishing their vineyards. As a result, a great many vineyards are planted with French grape varieties. In addition, a programme of capital investment by various organisations has helped to get Romania back online, and Australian and New Zealand winemakers have improved the quality of the wines. The four main regions are Tarnave, Dealul Mare, Murfatlar and Cotnari. At present, the home market is important for wine consumption; the UK and other European markets also account for about 30 percent of sales.

ALONG THE BLACK SEA

Moldavia This region was part of Romania until 1944 and its wine styles are similar to those of its European neighbours. With help from 'flying winemakers', the quality level has gone up. The principal grape varieties used include Feteasca for white wines and Cabernet Sauvignon and Saperavi for reds.

Ukraine This large vineyard area occupies much of the northern shore of the Black Sea. The country produces good-quality liqueur-style wines, similar to Port, from the Muscat grape, while Odessa is a centre for the production of sparkling wine.

Russia and Georgia Russia's wine production is concentrated in the south, with local and international grape varieties being planted. Meanwhile, Georgia is home to a flourishing sparkling wine production industry, which feeds high local demand.

Serbia–Macedonia These two provinces stretching down to Greece produce over half of the wines of Yugoslavia. Most of them are consumed locally, being full, fruity everyday drinking wines. The white Smedervka and red Prokupac and Modri Burgundec wines are the best known.

Slovenia This region centres on the towns of Ljutomer and Maribor and is noted for its fine white wines. The Laski-Riesling grape is planted all over the hills to supply the local co-operatives with the country's most exported wine. This part of Yugoslavia once belonged to Austria; and other white wines made in the German style are Sipon, Renski Riesling and Traminer.

Croatia The Dalmatia coast reaching around the Adriatic Sea to the Italian border is planted with red grape varieties. The hot summers are tempered by sea breezes so that the big, full alcoholic wines are made from Pinot Noir, Cabernet, Plavac and Merlot grapes. Opoi is a light red, and whites from the hotter inland areas are also full, round wines. Vranac is made from a local red grape in Montenegro and is being exported in two styles.

ENGLAND

Wine has been made in England since the Romans introduced the vine, and the Domesday Book records 83 established vineyards, most of which belonged to the religious orders. In the Middle Ages the light delicate native wine was widely drunk until the acquisition of Bordeaux brought French wines to England. In the early eighteenth century a treaty with Portugal brought more rival wines and the English product never regained its popularity. However, a few vineyards continued to flourish in the care of various noblemen.

It was not until 1925 that any scientific research was made into which grape varieties would suit the English climate and ripen enough to produce wine on a commercial basis. The climate in the south of England is not unlike that of parts of Germany and consequently many of the grape varieties and crossings of Germany are suitable for England. The early ripening Müller-Thurgau grape does well and in good years makes flowery, fruity dry wine that is ready for early drinking. Two varieties now being successfully cultivated are the Seyval Blanc, which is a hybrid produced by the Seyve Villard nurseries in France, and the Schönburger, which is a new variety bred from the Muscat grape from the Geisenheim Research Station in Germany.

The style of wine being produced in English vineyards is evolving. Due to the climatic conditions, the share of red wine is about 10 percent. Plantings of Pinot Noir, Pinot Meunier and Chardonnay by some of the leading estates have resulted in very good sparkling wines. Nyetimber and Ridgeview Wine Estate have proved that the production of classic bottled fermented sparkling wine is one area that will continue to expand. The success of these wines at international competitions proves that sparkling wine from the UK is here to stay and, as more people taste the product, they will discover how good it is. Sales of rosé wines continue to grow, and English winemakers are also making organic wine.

Between 1984 and 2004 the total hectares in production have grown from 356 ha to 722 ha. Wineries include: Barkham Manor, Stanlake Park, Nyetimber, Denbies Wine Estate, Lamberhurst and Three Choirs.

FRANCE

Wine is an integral part of life in France. From an early age a French child will drink a little wine in water at meal times, the French housewife uses it as a culinary aid, and Frenchmen sit for hours in small cafés quietly drinking the local product. The truly great wines of France stand unrivalled in the world of fine wine and are made with such loving care and skill that they can be compared with works of art. However, these wines represent a very small proportion of France's production, which covers every style and quality of wine. The small grower who has to store his pallets of new bottles out on the village street is as proud of his simple red wine as the owners of a château are of their famous wine.

All French wines are graded by quality and the finest of them are described by the name of their place of origin. The Institut National des Appellations d'Origine, known as the INAO, is the body that authorizes a region to call its wines after their place of origin by granting it the status of *Appellation d'Origine Contrôlée* (name of controlled origin), which is often referred to as an appellation or AC.

To qualify for the use of an AC, wines must be produced from stated grape varieties grown within the authorized area. The INAO sets a maximum yield per hectare and a minimum alcoholic strength for each appellation. Each AC region has a general appellation that can be used for any wine that meets the basic requirements. If that same wine is able to meet even stricter requirements it is entitled to one of the higher classifications within the AC. For example, the general appellation for the Rhône Valley is 'Côtes du Rhône'. Better wine may have the grading 'Côtes du Rhône Villages' and if it is of sufficient quality and grown in the correct locality it is entitled to be labelled 'Chateauneuf-du-Pape', 'Hermitage', 'Tavel' or the other names listed in the appellations of the Rhône. A winemaker will obviously market his wine with its best possible appellation, so the more specific the *Appellation Contrôlée* mentioned on the label, the better the wine. The inclusion of a village or vineyard name is an indication of quality.

Certain regions produce good quality wines that are not quite of AC standard and these are given the rating VDQS – *Vins Delimités de Qualité Supérieure*. The vast majority of these come from the Midi. The winemakers hope that their wines will eventually be upgraded to appellations, which provides an incentive for maintaining a good standard. The best-known come from the Aude, Gard, Herault and Tarn regions in Southern France and are straightforward flavoursome wines that represent good value. Vin de table is everyday drinking wine, most of which is consumed within France.

ALSACE

The province of Alsace lies in the north-east corner of France, on the German border. Alsace has always been wine country and the archives of the city of

Colmar include detailed records of over 1,200 vintages. Although famous during the Middle Ages, the wines of Alsace were virtually unknown while the province was under German sovereignty, as they were used for blending with German wines. Since 1945 the growers of Alsace have devoted themselves to replanting top quality vines and instituting strict controls over all aspects of viticulture and vinification. Today Alsace is one of the world's most consistent producers of good-quality white wine and 30 percent of all Appellation Contrôlée white wine is produced in Alsace. Germany takes over half of all Alsace wine exports and much of the wine is sold from the 'cellar door' to Germans, Swiss and Belgians who visit this beautiful region.

Climatically, Alsace is near the limit of vine cultivation as it is so far north, but the Vosges mountains, which border it on the west, form a natural barrier to protect the region from rain and cloud cover. Consequently the 96km strip of vineyards nestles on the lower slopes of the mountain range and enjoys warm summers and long sunny autumns. In contrast to other wine-producing areas, Alsace has rich soil, but frost, hail and birds are real dangers. Most vineyards are less than two and a half acres in size, so much of the wine is made by the co-operative wineries or by producer-dealers (*négociants*) who buy grapes to supplement their own vineyard supplies.

The best wines come from the south of Alsace and are much softer and richer than those from north of Barr. There are two appellations, 'Alsace' and 'Grand Cru Alsace'. To gain Grand Cru status the wines must come from vineyards whose slopes had been regarded as exceptional. Grand Cru must come from one grape variety. The permitted grape varieties are Gewürztraminer, Muscat, Pinot Gris and Riesling.

The wine may be sold under a brand name but the vast majority of it is marketed under the name of the grape used to produce the wine. The law requires that if a grape variety or vintage is stated on the label, the wine must be composed entirely of that grape variety or vintage and the label must carry the name and address of the bottler. All Alsace wine must be sold in the characteristic tall, green, flute-shaped bottles.

Riesling This variety is considered to produce the best Alsace wine. It makes racy, delicate wine with fine grape aroma and fruity flavour. This wine complements fish dishes.

Gewürztraminer This rich, spicy wine has an almost overpowering fruitiness and in a good year can have up to 15 percent alcohol. It is an excellent accompaniment to highly seasoned food and strong cheese. This is the best known of the Alsace wines because of its distinctive spiciness.

Muscat This wine has a very pronounced perfume characteristic of the grape variety. Although it makes sweet wine in other parts of Europe, the Alsace Muscat is bone dry. The best have a gentle, delicate flavour and when served chilled make a delicious aperitif.

Pinot Gris An EU ruling has asked the growers to fade out the word 'Tokay', in order to avoid conflict with Tokay produced in Hungary. This grape is a late ripener with good yields and produces wines of intense flavour and pleasant acidity and good ageing potential.

Pinot Blanc This is a high-yielding variety, also known as Klevner. It produces straightforward wines that are dry, clean and crisp.

Sylvaner This grape variety is grown predominantly in the north of Alsace. It is good everyday drinking wine.

Edelzwicker This term denotes a blend of several varieties, the most used being Tokay d'Alsace, Sylvaner and Chasselas. Many of these blends are sold under brand names.

Reserve, Cuvée Exceptionelle These terms are used at the discretion of the maker to indicate top-quality wines that will repay keeping.

Vendage Tardive This term means that the grapes have been harvested late in the season so that the wine will have a more concentrated sweetness. It is the equivalent of the German term 'spätlese'.

Selection de Grains Nobles Grapes that have been affected with noble rot and will be sweet. Only produced in outstanding years.

Eaux-de-vie Orchard fruits and wild berries from the mountain forests are used to produce the many famous *alcools blancs* of Alsace.

BORDEAUX

In south-west France, the Dordogne river in the north and the Garonne river from the south converge to become the broad Gironde, which flows to the sea via its long estuary. The whole of the department of the Gironde has been dedicated to vines since Roman times when it was known as Aquitainia. For centuries the Duchy of Aquitaine was almost a mini-kingdom and when Eleanor of Aquitaine married Henry Plantagenet in 1152 this much-prized region became English territory.

The English took to drinking the pale delicate red wine they named *clairet*, and by the fourteenth century over three-quarters of Bordeaux wine exports went to England. English merchants have lived in Bordeaux ever since and the wine is still referred to as claret.

The most important regions of Bordeaux with their own appellations are as follows:

Médoc	Entre-deux-Mers	St Émilion
Haut Médoc	Premières Côtes	Pomerol
Graves	Cérons	Fronsac
Barsac	Louplac	Bourg
Sauternes	Sainte-Croix-du-Mont	Blaye

The châteaux of Bordeaux have been officially classified since 1855 when the wine brokers drew up a list of the finest wines based on soil, prestige and price. However, only the Médoc and Sauternes regions were recognized to produce quality wines at this time, so that Graves and St Émilion had to wait until the 1950s to have an official rating and Pomerol has still not been classified.

Any wine grown within the Bordeaux area is entitled to the AC 'Bordeaux' or 'Bordeaux Supérieur' according to the degree of alcohol it contains. Many regions, such as Médoc and Graves have the right to use their own names as the AC for their wines and some communes (villages) within these regions produce wines of such quality that they can use the village name as the AC for the wine. So, wine from the commune of Pauillac in the Haut Médoc can be labelled *Appellation Pauillac Contrôlée*. However, if the wine is not considered good enough for such a prestigious AC, then it can be labelled Haut Médoc, 'Bordeaux Supérieur' or just 'Bordeaux'.

Médoc The Médoc is a strip of land that borders the south side of the Gironde estuary. The vines are only planted along the river on a narrow, gravelly, sandy strip of land that varies in width from 5 to 10 km. Médoc wine is made with a high proportion of Cabernet Sauvignon grape, which takes many years to mature, so the wines are very long-lived. Most of the wine for the basic appellation 'Médoc' comes from the north, while wine from the southern part is entitled to be labelled Haut Médoc. Within the Haut Médoc there are six communes that have their own appellations:

St Estèphe These are robust full-bodied clarets with plenty of tannin so they need time to develop fully. The best-known châteaux are Cos-d'Estournel and Montrose, and the Cru Bourgeois from here are very good wines.

Pauillac This is the most prestigious commune as it contains three of the First Growth châteaux: Lafite, Latour, Mouton-Rothschild. The wines have a powerful fruity bouquet and a rich velvety texture when mature.

St Julien The high gravel content of the soil means that virtually all vines grown here make good wine. It is gentle and supple wine when mature. The best known châteaux are Léoville-Lascases and Talbot.

Margaux In good years the wine is excellent but poor years can produce thin wine. At its best it has exceptional finesse and elegance with a perfumed bouquet. The famous châteaux Margaux and Palmer are in this commune.

Moullis and Listrac These two communes lie behind St Julien but are situated away from the river, so the wines are much heavier than those of St Julien. This is a good area for Bordeaux Supérieurs and Crus Bourgeois.

In the 1855 Classification, châteaux of the Médoc are listed as First, Second, Third, Fourth and Fifth Growths. These 61 châteaux were chosen from almost 2,000 vineyards so that even a Fifth Growth must be regarded as a very fine wine. They can be identified by the phrase 'Cru Classé' on the label. Since 1932 when the 'Crus Bourgeois' came into being they have been trying to gain legal status for themselves. Since 2003 this group will have the same legal status as the 1855 classification. The new terms are: 'Cru Bourgeois', ''Cru Bourgeois Superieur' and 'Cru Bourgeois Exceptionnel'.

Of 490 properties that registered for the classification only 247 were included. Since the list was produced a large number of proprietors have questioned the decision and they are awaiting a court ruling about the decision. It is believed that the classification will be renewed every 10 years, and this will ensure that the owners maintain the accepted standard of the wines.

GRAND CRUS CLASSES OF THE MEDOC The Official Classification of 1885

First Growths

PROPERTY	COMMUNE
Ch. Lafite-Rothschild	Pauillac
Ch. Latour	Pauillac
Ch. Margaux	Margaux
Ch. Mouton Rothschild	Pauillac
Ch. Haut-Brion	Pessace-Leognan

Second Growths

Ch. Rauzan-Ségla	Margaux
Ch. Rauzan-Gassies	Margaux
Ch. Léoville-Lascases	Saint-Julien
Ch. Léoville-Porféyré	Saint-Julien
Ch. Léoville-Barton	Saint-Julien
Ch. Dufort Vivens	Margaux
Ch. Gruard-Larose	Saint-Julien
Ch. Lascombes	Margaux
Ch. Brane-Cantenac	Margaux
Ch. Pichon-Longueville -Baron	Pauillac
Ch. Pichon-Longueville -Lalande	Pauillac
Ch. Decru-Beaucaillou	Saint-Julien
Ch. Cos-d'Estournel	Saint-Estephe
Ch. Montrose	Saint-Estephe

Third Growths

Ch. Kirwan	Margaux
Ch. d'Issan	Margaux
Ch. Lagrange	Saint-Julien
Ch. Langoa Barton	Saint-Julien
Ch. Giscours	Margaux
Ch. Malescot-Saint-Xupery	Margaux
Ch. Boyd-Cantenac	Margaux
Ch. Palmer	Margaux
Ch. La Lagune	Haut-Medoc
Ch. Desmirail	Margaux
Ch. Cantenac-Brown	Margaux
Ch. Calon-Ségur	Saint-Estephe
Ch. Ferrière	Margaux
Ch. Marquis-d'Alesme -Becker	Margaux

Fourth Growths

PROPERTY	COMMUNE
Ch. Saint-Pierre	Saint-Julien
Ch. Talbot	Saint-Julien
Ch. Branaire-Ducru	Saint-Julien
Ch. Duhart-Milon -Rothschild	Saint-Julien
Ch. Pouget	Margaux
Ch. La Tour-Carnet	Haut-Médoc
Ch. Lafon-Rochet	Saint-Estephe
Ch. Beychevelle	Saint-Julien
Ch. Prieuré-Lichine	Margaux
Ch. Marquis-de-Terme	Margaux

Fifth Growths

Ch. Pontet-Canet	Pauillac
Ch. Batailley	Pauillac
Ch. Haut-Batailley	Pauillac
Ch. Grand-Puy-Lacoste	Pauillac
Ch. Grand-Puy-Ducasse	Pauillac
Ch. Lynch-Bages	Pauillac
Ch. Lynch Moussas	Pauillac
Ch. Dauzac	Labarde
Ch. D'Armailhac	Pauillac
Ch. du Terte	Margaux
Ch. Haut-Bages-Libéral	Pauillac
Ch. Pédesclaur	Pauillac
Ch. Belgrave	Haut-Médoc
Ch. Camensca	Haut-Médoc
Ch. Camensca	Haut-Médoc
Ch. Cos-Labory	Sainte-Estephe
Ch. Clere-Milon -Rothschild	Pauillac
Ch. Croizet-Bages	Pauillac
Ch. Cantemerle	Haut-Medoc

Graves South of the Médoc and on the left bank of the Garonne River lies the region of Graves which takes its name from the coloured quartz pebbles that abound there. Red wines are produced in the north around the town of Bordeaux and are not unlike the wines of the Médoc, often being described as sandy. The wine of Château Haut Brion was so good even in 1855 that it was included as a First Growth even though Graves was not known as an area for fine wine. Pessac-Leognan was created in 1987. This appellation includes all the top properties included in the 1959 classification as well as other top château. Dry white wines are made from the Sauvignon Blanc grape and the best are full-bodied smokey wines listed in the 1959 Classification. Sweeter white wines are made further south in the areas closer to Sauternes.

CLASSIFIED GROWTHS OF THE GRAVES

Red Wines
Classified in 1953 and confirmed in 1959

PROPERTY	COMMUNE
Ch. Bouscaut	Pesscac-Leognan
Ch. Haut-Bailly	Pesscac-Leognan
Ch. Carbonnieux	Pesscac-Leognan
Domaine de Chevalier	Pesscac-Leognan
Ch. Fieuzal	Pesscac-Leognan
Ch. Olivier	Pesscac-Leognan
Ch. Malartic-Lagravière	Pesscac-Leognan
Ch. La Tour-Martillac	Pesscac-Leognan
Ch. Smith-Haut-Brion	Pesscac-Leognan
Ch. Haut-Brion	Pesscac-Leognan
Ch. La Mission-Haut-Brion	Pesscac-Leognan
Ch. Pape-Clément	Pesscac-Leognan
Ch. La Tour-Haut-Brion	Pesscac-Leognan

White Wines
Classified in 1959

PROPERTY	COMMUNE
Ch. Bouscaut	Pesscac-Leognan
Ch. Carbonnieux	Pesscac-Leognan
Domaine de Chevalier	Pesscac-Leognan
Ch. Olivier	Pesscac-Leognan
Ch. Malartic-Lagravière	Pesscac-Leognan
Ch. La Tour-Martillac	Pesscac-Leognan
Ch. Laville-Haut-Brion	Pesscac-Leognan
Ch. Couhins	Pesscac-Leognan
Ch. Couhins-Lurton	Pesscac-Leognan

Sauternes The region of Sauternes lies south of Graves. The Semillon and Sauvignon grapes are used to make naturally sweet white wine. In the autumn, morning mists give way to long sunny afternoons that allow the grapes to ripen fully. The humid mornings encourage the development of a fungus – *botrytis cinerea* – that settles on the grapes. This noble rot gradually dehydrates the fruit so that it shrivels and turns pinkish grey, but the few drops of juice that remain have a very high concentration of sugar. There is a great risk that the whole crop will be lost, because the fungus makes the skin porous and if it were to rain the grapes would quickly absorb the water which would dilute the sugar and might even explode them, making them useless. To reduce this risk the vineyards are hand-picked to remove the grapes as soon as they become shrivelled. At Château d'Yquem the pickers may pick the crop 10 times in a vintage lasting three months. When weather conditions are favourable the district makes excellent wine but in some years

it is thin and lifeless. In 1964, 1972 and 1974 Château d'Yquem made no
wine at all under its own label and the standard of winemaking is so high
that each vine produces only about one glass of wine a year. When wine is
made from these grapes the slow fermentation stops spontaneously once the
alcohol level reaches 14°–17° and the remaining sugar gives the Sauternes its
natural richness. Then the wine is matured in oak. The production of
Sauternes is labour-intensive and time-consuming and its cost is reflected in
the price of the wine. In a good year it has a magnificent full luscious flavour
that continues to develop for many years. Château d'Yquem has long been
acknowledged the finest of the Sauternes although many of the Premier Crus
represent excellent value in a good year.

Barsac This region just north of Sauternes produces similar wine but the
bouquet is more intense and the finish a little drier. The best-known châteaux
are Climens and Coutet.

SAUTERNES AND BARSAC The 1855 classification

First Great Growth		Second Growths	
Premier Grand Cru		*Deuxièmes Crus*	
Ch. d'Yquem	Sauternes	Ch. de Myrat	Barsac
		Ch. Doisy-Däene	Barsac
First Growths		Ch. Doisy-Dubroca	Barsac
Premier Crus		Ch. Doisy-Vedrines	Barsac
Ch. La Tour-Blanche	Bommes	Ch. d'Arche	Sauterens
Ch. Lafaurie-Peyraguey	Bommes	Ch. Filhot	Sauternes
Ch. Clos Haut-Peyraguey	Bommes	Ch. Broustet	Barsac
Ch. Rayne-Vigneau	Bommes	Ch. Nairac	Barsac
Ch. Suduiraut	Preignac	Ch. Caillou	Barsac
Ch. Coutet	Barsac	Ch. Suau	Barsac
Ch. Climens	Barsac	Ch. de Malle	Preignac
Ch. Guiraud	Sauternes	Ch. Romer-du-Hayot	Fargues
Ch. Rieussec	Fargues	Ch. Lamothe	Sauternes
Ch. Rabaud-Promis	Bommes	Ch. Lamothe Guignard	Sauternes
Ch. Sigalas-Rabaud	Bommes		

Cérons, St Croix-du-Mont, Loupiac Cérons lies on the south bank of the
Garonne river within the Sauternes region. St Croix-du-Mont and Loupiac lie
along the north bank of the same river. These three areas are entitled to their
own appellations and all produce white wines similar to Sauternes although
not as rich; they represent good value wines for the money.

Premières Côtes de Bordeaux The strip of land running along the north bank of
the Garonne produces red and white wines entitled to this Appellation
Contrôlée. Traditionally the wines have been sold in bulk to the négociants in
Bordeaux but many of these wines are now bottled under their own vineyard
names.

Entre-Deux-Mers This area stretches between the two rivers and is the largest region of Bordeaux. Only the white wines are authorized to bear the AC Entre-deux-Mers and reds from this region are sold under the AC Bordeaux. There are 15 large co-operatives and much of the dry white wine produced is used for blending purposes.

St Emilion Situated on the north bank of the Dordogne River, this is one of the oldest wine regions of France. The high proportion of merlot grapes produces soft full wines that are easy to drink as they contain less tannin. They will mature before the wines of the Médoc. The most famous châteaux are Cheval Blanc, Ausone, Canon and Bel-Air. The 1955 official classification lists 12 Premiers Grands Crus and 72 Grand Crus.

1955 CLASSIFICATION

The wines of this region were classified in 1955 and every 10 years they re-classify the wines. This ensures that the wine growers maintain a high standard of wine making. The 1995 official classification lists Châteaux Ausone and Cheval Blanc as (A) and 11 other châteaux as (b)

Premiers Grands Crus Classes (A)
Ch Ausone
Ch Cheval Blanc

Premiers Grands Crus Classes (B)

Ch Angelus	Ch Figeac
Ch Beau-Sejour-Becot	Ch La Gaffeliere
Ch Beausejour-Duffau-Lagarosse	Ch Magdelaine
Ch Belair	Ch Pavie
Ch Canon	Ch Trottevieille
Clos Fourtet	

Fifty-five châteaux were graded as Grand Crus Classe. Satellite districts are becoming important. They are St-Georges-St-Emilion, Montagne-St-Emilion, Lussac-St-Emilion and Puisseguin-St-Emilion.

Pomerol This is a relatively small area producing tiny quantities of wine. The soil is better suited to the Merlot vine and Cabernet Franc is grown rather than Cabernet Sauvignon. The wines of this region have never been classified, but the top wine of Châteaux Petrus more often than not sells for more than the Grand Cru of the Medoc. Châteaux Petrus may produce 4,000 cases of wine where Châteaux Mouton Rothschild may produce 33,000 cases. In 1979 the first wine of Châteaux le Pin was made and, from this 'garage' wine, only 600 cases were produced, which command a very high price. To the north lies the region of Lalande-de-Pomerol, which produces very good wines.

Fronsac This small region to the west of Pomerol produces red wine that can be sold under the appellations 'Côtes de Fronsac' or 'Côtes Canon Fronsac'. These big fruity wines resemble those of St-Émilion although they lack the finesse of their neighbours; the Fronsac wines are well worth drinking.

Bourg and Blaye Facing the Médoc across the Gironde estuary are the two old towns of Bourg and Blaye. Quality can vary and much of the white wine is sold for blending purposes. However, as the prices of well-known clarets escalate these red wines can represent good value and many of the petits chateaux sold abroad come from these regions.

BURGUNDY

This beautiful part of central France noted for its gourmet food and superb wines stretches for about 200 km although it is no more than a few kilometres in width. In the Middle Ages the wines of the region were highly regarded at Court but during the French Revolution the great vineyards, most of which had been owned by the Church, were broken up into smallholdings for local citizens. Thus there are no great châteaux in Burgundy and the pattern of small ownership has persisted so that although the great vineyards still exist they are divided amongst several owners; for example the 50-hectare Clos de Vougeot vineyard has 80 owners. Not all growers are good winemakers so it is possible to get wines of the same year from the same vineyard that vary in character, quality and price. Most growers sell their wine to négociants who blend, mature and market the wine. A reputable négociant will buy quality wine to sell under his own label. The area available for the production of Burgundy is limited and the recent increase in demand has caused severe price rises. Here is a brief explanation of the appellations of Burgundy.

General Appellation Wine from grapes harvested anywhere within the authorized Burgundy area may be sold under the appellation 'Bourgogne' or 'Bourgogne Grand Ordinaire'. Wine made from a mixture of Pinot Noir and gamay grapes is entitled to the AC 'Passetout-grains' whilst wine from the aligoté grape bears the AC 'Bourgogne Aligoté'.

Village Appellations Villages may legally give their names to wine from grapes harvested within their local area known as the commune. Vineyards near the town of Beaune may label their wine as *Appellation Beaune Côntrolée*. Some villages have hyphenated the name of the nearest most famous vineyard to the village name, as in Gevrey-Chambertin. This does not mean that wine bearing this appellation has any connection with the famous vineyard; it simply comes from the same local area.

Climats Certain plots — *climats* — of the vineyards produce superior wines. Their names may appear on the labels after the name of the commune as in 'Beaune Grèves'. The very best of these may use the words *Premier Cru*.

Vineyard Names Some climats are so highly regarded for their top-quality wines that their names alone have become the appellation. There are about

20 of these Grand Crus of Burgundy and their wines will simply be labelled with the vineyard name such as Chambertin.

Chablis The most northerly area produces fine dry white wines from the Chardonnay grape. Good Chablis is a pale straw colour and possesses a flavour often described as flinty, which makes it the perfect accompaniment to seafood. Frost is a real danger in late spring and a small crop will mean higher prices for this sought-after wine. A label will bear one of the following appellations:

Petit Chablis	The basic wine of the area
Chablis	A blend of wines from several vineyards
Chablis Premier Cru	Wine from the superior climats
Chablis Grand Cru	Wine from the climats of: Vaudésir, Bougros, Les Preuses Valmur, Les Clos, Blanchots, Grenouilles

Côte de Nuits This area stretches on either side of the Route National 74 from Dijon to Nuits-St-Georges. The fruity red wines are noted for their perfumed bouquet and great elegance. They command exceptionally high prices and mature more slowly than the wines of the Côte de Beaune. These two areas together are known as the Côte d'Or and contain most of the Premier Cru climats for red wine.

The Grand Cru climats are:

Chambertin	Ruchottes-Chambertin	Echezeaux
Chambertin clos-de-Bèze	Bonnes Mares	Grande Rue
Chapelle-Chambertin	Clos des Lambrays	Grands-Echezeaux
Charmes Chambertin	Clos-de-la-Roche	Richebourg
(or Mazoyeres Chambertin)	Clos-St-Denis	La Romanée
Griotte-Chambertin	Clos-de-Tart	Romanée-Conti
Latricieres Chambertin	Musigny	Romanée-St-Vivant
Mazis-Chambertin	Clos-de-Vouget	La Tache

Côte de Beaune The town of Beaune is the centre of the Burgundy wine trade and the surrounding area is dotted with wine villages. Red wines are softer and lighter than those from further north. The communes of Aloxe-Corton, Meursault, Puligny-Montrachet and Chassagne-Montrachet produce powerful white wines full of flavour and perfume that are among the world's finest.

The Grand Cru climats are:

Corton	Montrachet	Criotes-Batard-Montrachet
Corton-Charlemagne	Chevalier-Montrachet	
Charlemagne	Bâtard-Montrachet	

Côte Chalonnaise This area lies south of the Côte de Beaune. The communes of Rully and Montagny make fresh white wine and Mercurey and Givry produce light-bodied fruity reds that are best drunk young. Sparkling wine is made by the méthode champenoise and is entitled to the appellation 'Crémant de Bourgogne'.

Mâconnais The Mâconnais lies on the left bank of the River Saône and makes pleasant red wines from Gamay grape. It is better known for its fresh young white wines made from the Chardonnay grape. The best known of these are Pouilly-Fuissé and St Véran although good quality whites also come from Lugny, Clessé and Viré.

Beaujolais The Gamay grape and the granite soil of the area south of Macon combine well to produce the fresh fruity red wines known as Beaujolais. In a good vintage year the best of them will continue to develop into well-balanced, flavoursome wines for a few years. Some of it is ready to be released for sale by the third Thursday of November each year and this wine is known as Beaujolais Nouveau. Sale of this wine has declined in the past ten years. Some 39 villages producing superior Beaujolais are entitled to the appellation 'Beaujolais Villages'. Premium quality Beaujolais comes from the following communes which all have their own appellation:

St Amour	Moulin-à-Vent	Morgon
Juliénas	Fleurie	Brouilly
Chenas	Chiroubles	Côte de Brouilly
Regnie		

CHAMPAGNE

Many wine-producing areas in the world have tried to emulate the success of Champagne by producing good-quality sparkling wine, but only vines from this small region just north of Paris are able to make wine of inimitable finesse. This is possible because of the area's geological composition and micro-climate, the use of superior grape varieties and a special method of production. Whilst each of these factors occurs elsewhere, only in Champagne do they coincide to produce the unique wine.

Some seventy million years ago what is now northern France and southern England was part of a sea that dried up leaving a sediment of chalk up to 1,000 feet deep and violent upheavals since then have forced great outcrops of it up to the surface. The chalk slopes of Champagne and the white cliffs of Dover are part of this phenomenon. The chalk provides effective drainage whilst retaining enough moisture to nourish plants, and it holds the sun's warmth for a much longer period than most subsoils, thus supplying the vital ingredient for vine cultivation in this very northerly region. Champagne has a continental climate with very cold winters and short hot summers so the vines must get as much heat as is possible to ripen the fruit. The gravelly topsoil is only about one foot thick and it is rich in minerals. The best vineyard sites are located between 137m and 165m above the plain, where the vines are exposed to the maximum amount of sun and light and protected from the winds and severe spring frosts.

Although there are five grape varieties authorized for the region, most champagnes are made from Pinot Noir and Pinot Meunier and the white Chardonnay. The purple black Pinot Noir has a colourless sugary juice that gives body and long life to the wine whilst the small gold Chardonnay contributes the finesse and perfume. Each vineyard is classified on a percentage scale with the best growths being rated as one hundred percent and the fruit from these vineyards being bought for one hundred percent of each year's declared grape price. The Champagne region is divided into three areas of production:

Montagne de Reims Pinot Noir vines are planted on the gentle slopes near Reims.

Vallée de la Marne The vineyards lie on either side of the River Marne and grapes from here are said to contribute a particularly fine bouquet.

Côte des Blancs This area south of the River Marne is principally devoted to growing Chardonnay grapes.

Champagne is a blended wine and the general pattern is for the big houses (*grandes maisons*) to buy grapes or still wines which are then blended in their cellars in Ay, Reims or Épernay to their own specifications, so providing continuity of style from year to year. Recently, however, growers have been grouping together to form co-operatives that now make champagne to be sold under the co-operative label, whilst some particularly independent growers are making their own champagne from their own grapes. There is a ready market within France for these wines and the trend has severely reduced the quantity of grapes available to the champagne houses. Champagne is expensive; it is a labour-intensive product, large stocks must be held in reserve, and the méthode champenoise is a costly procedure even requiring special bottles and corks to package the wine safely. Many of the houses are modifying techniques in an attempt to curb increasing costs. One factor beyond their control is the weather and a late spring frost or wet summer can have a devastating effect on the quantity and quality of grapes. Thus the balance between supply and demand is always a delicate one with champagne and any imbalance is immediately reflected in the price. France is the largest consumer of champagne, and Britain is the most important export market.

PRODUCTION

Picking It is critical that the grapes be picked at the correct ripeness. *Épluchage* is the name given to the procedure of removing rotten grapes in order to improve the quality of the wine; this practice, however, is fast disappearing because of labour costs. Immense care must be taken in the handling of grapes to avoid damaging them.

Pressing The more rapidly the grapes are pressed, the less danger there is of the skins of the red grapes colouring the juice. They are put into a wooden press, known as a Marc, which holds 4,000 kilos of grapes and can produce 3,000 litres of juice, although the law only allows 2,666 litres of juice to be known as the *vin de cuvée*, and all the best champagne is made from it. The next 666 litres are known as the *vin de taille* and most Buyers' Own Brands are from this pressing. The remainder is the *rebêche* and is distilled for Marc de Champagne or consumed locally.

Débourbage It is essential that all impurities in the must be given time to fall to the bottom of the cask, so that the clean must may be drawn off. In very hot weather, the must may be passed through refrigerated pipes to prevent premature fermentation.

First Fermentation For about two weeks the must bubbles violently as the yeasts begin converting the sugars to alcohol. From then on, if a fine bouquet and real finesse are to be obtained, the fermentation has to be slow, regular and complete. The ideal temperature is 12-20°C. Some firms are now using stainless steel or glass-lined cement vats to give better temperature control, and others have air conditioned their above-ground *celliers*.

Topping Up Casks or vats must be frequently topped up to prevent bacteria altering the character of the wine.

Racking and Fining Two or three racks and a fining with bentonite or isinglass are carried out during winter to prevent the still wine from becoming cloudy.

Preparation of the Cuvée Great skill is required when blending the still wines together. The houses maintain large reserves of previous vintages to give character and flavour to wine. This is the most critical phase of the whole méthode champenoise. Even in a vintage year blending is necessary, because the wines from different vineyards and of different grape varieties must be added in varying proportions to achieve the desired balance of flavours.

Liqueur de Tirage A small amount of cane sugar and old wine is added along with special yeasts of a type that will fall easily, work in highly alcoholic surroundings and at low temperature. This ensures that every bottle will undergo a secondary fermentation.

Sealing The bottles are sealed by hand with corks and agrafe clips or mechanically with crown corks. The bottles are then stacked on their sides in underground chalk caves.

Second Fermentation This is best carried out at 10-12°C and will take three to six months. An inferior champagne fermented at 18°C would take only eight days. The yeast turns the sugar into alcohol and carbon dioxide, which dissolves into the wine, creating the desired stream of bubbles known as the *mousse*. A long, slow fermentation produces a fine, lasting mousse. The gas exerts an extremely high pressure on the bottles and so the glass must be strong enough to resist it.

Ageing The best wines are aged for three to five years, but the legal minimum period is fifteen months. During this time the alcohol reacts with the acids in the wine to produce the sweet-smelling esters that give fine champagne its exquisite bouquet, and a long rest period results in a well-balanced wine.

Rémuage The bottles are placed in a rack with oval holes (the *pupitre*) their necks being tilted slightly downwards. The specialist cellar worker, known as the *rémueur*, grasps the bottom of the bottle and gives it a slight shake, then a turn and a tilt. He does these actions to each bottle in the rack every three days for about six weeks and at the end of this time the bottles will all be standing vertically, with necks downwards. The purpose of this is to drive the sediment down on to the cork. This is a highly skilled art, handed down from generation to generation, as the finer, more easily disturbed sediment has to be moved down on to the cork first so that the heavier, granular sediment can fall on top of it and so prevent clouding of the wine. Many champagne houses use gyro pallets to perform this expensive task.

Resting Bottles are stacked upside down in the cellar, with the neck of one resting in the bottom of another. The champagne can remain like this for many years, continuing its slow ageing process. The very best vintage champagnes stay like this until ready for consumption, when the rest of the process is carried out.

Dégorgement The neck of the bottle is dipped in a freezing brine solution, so forming a small block of ice that contains the deposit inside the neck. The pressure built up in the wine expels the ice when the cap is removed. This process is done mechanically in most houses.

Dosage The *liqueur d'expédition* is wine of the same blend with a mixture of cane sugar and old wine added to it. A small proportion of high-class grape brandy may be included to stop further fermentation. This dosage is added to top up each bottle and give the champagne the desired sweetness. It also serves to mask any flaws in wine made from cheaper grapes.

Recorking A compounded cork of three sections is wired down to resist the pressure of the carbon dioxide contained in the wine.

Shaking Bottles are given a good shake up, either by hand or machine, to distribute the dosage evenly.

Resting The wine is rested for four to six months to allow it to marry and settle down.

Packaging The bottles are cleaned, labelled and despatched. Most houses only ferment in magnums, bottles and halves and all other sizes are decanted from bottles under pressure. The names of the large bottle sizes are:

Magnum	2 bottles
Jeroboam	4 bottles
Rehoboam	6 bottles
Methuselah	8 bottles
Salmanazar	12 bottles
Balthazar	16 bottles
Nebuchadnezzar	20 bottles

STYLES OF CHAMPAGNE

Brut or Nature	Only a minute amount of sweetening is added in the dosage to remove the astringency of complete dryness.
Extra Sec or Goût Anglais	Dry champagne.
Sec or Goût Américain	Medium sweet champagne.
Demi Sec	Sweet champagne.
Doux or Rich	Exceptionally sweet champagne.

Non-Vintage The aim of each house is to maintain a consistent style of unvarying quality. Among the dozen or so well-known non-vintage champagnes there are soft feminine wines, some drier and more austere ones and others sweeter or full-bodied. The quality of the grapes is the major factor determining the price of a champagne – if these come from 100 percent Grand Cru vineyards, then they will be more expensive than if they come from a lesser vineyard.

Vintage When good weather conditions allow the production of top-quality wine, a 'vintage' year is declared by the champagne authorities. Each house aims to produce a champagne unique in style to that vintage year and only the highest quality wines are used although up to 20 percent of the wine in the bottle may come from other years.

Rosé Most rosé is made by blending some of the still red wine of the Champagne region with the white wine. It is more full-bodied but not necessarily sweeter than golden champagne, as the red wine provides a touch of astringency. This style was popular in late Victorian times and some houses still produce a vintage rosé as a prestige product.

Crémant These champagnes have less mousse, because less sugar is added in the *liqueur de tirage*. Consequently, not as much carbon dioxide is created as a result of the secondary fermentation in bottle. The term is now being used for sparkling wines of other regions.

Blanc de Blancs This champagne is made entirely from white grapes. It is a particularly elegant wine noted for its delicacy and finesse, and is marketed as a premium quality vintage champagne.

Blanc de Noirs Some champagne made entirely from black grapes is produced but most of it is consumed locally.

Deluxe Most houses market a premium champagne that is beautifully packaged and highly priced. Some are made solely from grapes from 100 percent Grand Cru vineyards, others are made entirely of wine from the first pressing and most are vintaged. There are no legal requirements for these wines so there is much variation in style, quality and age of the wines.

Still Champagne The appellation for still wines from the Champagne region is '*côteaux champenois*'. Previously known as '*vins natures*' these red and white still wines have been made in this part of France from the third century AD. The most widely available reds come from Bouzy and Sillery.

STORAGE AND SERVICE

Champagne is a delicate wine that must be stored correctly if it is to be served in prime condition. All fine champagnes will repay keeping; non-vintage wine laid down for a few years will develop to flavoursome maturity. Even six months' quiet rest at home before consumption will benefit champagne, providing the following conditions are available: a temperature of around 11°C (a few degrees on either side of this is acceptable but it is important to avoid seasonal and daily fluctuations); horizontal storage in a dark place away from vibration (light will seriously damage the wine).

Champagne should be served at a temperature of 6–8°C. If it is too cold it loses its taste, if too warm it is heavy and the sparkle does not keep. Champagne should be cooled as gradually as possible. The least cold parts of the refrigerator may be used but the best method is to put a bottle in an ice bucket in a mixture of water and ice. It will take about 25 minutes to reach the ideal drinking temperature. Tulip-shaped glasses will preserve the bouquet and allow the mousse to rise in a fine long-lasting stream; the glasses must be dry, as any dampness will flatten the champagne. The cork is best covered with a napkin and twisted gently before being eased from the bottle.

LOIRE

The valley of the Loire is one of the most picturesque regions of Europe as its natural rural beauty is enhanced by the graceful châteaux built by French royalty on the banks of the river. The wines of the Loire valley have always been in demand in France and there is a world-wide market for the fresh dry white wines. The valley can be divided into four main vineyard areas, which stretch across northern France from west to east.

Nantais District The area surrounding the city of Nantes in Brittany is the home of Muscadet, one of the most popular wines of France. The best wine is entitled to the appellation 'Muscadet de Sèvre-et-Maine' and its clean crisp acidity complements seafood. The wine comes from the Muscadet grape and is invariably sold young. It must be bottled quickly to keep the pale gold colour and some of the wine is sold *sur lie*. This means it has gone straight from the cask to the bottle without being filtered, so that it has freshness and pétillance.

Anjou–Saumur District Anjou produces rosé wine, the most flavoursome of which is made from the Cabernet grape and marketed as 'Cabernet d'Anjou Rosé'. The best wines of the region are white and the appellations 'Anjou' and 'Saumur' signify the generic wines. Côteaux du Layon and Côteaux de l'Aubance produce quality sweet white wines from botrytis-affected Chenin Blanc grapes, whilst in Savennières the same grape makes perfumed dry white wine. The Saumur area has a deep chalky soil and is the centre of a fine sparkling-wine industry. Still wine from the Chenin Blanc grape is fermented in bottle in exactly the same way as Champagne and marketed as 'Crémant de la Loire'.

Touraine District The vineyards surround the city of Tours. Around the wine villages of Chinon and Bourgueil the Cabernet Franc grape produces soft, light-bodied red wines. The most interesting wines of this district are those of Vouvray — these light white wines have a honeyed character whether they are made dry, sweet or sparkling and the best of them have the unusual ability to improve in bottle for up to fifty years.

Central Vineyards This district is located in the centre of France and has a continental climate so that in some years the crop is very small or highly acid because of unfavourable weather. Sancerre and Pouilly-Fumé both come from here. These wines made from the Sauvignon Blanc grape have a distinctive aroma and are essentially straightforward wines best drunk whilst young.

RHONE

The valley of the Rhône river, running as it does from north to south, has been a natural route into Europe for over 3,000 years. Greek traders first brought the vine to Marseilles about 600 BC; cultivation spread along the Rhône and was encouraged centuries later by the Roman invaders. Today the vineyards stretch for about 200 km from Vienne to Avignon along the main route to the famous Mediterranean beaches. This is also the land of olives, herbs and garlic for the magnificent cuisine, which complements the excellent wine. Much of the wine is sold under the general appellation 'Côtes-du-Rhône' and some villages are entitled to market their produce as 'Côtes-du-Rhône Villages'. The following areas have their own appellations.

Cóte Rotie This small district has some of the steepest slopes in France so that vines must be cultivated entirely by hand. The wine is made from a mixture of black Syrah and white Viognier grapes, which produces a perfumed red wine of great elegance that is somewhat softer than the wines of Hermitage.

Condrieu and Château Griliet The Viognier grape is used to make dry white wine with a delicate, flowery bouquet. Output is limited because the yield is small. Château Grillet has the distinction of being the only single estate to have its own appellation; it is also the smallest in France.

Hermitage The hill of Hermitage is one of the landmarks of the Rhône and the granite subsoil allows the Syrah grape to produce strong, rich red wines that need years to develop and in a good year must rate among the finest wines of France. There is also a golden dry white Hermitage noted for its longevity.

Crozes–Hermitage and St Joseph The communes at the foot of the hill of Hermitage and around Tournon make light red wines using modern production methods so that wine can be bottled and sold within a year of the vintage.

Cornas Red wine from the Syrah is made by traditional methods and given two years in cask so that the best are similar to the wines of Hermitage.

St Péray This is the best sparkling wine of the Rhône valley and is made by the méthode champenoise from the Marsanne grape, producing a full-bodied wine. Sparkling wine is also made near Die from the Clairette grape.

Châteauneuf du Pape This district is named after the ruined castle that stands above the village. In the fourteenth century this was the summer home of the schismatic Popes who lived in Avignon rather than Rome. The vineyards are covered with large cream-coloured boulders. These absorb the heat of the sun in the day and then reflect it back on to the vines at night so that the grapes ripen thoroughly. Thirteen different grape varieties may be used for the wine. Made by the traditional methods it is big, alcoholic, tannic wine, but some estates use modern methods to produce a lighter, well-rounded wine that matures earlier. Quality wine bottled locally, rather than sold in bulk to a négociant, comes in a burgundy-shaped bottle with the old Papal arms embossed on the glass.

Gigondas and Vacquerays Gigondas The latter area in the southern Rhône was the first, and Vacquerays the second area, to gain full Appellation status. With a mix of Grenache, Syrah, Mourvedre and Cinsaut in the blend, the wines are similar to Châteauneuf du Pape. Good producers from these two areas are now producing outstanding wines. Lirac has not quite gained the recognition that Gigondas and Vacquerays have, but still produces good reds, rosé wine, and some white wine.

Tavel This area, with its sandy soil, makes very good rosé by bottling it early to keep plenty of fruit in the wine. It is meant to be drunk within two years of the vintage and most of the wine is made by the local co-operative.

Beaumes de Venise The co-operative in Beaumes de Venise makes a sweet fortified wine from the Muscat grape. It is known as a Vin Doux Naturel. The grapes are harvested late to concentrate the sugar, and brandy is added to stop fermentation and retain the natural sweetness. These wines are meant to be drunk whilst young and are best served chilled with dessert. This region also produces very good red wines.

Rasteau Winemakers here are producing very good Vin Doux Naturel wines similar to Beaumes de Venise. There are also very good Côtes du Rhone Villages wines being made by quality producers.

OTHER REGIONS OF FRANCE

Jura and Savoie This region is in eastern France near the Swiss border. 'Vin jaune' is made by leaving white wine untouched in wooden casks for six years. During this time a 'flor', or veil of yeasts, spreads across the surface of the wine. Louis Pasteur's discovery of bacteria was a result of his research into this phenomenon. The strong, very dry, gold wine is best served chilled as an aperitif. The dessert wine 'vin de paille', or straw wine, comes from fruit that is laid out on straw mats after picking so that the moisture evaporates leaving shrivelled grapes full of sugar.

South–West France The red wines of Bergerac, Madiran, Buzet and Gaillac resemble to some degree those of Bordeaux and as the prices of the latter increase there is much interest in the nearby appellations. The 'Black Wine' of

Cahors is no longer as meaty as it was in previous decades but it is still a deep-coloured, rich, tannic wine. The best sweet white wines come from Monbazillac near Bordeaux and from Jurançon in the foothills of the Pyrenees.

The Midi The region known to the French as Le Midi around the Mediterranean coast from the Spanish border to Nice, near the Italian border. Once recognised as the region that accounted for vast quantities of unwanted wine it has, over the past 15 years, seen major changes in the production of quality wine.

Roussillon Banyuls, near the Spanish border, produces a range of sweet Vin Doux Natural wines. The seaside resort town of Collioure is producing AC wines, both red and white. The grape varieties used are Grenache, Syrah, Mourvedre and Carignan. Around the coast past Perpignan, winemakers are producing the AC wines of Fitou, Corbieres, and Minervois.

The Languedoc–Roussillon This area, the western part of the coast to the Rhone river, is the largest wine region in France. It produces good, sound wine labelled as 'Vin de Pays D'Oc'. In fact, a number of leading wineries label their wines at the Vin de Pays level, but the quality of their wine is outstanding. Mas de Daumas Gassac is certainly one of the most famous. Muscat is planted in a number of regions, producing the sweet wines of Frontignan and Lunel.

Provence was previously known as a rosé region, but its wine industry has moved on. Although there are some very desirable rosé wines made, this region also produces outstanding red and white wines. In particular, wines from Bandol are making a mark in world wine markets.

GERMANY

The River Rhine rises in the Swiss Alps just a few miles away from the source of the Rhône. Along its banks old fortress-castles guard the crests of the vine-covered hill slopes that are capable of producing some of the world's finest sweet white wines.

The cultivation of the vine spread up the Rhône valley from Marseilles into the valleys of the rivers Rhine and Mosel in early times. In the third century AD, the Roman Emperor ordered the destruction of the vineyards of these areas, but fortunately the Emperor Probus, who ruled in AD 276–282, ordered them to be replanted. Some of the more important vineyards in this region were laid out in the twelfth century.

The chief quality of the best of German wine, whether from the Rhine or its tributary the Mosel, is balance. The amount of acid must be just enough to heighten the taste of grape sugar and flavouring substances and leave a long, lingering, spicy finish. Too much sugar makes flat, uninteresting wine; too much acid can mean tart, almost sour wine. The Rhine is as far north as the vine can be profitably cultivated, so the grower has a constant battle with the weather to produce ripe enough grapes.

The Riesling grape is widely planted in areas where high-quality wine can be produced, because it gives character and longevity. However, it is difficult to cultivate, so many growers plant other varieties and blend a proportion of Riesling into their wine, although wine that bears the name of a grape must be made from 85 percent of this variety. The Müller-Thurgau is a cross variety developed in Germany especially for local conditions. It produces a heavy crop that ripens two weeks earlier than the Riesling and makes flowery, fruity wine ready for early drinking. The Sylvaner variety makes good blending wine whilst the Spätburgunder, a relation of the French Pinot Noir, produces Germany's red wines. Both the Riesling and Müller-Thurgau are suitable for developing the fungus botrytis, which dehydrates the grapes, thus concentrating the natural sugars in the shrivelled fruit.

German wines are traditionally referred to as Hocks or Moselles. The latter name is the French spelling for the name of the river. Hock is an abbreviation of Hochheim, a town on the Rhine that for centuries was the port for shipping the Rhine wines to other parts of Europe, especially England. The term is generally used for all wine produced along the Rhine and marketed in brown bottles.

Mosel–Saar–Ruwer High-quality wine comes from this region because the slate covering the hillsides holds in moisture and reflects the heat it has absorbed through the day back on to the vines. The Riesling grape is difficult to cultivate as it ripens late and bears a small crop, but it is widely planted here to produce very elegant wine. The pale green-gold whites of the Mosel, marketed in green bottles, are gentle wines with low alcohol and a refreshing acidity, often producing a tingle or *spritzig* on the tongue. Wine from the Saar is a little more austere whilst the Ruwer produces some of Germany's finest most delicate wines.

Rheingau This pocket of land on the right bank of the Rhine has a micro-climate that affords it the most sunshine and least frost of any part of west Germany. Here the aristocratic Riesling grape produces firm, steely wine with an intensely fragrant bouquet and a richness that lingers in the mouth. The best vineyards face south on to the river and benefit from the sunshine reflected from its surface. Morning river mists rise through the vines providing humid conditions ideal for development of the noble rot that is necessary to produce the great sweet wines.

The best of the Rheingau single vineyards make wine of such high quality that they are marketed under their own names and referred to as 'Estates' – Schloss Vollrads, Schloss Johannisberg and Schloss Rheinharthausen command very high prices for their wines. Up on the hill behind the town of Hattenheim is the state-owned estate known simply as the 'Steinberg'. The government owns vineyards in many wine-producing areas but this is the undisputed jewel of the State Domain. Kloster Eberbach is an old monastery that has been converted to a winery and cellars for the Steinberger wine. It is also the home of the German Wine Academy, which holds wine courses for anyone interested in learning about German wine. The Research Station at Geisenheim is acknowledged as one of the world's foremost authorities in viticultural studies.

Nahe The area around Bad Kreuznach on the River Nahe has a great range of soils and the Riesling, Sylvaner and Müller-Thurgau grape varieties are all planted here. The crisp clean wines have plenty of fruit and are sometimes described as a bridge between the delicate Mosels and the spicy Rheingaus.

Rheinhessen The undulating country between the Nahe and Rhine rivers has rich soil suited to market gardening and the Sylvaner grape. This is a bland variety, so plantings of Müller-Thurgau increased in the mid to late 1900s to give the wines more character. Co-operatives bottle most of the wine to be exported as Liebfraumilch. This must not be confused with a wine called Liebfrauenstift which comes from the vineyards around the Liebfrauenkirch – 'The Church of Our Dear Lady' – in Worms.

Rheinpfalz The dry sunny climate of this area situated just north of Alsace produces full-bodied, grapey wines. The co-operatives make wine for early drinking and most of it is sold under grosslage names.

Hessische–Bergstrasse Most of the vineyards in this very small region near Worms are owned by the State. They produce bland wine meant for immediate consumption.

Baden The Baden vineyards stretch along the River Rhine facing the region of Alsace. The Müller-Thurgau grape planted here produces fruity whites and the Spätburgunder makes a good red wine. This area has some of the most modern and largest co-operatives in Europe and 90 percent of the wine is produced by them, mainly for the local market. The best vineyards are in Kaiserstuhl and Ortenau.

Ahr This is the most northern red wine district in the world. These light red wines are low in alcohol and are made from the spätburgunder grape.

Wurttemberg Situated around the city of Stuttgart, this region produces more red than white wine. They are mixed together to make the pink Schillerwein, which the locals consume in great quantity.

Mitteirhein The area around Bonn and Koblenz provides much of the wine for Sekt. It is particularly difficult land to cultivate because of steep slopes and high winds.

Franken Würzburg is the centre of the Franken region. The Sylvaner grape makes fine dry steely whites that still have a fruitiness. Franconian wine is marketed in the squat Bocksbeutel and is sometimes referred to as Steinwein.

Saale–Unstrut and Sachsen Both places have suffered from the communist rule of earlier decades. However, the vineyards are improving.

CLASSIFICATION OF GERMAN WINES

Table wine		Quality wine	
Tafelwein	Deutscher Tafelwein	Qualitätswein bestimmer Anbaugebiete (QbA)	Qualitätswein mit Prädikat (QmP)

Tafelwein Wine marketed as Tafelwein may come from any country within the EU. Germany imports large quantities of wine that is blended, bottled and packaged for local consumption and export. The label must show a phrase similar to 'Produce of EU', which is usually in small print.

Deutscher Tafelwein Ordinary table wine made exclusively from grapes harvested in Germany with a minimum alcohol content of 8.5 ABV. It may also carry the name of a district (Bereich) or village.

Quality Wines A Qualitätswein must originate in one of the 13 authorized regions and be made from approved grape varieties grown in approved vineyards. Every year a tasting panel in each region carries out a check on the grower's wine to ensure its authenticity of style and allocate it one of the grades of Qualitätswein:

(a) Qualtätswein bestimmer Anbaugebiete or QbA

(Quality wine from an authorized region). These everyday drinking wines must show on the label the name of the authorized region and the term 'Qualitätswein'. The label may show a vineyard – Einzellage or Grosslage – name if 85 percent of the grapes come from there.

(b) Qualitätswein mit Prädikat or QmP (Quality wine with predicate). The predicate is one of the five categories listed below. These are the fine German wines. For a wine to be awarded this classification it must come from a single district in one of the authorized regions. The label must show the term 'Qualitätswein mit Prädikat' and the name of the authorized region.

Prädikat wines are divided into these five styles depending on the degree of sweetness:

Kabinett light, fairly dry white wine

Spätlese wine from late-harvested grapes with the resulting high sugar content

Auslese superior rich wine from fully ripe or botrytis-affected grapes, which give a full ripe bouquet

Beerenauslese finest quality wine made from individually picked, overripe grapes that have usually been botrytis affected. This amber-coloured wine can keep for almost a century.

Trockenbeerenauslese very expensive luscious wine, made from hand-picked shrivelled grapes, showing excellent balance and a full-scented bouquet. The word 'trocken' means dry and refers to the dried-up grapes.

Eiswein rare sweet wine made from hand-picked fully ripe grapes that have been left on the vines into early winter, then picked once the water content has frozen to ice. They are pressed immediately so that only the sugar, aromatic and flavouring substances are obtained thus producing intensely sweet fragrant wine. An Eiswein must be labelled as one of the last three categories, for example, 'Auslese Eiswein'.

Anbaugebiete These are the 13 authorized regions of wine production discussed above and each has its own particular characteristics.

Bereich Each region is divided into large districts. The Rhinegau has only one district but the Mosel has three. The basic QbA wine is sold under this district name, for example 'Bereich Nierstein'.

Grosslage This is a collection of vineyards with the same climatic conditions, soil and terrain. Wine from one vineyard can be blended with wine from other vineyards within the same grosslage. The 'middle class' wines of the district are sold with this name, for example 'Niersteiner Gutes Domtal'.

Village Names The village amidst a collection of vineyards (Grosslage) is a centre for the local winemaking community and so a village name is attached to the grosslage name, as in 'Piesporter Michelsberg' – Piesport being a village amongst the Michelsberg vineyards.

Einzellage This is an individual vineyard. One vineyard may have several owners, so the quality and character of wine from one einzellage may vary considerably depending on the skill and care of the producer. The finest wine is marketed under the einzellage name but it is also entitled to use the grosslage name. As the name of the grosslage is often the same as the most famous individual vineyard in it, it is difficult to tell whether a wine is from an einzellage or grosslage just by looking at the label.

AP Number This number is awarded by the inspection board of the region after tasting the wine and consists of a series of codes. All quality wine must carry its AP number on the label. Here is an example:

19	317	034	04
number of the inspection board	number of village community where the vineyard is located	number of the bottler	year of bottling (not year of vintage)

Erzeugerabfüllung This term means the wine has been bottled by its grower rather than sold in bulk to a shipper.

Weinkellerei This is a wine cellar or winery. A large-scale wine estate is known as a Weingut.

Liebfraumilch The name can only be used for a QbA wine made from grapes grown in the Rheinhessen, Rheinpfalz, Rheingau and Nahe. Most of these mild, fairly sweet wines are sold under brand names.

Sekt The highest-quality sparkling wine is QbA Sekt, which must be made from 60 percent German wine. Much wine is imported and made into sparkling wine by the Charmat method and marketed as Schaumwein or Sekt.

Trocken or Diabetiker-Wein Trocken means dry, Halbtrocken means off-dry. These are terms to let the consumer know whether they are dry or sweet. Since the 2000 vintage the terms 'classic' and 'selection' have simplified matters. 'Classic' wines enable everyone to easily find uncomplicated, dry varietal wines for everyday enjoyment at an affordable price. 'Selection' wines are premium-quality, dry varietals available in limited quantities and so priced.

Picturesque script and unfamiliar words make German wine labels a mystery. The name given to quality wines has up to four parts to it. The first word is the village name which always has the suffix 'er'; the second is either the einzellage or grosslage name, which is the clue as to whether the wine is from a prestigious single vineyard, or from the local collection of vineyards; the grape variety is third and, if not stated, it means the wine is a blend with no outstanding character; the last word is the grading of quality wine awarded to it. In this example, the quality and price of one of these wines would be higher than the other.

JOHANNISBERGER	KLAUS	RIESLING	SPATLESE
village	Einzellage	grape variety (single vineyard)	grading of quality wine
JOHANNISBERGER	ERNTEBRINGER		QbA
Village	Grosslage (general vineyard area)		grading of quality wine

There are over 3,000 registered single vineyards in Germany. The names of the better known are included here to help the reader interpret the labels of the German wines most often seen outside the country.

BEREICH District name	GROSSLAGE Collection of vineyards	VILLAGE	EINZELLAGE Single quality vineyard within the grosslage
Mosel–Saar–Ruwer			
Bernkastel	Badstube	Bernkastel	Doktor
	Kurlürstlay	Bernkastel	
	Michelsberg	Piesport	Goldtröpfchen
		Trittenheim	Altärchen
	Munzlay	Graach	Domprobst
		Zeltingen	Sonnenuhr
	Nacktarsch	Kröv	
	Schwarzlay	Erden	Treppchen
Saar-Ruwer	Römerley	Kasel	Hitzlay
	Scharzherg	Wiltingen	Hölle
		Ockfen	Bockstein
Zell-Mosel	Schwarze Katz	Zell	
Rheingau			
Jooannisberg	Burgweg	Rüdesheim	Rosengarten
		Geisenheim	Rothenberg
	Daubhaus	Hochheim	Hölle
	Deutelberg	Erbach	Marcobrunn
		Hattenheim	Wisselbrunnen
	Erntebringer	Johannisberg	Klaus
	Honigberg	Winkel	Hasensprung
	Steinmacher	Eltville	Sonnenherg
		Kiedrich	Grafenherg
Nahe			
Kreuznach	Kronenberg	Bad Kreuznach	Kauzenberg
Schloss Bockelheim	Burgweg	Schlossbockelheim	Kupfergrube
Rheinisessen			
Nierstein	Auflangen	Nierstein	Olberg
	Gutes Domtal	Nierstein	
	Krötenbrunnen	Oppenheim	
	Rehbach	Nierstein	Pettenthal
Rheinpfalz			
Mittelhaardt-Deutsche Weinstrasse	Honigsackel	Ungstein	
	Mariengarten	Deidesheim	Herrgottsacker
		Forst	Pechstein
		Wachenheim	Gerümpel

ITALY

The early inhabitants of Italy were drinking wine in the tenth century BC, well before the founding of Rome, although the Greeks brought 'modern' viticulture to Naples about three centuries later. Wine was such an integral part of daily life that Bacchus in Rome and Dionysus in Sicily were worshipped as gods of wine. The Italians are now one of the world's leading wine producers and consumers of wine.

The *Denominazione di Origine Controllata* (DOC) is only awarded once growers have supplied proof that a genuine typical wine style exists within a specified boundary and that grape varieties, yield per hectare, annual production and winemaking methods are all of a sufficiently high standard to warrant the DOC. A National Committee supervises over 200 DOC wines to ensure that they are grown, produced, aged, bottled and labelled according to regulations.

Growers in some areas have organized consortiums to maintain standards and promote their wine. A *Consorzio* issues a seal that can be found on the neck of a bottle guaranteeing the quality of the wine. *Denominazione di Origine Controllata et Garantita* are awarded to wines from geographically controlled areas and are officially guaranteed as Italy's best wines. Twenty-four wines were given this title in 2004. Ordinary table wines are known as Vini da Tavola and a DOC wine may be named after a grape variety or its region of origin.

Indicazione Geografica Tipica is a new title, which carries the grape variety and means it is from a recognised large production area with more tolerant quality levels than DOC (for example, IGT Toscano).

Generally, the best wines come from Northern Italy, especially the provinces of Piedmont and Tuscany. Certain communes within a region are allowed to use the word *classico*, and *superiore* indicates that the wine has a slightly higher alcoholic content and has been allowed to age before release. *Amabile* refers to a semi-sweet style and *abboccato* to sweet wine.

Piedmont The province of Piedmont lies in the north-west of Italy and borders France. The highly regarded red wine is Barolo a full-bodied, flavoursome red wine that will mature for many years. Barbaresco is similar but slightly softer, whilst Gattinara is reckoned by many to be more elegant than Barolo in a good year and demand exceeds its production. These wines are all made from the Nebbiolo grape and are named after places. The Barbera grape makes dark tannic wines that vary in quality and may be *frizzante*, which is the Italian word for the tingling sensation on the tongue. The best are named after the grape with place name attached, as in Barbera d'Alba, and will soften with bottle age. Asti is the centre of Italy's sparkling wine industry, which uses the Moscato grape to produce the sweetish fragrant wine by the Charmat and transfer methods. The best is sold as Asti Spumante while Moscato d'Asti is cheaper and sweeter. Many large companies produce a dry sparkling wine by the méthode champenoise which is marketed under a prestigious brand name.

Tuscany The large area around Florence and Siena is the home of 'Chianti'. This, the most famous of all Italian wines, is now made from red grapes. In the past, the wine was made from Sangiovese grapes, with Canaiolo Nero and white Trebbiano also used. With the change in the law in the mid-1990s, a percentage of Cabernet Sauvignon can be added to the blend. Chianti can be made from seven different zones in Tuscany: Chianti Classico, Chianti Montalbano, Chianti Colli Fiorentini (Florentine hills), Chianti Rufina, Colli Senesi (Siena hills), Colli Pisane (Pisa hills) and Colli Aretini (Arezzo hills). Basic Chianti is now considered an everyday drinking wine with no ageing potential. Chianti Classico is produced from the heart of the region and winemakers in the Consorzio place the insignia of a black cockerel on the neck label. Wines that have been aged in barrel for a period of at least three years can be called Reserva.

Brunello di Montalcino is produced in the vineyards around Montalcino. A superior clone of Sangiovese is used to produce this wine. Changes to the length of time in oak (from five years to two years) has brought about a change to the wine. It still has to be aged in bottle for a further two years, bringing the total ageing to four years. A younger version called Rosso di Montalcino requires only one year of ageing. These wines are two of the higher quality types from Italy.

Veneto Another region that has raised the quality of its wines is Valpolicella. While many co-operatives still produce sound wine, top wine producers such as Masi and Allegrini are fine examples of the best from this region. Valpolicella comes in different quality levels: Valpolicella, Valpolicella Superiore, Valpolicella Classico, Valpolicella Amarone, Recioto (a sweeter version) and Ripasso.

Bardolino is the other popular red wine from this region, while Soave is the pale, dry white wine. This region has also planted Pinot Grigio grapes because demand for wine from this grape is rising.

Trentino–Alto Adige The vines in this region bordering Austria are set against a background of the Dolomites, creating one of the most picturesque sights in Italy. The Italian-speaking Trentino growers produce wines named for the classic grape varieties from which they are produced: Cabernet, Merlot, Riesling, Traminer and Moscato. The German Alto Adige growers produce the finer red wines that are exported to Germany, Switzerland and Austria.

Emilia–Romagna The area around Bologna, Parma and Modena is noted for its large wine production. Sangiovese is a dry, ruby red wine of excellent balance, Albana di Romagna is a golden, fresh white wine (either dry or semi-sweet) and good Trebbiano is a dry fairly acid wine that goes well with fish. Lambrusco is a semi-sparkling red that froths in the glass when poured and has a pronounced prickle in the mouth.

Lombardy The far north of Italy is a heavily industrialized region but some wines are grown on the steep terraces leading to the Alps. The red wines Sassellas, Grumello and Inferno are highly esteemed but most of them are drunk locally or exported to Switzerland.

Friuli-Venezia Wines from the environs of Trieste are named after the Pinot, Cabernet and Riesling grape varieties. The best-known wine is Tocai, a pale dry wine with a slightly bitter taste that complements the local seafood. This grape variety is in no way connected to the Hungarian grape of the same name, which makes a dessert wine.

The Marches On this part of the Adriatic coast the Verdecchio grape produces pale straw-coloured wine with a pronounced lemony dryness. The best-known is Verdecchio dei Castelli di Jesi and is marketed in an elongated curved bottle.

Umbria This small region in central Italy is the home of the light, delicate white wine named after the town of Orvieto. The grapes, mainly of the Trebbiano variety, remain in open casks in the underground cellars until they begin to rot, so concentrating the sugar to produce amabile and abboccato Orvieto. Good dry Orvieto is crisp and flowery with an underlying sharpness.

Latium The hills around Rome produce the clear, golden Frascati wines. The juice is left in contact with the skins of the grapes for a longer period than most Italian whites, so Frascati has a good grapey aroma and flavour. It is made in secco, amabile and abboccato styles. 'Est! Est! Est!', more notable for its name than for its quality, is light white wine made dry or sweet.

Campania, Basilicata, Apulia, Calabria These regions used to produce vast quantities of wine which were transported up to Turin to be processed as the base for vermouth. With a drop in sales of vermouth in some markets, producers replanted with quality grapes. Wines to look out for are Salice Salentino and wines made from Primitivo and Negroamaro grape varieties. These wines will be labelled as IGT.

Sicily Vines are grown on the slopes of Mount Etna. The red is a fine velvety wine while the full-bodied white has a fresh grapiness.

Marsala is a dessert wine from north-west Sicily, made from a blend of aromatic white wine, brandy and heated must and matured in a solera system. It is probably best known as an ingredient of zabaglione, the frothy dessert made from egg and Marsala wine. Marsala Fine varies in style from dry to sweet and requires a minimum of four months' ageing and must be no less than 17 percent ABV. Marsala Superiore styles range from dry to sweet. They must be a minimum of two years old and no less than 18 percent ABV. The name Marsala Speciale is given to Marsala with added flavours such as almond, coffee or fruit. Marsala Vergine is much drier than the others and is normally served lightly chilled as an aperitif. It is aged for a minimum of five years and must contain at least 18 percent ABV.

PORTUGAL

Portugal is a small country with a big future in wine. The inland climate is moderate, and Adriatic breezes along the coast bring enough rain to ensure there is a good harvest every year. The mountain ranges also play a part. The result is a range of wines from light, fresh fruity whites to full-bodied, rich reds.

Grape varieties include Touriga Nacional, Trincadeira and Castelao, which produce red wines, and Fernao Pires, Loureiro, Antao Vaz and Roupeiro, which produce white wines. Portuguese wines are classified by a similar system to French wines: *Denominaçao de Origem Controlada* (DOC) is the highest category, with I*ndicacao de Proveniencia Regulamentada* (IPR) indicating a wine with DOC potential. *Vinho Regional* indicates a wine from a defined region, and *Vinho de Mesa* is used for table wine.

Minho The far north produces wines known as *vinhos verdes* (green wines), picked early and drunk when very young. The wines cause a slight tingling sensation on the tongue, known as pétillance, as a result of their very high acid content. Mainly yellow in colour but with a suggestion of slight green, they are classified as a semi-sparkling wine with a lower alcohol content. The appellation region of Vinho Verde is from south of Porto up to the Spanish border. In the extreme north, the Alvarinho grape produces an individual style of wine that will keep for three to five years.

Douro The Douro River is best known as the home of port. Many port producers make top-quality red and white wines from local grape varieties: Tinta Roriz (Tempranillo) and Touriga Franca for reds, and Rabigato and Malvasia Fina for whites. Vila Real is the centre of the Mateus Rose winery.

Daõ The mountainous inland region around the Dao river has a mild climate and granite soil that encourages quality wine. The wines produced are both red and white; the reds are firm-flavoured with a soft, vanilla character. The whites (the best grape is the Encruzado) are crisp, fresh and balanced. Other important DOC regions of Portugal's centre are Bairrada, Beira Interior and Tavora/Varosa.

Lisbon and the Tagus Valley The vines that grow in the beach area around Lisbon are ungrafted stock because the phylloxera virus could not penetrate the sand. Bucellas is improving its quality. Other important DOC regions are Obidos, Alenquer, Arruda, Torres Vedras and Ribatajo. Estremadura and Ribatejano are are now producing better-quality wines.

The South Setúbal is known for its dessert wines made from red and white Moscatel grapes. Other DOC regions are Palmela, Alentejo, Lagos, Portimao, Lagoa and Tavira. The Vinho regional wines are labelled Terras do Sado, Alentajano and Algarve.

For information on wines from the island of Madeira, see page 225.

SOUTH AFRICA

The break-up of the Co-operative Wine Growers Association, known previously as the KWV, has resulted in a wider range of South African wines on world markets. Mergers of larger co-operatives and wine merchants mean the newly formed countries will be in a position to meet the demands of the large gobal retailers. However, small family growers are also gaining wider recognition for the quality of their wine.

Vines were first introduced to South Africa over 300 years ago by Jan van Riebeeck, commander of the first Dutch settlement at the Cape of Good Hope. Many of the settlers were French Huguenots who had fled Europe to escape religious persecution. They extended the vineyards and improved the quality of winemaking so that by 1711 South African wines were becoming known abroad, especially the wines of Constantia. To help protect the industry after a fall in the export market the growers formed the Co-operative Wine Growers Association (KWV).

In 1973 a system of control of origin was installed to ensure that wines were derived from the location stated on the label, and to maintain quality levels. The classification is administered by the Wine and Spirit Board appointed by the Minister of Agriculture. A seal appears on each bottle guaranteeing the reliability of all the information relating to region of origin, grape variety and vintage

The regions now produce wines with the tradition of the old-world style combined with influences from newer winemakers and techniques.

South Africa has five wine regions with so far 18 diverse districts or wards and individual estates. The number of regions is increasing as new vineyard areas and estates are created.

The well-known regions (wards) are:

Constantia This district is located close to Cape Town. Chenin Blanc grapes, known as Steen, are grown here as well as Pinotage, Cabernet Sauvignon and Shiraz. The first wines were made in Groot Constantia in 1679 and this vineyard, now owned by the state, is noted for its red wines.

Durbanville This district is located in the hills to the north of Cape Town. However, the city is expanding in this direction. The mild climate and red granite soil mean this area is suited to the production of quality red wine and liqueurs. The two properties defined as wine estates are Meerendal and Diemersdal.

Stellenbosch This small district, around the towns of Stellenbosch and Strand, is considered the hub of the wine industry. White wines are produced on the sandy soil in the west whilst red wines come from the mountain slopes in the east. The region has the greatest concentration of top wine estates in the Cape, with names like Le Bonheur, Delheim, Neil Ellis, Meerlust, Simonsig and Warwick.

Paarl Situated 60 km from Cape Town, the area lies within the fertile valley of Berg River at the foot of the Paarl Mountains. The diversity of soil and climate favours a range of wines. Leading producers are Backsberg, Fairview, Nederburg, and Simonsvlei. Cabriere Estate is an established winery producing Cap Classique sparkling wines from Pinot Noir and Chardonnay. Wellington is another small ward within the region, with many nurseries producing most of South Africa's vine cuttings.

Tulbagh This is a small area surrounding the town of Tulbagh producing white and sherry style wines.

Swartland An area that is improving the quality of its wine.

Piketberg and Olifants River New winemakers are increasing vine plantations here.

The Breede River Valley This is a region with three districts:

Worcester The biggest wine-producing region with high brandy and dessert wine production.

Robertson Hot and dry with some lime-rich soil, uncommon in the Cape, the region is good for Chenin Clanc and Colombard grapes used for brandy. Chardonnay, Sauvignon, Shiraz, Merlot and Cabernet Sauvignon are also grown here.

Swellendam Stretches from the coast inland to the town of Bonnievale. Local co-operatives produce dry white wine and wine for distilling into brandy.

Overberg This is the most southerly wine region, recognised as a cool climate zone. The ward of Elgin is well known for Sauvignon Blanc from the Iona winery. Nearby, within the ward of Walker Bay, the family-run estate of Beaumont has a reputation for its Chenin Blanc. Walker Bay is also known for its Pinot Noir.

Little Karoo A semi-arid region producing some of the country's finest fortified wines.

SOUTH AMERICA

ARGENTINA

Italian immigrants of the nineteenth century cultivated and developed the vineyards in Argentina. The most widely planted variety is the red and white Criolla grape. The wine region is in the west of the country in the foothills of the Andes mountains and stretches from the Salta province in the north through the provinces of Catamarca, La Rioja, San Juan and Mendoza to Rio Negro in the south. Mendoza used to be a huge inland desert, but canals now irrigate the vineyards with water from the melting snows of the Andes. This province provides 90 percent of Argentina's table wine and includes some huge wineries. The San Juan province is also irrigated and the hot climate is well suited to the production of base wine for vermouth. Rio Negro, to the south of Mendoza, is much cooler and produces good quality white wine and sparkling wine.

BRAZIL

The characteristic 'foxy' taste of the native American vine, Labrusca, flavours the wine, and it is used to make most of the everyday wine. Brazil makes a range of table, fortified and sparkling wines and imports wine to make vermouth.

CHILE

The production of wine in Chile has soared since 1996. Cabernet Sauvignon, Merlot and Marmenere lead the way in red plantings, with the local Pais grape holding its own. Planted white grapes are Chardonnay and Sauvignon Blanc.

Limari Valley An emerging area north of Santiago where grapes have been planted since 1993 and used to make a pisco, a local brandy.

Aconcagua Valley A hot region north of Santiago, it receives water from the River Aconcagua. Cabernet Sauvignon, Carmenere, and Syrah are planted.

Casablanca Valley A cool climate where Sauvignon Blanc grows well; in some areas Gewürztraminer, Riesling and Pinot Noir thrive; in the hotter, the late-ripening variety Carmenere is planted.

San Antonio Valley South of the Casablanca valley, this is a region for grapes that ripen earlier, like Pinot Noir and Chardonnay.

Maipo Valley Cuttings from these pre-phylloxera varieties are still used in Chile. Many of the top wine-producing companies are situated here.

Rapel Valley Divided into two main regions, the Cachapoal and Colchagua valleys. Both areas have a high potential for the production of quality wines.

Curico Valley The heartland of Chilean viticulture. Leading wineries include Torres.

Maule Valley Chile's biggest wine-growing region.

Itati and Bio Bio These valleys in the south are increasingly important.

SPAIN

Spain is mentioned as an exporter of wine in the early records of civilization and her vines were bearing so prolifically by the first century BC that the Roman conquerors limited new plantings in Spain to protect Italian wine growers. In recent years, the Spanish wine industry has successfully redefined itself to appeal to the changing taste of wine drinkers.

When Spain joined the European Union it adopted the EU industry regulations regarding Vino de Mesa (basic table wine) and Vino de la Tierra (regional wine).

The *Denominación de Origen* (DO) regions (there are more than 50) are the mainstay of the Spanish system, guaranteeing wines come from a specific area; *Denominación de Origen Calificada* identifies wines from Rioja and Priorat, and *Denominación de Origen de Pago* is used for single-estate wines. Spanish wines can also be classified by the period of time they spend in the barrel. Young wines bottled with little time in oak and the bottle are Joven; Crianza is used for wines with a minimum of six months ageing in oak and and six months in bottle. Reserva is for wines two years in oak with a further year in bottle. Gran Reserva is for three years in oak and a further two years in bottle before release.

There are eight main wine regions:

The Northwest Situated above Portugal and along the coast of the Bay of Biscay, where the climate is cool and wet with an Atlantic influence, the area has two DOs, Rias Baixas and Ribeiro.

The Upper Ebro This region includes Rioja, Navarra and Aragon.

   Rioja has three sub regions: Rioja Alta, Rioja Alavesa and Rioja Baja. Rioja Alavesa is considered the best region. Four Spanish grapes – Tempranillo, Garnacha, Graciano and Mazuelo – are used to produce Rioja and there is debate as to the advantages of using French varieties in the blend. The white Viura grape is used to make white Rioja. Plantings of Cabernet Sauvignon, Merlot and Syrah are experimental. New winemakers in Rioja are producing a wine more modern in style than before to appeal to current taste. Traditionally Rioja was aged in American oak barrels but many are using French oak.

   Navarra Situated north of Rioja. Rosé was the main wine from this region but now both red and white are made. Grapes similar to those grown for Rioja are used, and the wine has a similar character.

   Aragon South and east of Navarre, its sub regions of Carinena, Campo de Borja, Calatayud and Somontano produce wines to look out for.

The Duero Valley The DO regions of Bierzo, Cigales, Ribera del Duero, Rueda and Toro produce wines worth following – in particular, the whites from

Rueda and the reds from Ribera del Duero. Spain's most expensive wine, Vega Sicilia, is produced in Ribera del Duero. Winemaker Marques de Riscal has moved away from Rioja to Rueda for some of its white wines.

Catalonia The DO regions include Alella, Ampurdan-Costa Brava, Conca Barbera, Priorato, Tarragona and the region of Penedas, which has come alive in the last 40 years. The use of stainless steel fermentation vats and a better use of local grapes, combined with plantings of French grapes, have meant this region can produce wines for a changing market. Although Cava can be made in many parts of Spain, the bulk of the wine is made from grapes grown in this region. Cava, produced since 1872, is made in the same way as champagne – a second fermentation in bottle, with a short ageing period after the final blend.

The Levant This region centres on Valencia which still produces vast quantities of wine. Other DO regions are Alicante, Utiel-Requena, Yecla and Jumilla.

The Mesata The DO wines from Madrid are still trying to gain a higher quality level in their wines. To the west lies Extremadura, which produces bulk wine for distilling into Spanish brandy.

Castilla – La Mancha A large percentage of wine comes from this vast region to the south of Madrid. The most widely planted grape in Spain, the Arien (it accounts for over 30 percent of wine production) is planted here. It is used not only for producing varietal whites but also as a blending grape for the more beefy reds of the Valdepenas region. The four DOs are Mentrida, La Mancha, Valdepenas and Almansa.

Andalucia Historically, the first vines were planted around Cadiz and along the coast to Montilla, Huelva and Malaga. Sherry and sherry style wines are produced in this region, as well as table wine.

For more information on sherry see page 229.

USA

The early settlers found that America had an abundance of native vines 'Vitis labrusca', so these were used to make the first local wine. However, it had an unusual taste and eventually European vines 'Vitis vinifera' were shipped across to make wines that tasted like those of France and Germany. Unfortunately the European vines were not hardy enough to resist the 'foreign' diseases that attacked them. Most succumbed to mildew and those that survived it fell victim to phylloxera. This louse had lived among the American vines for centuries without doing apparent harm but the roots of European vines were highly susceptible.

Unfortunately, in about 1863, American vines carrying phylloxera were taken to France for experimental planting and within 30 years phylloxera had invaded almost every wine-growing area in the world. Ironically, it reached California around 1873 as a passenger on European vines imported for experimental planting, seriously damaging the vineyards. The solution to the problem was to graft European vines onto the American rootstock, so the louse could not damage the roots, but the grapes could be European varieties. American wines were just beginning to gain recognition when Prohibition delivered an even more devastating blow to the industry. After Prohibition was repealed, the commercial wine industry had to be almost entirely rebuilt. It takes many years for a vine to mature enough to produce quality wine, but by the 1960s the industry was functioning on a serious commercial basis. By the late 1970s the world became aware once again that the USA was a quality producer.

American wines can be grouped broadly into three categories: branded wines; generic wines, which have such names as California Burgundy (these names are not permitted in wines for export to the European Union); and varietal wines, which are named after the grape variety. The wines come either from the western region, dominated by California, or the eastern region centred around New York. If the word 'American' is on a label it means the wine is a blend from different states.

California This area has always had the climate and soil suitable for vine cultivation and when the Franciscan missionaries introduced one of the European 'Vitis vinifera' vines around 1769 it thrived so well that it became known as the mission grape. Many of the settlers who moved west were from wine-producing regions of Europe and possessed the skills necessary to found the wine industry. One such immigrant was Colonel Harászthy, a Hungarian refugee who opened the Buena Vista winery in 1857 in the Sonoma Valley. This was probably the largest winery in the world at that time and its wine was even sold in London. Haraszthy is thought to have brought the mysterious Zinfandel grape variety back from Europe on one of his research trips. Recent DNA testing has proved that it is the Primitivo grape, found in Italy. Zinfandel is also now being planted in other wine regions of the world.

Today California has more land under vine than Germany and provides over 90 percent of American wine production, including all the quality wine. It is also the home of the research department of the University of California at Davis, responsible for many of the advances made in the post-war wine industry. Winemaking changed from a cottage industry into a technological science largely funded by big business interests.

At most wineries fermentation takes place in large temperature-controlled stainless steel vats and much American wine never sees any oak casks at all but is stored outside in stainless steel tanks which are virtually refrigerators.

Classic grape varieties are used for quality wines, which may be all of one variety or a traditional blend such as Cabernet and Merlot. California's own grape, the Zinfandel, makes full-bodied inky wine that was used for years to give backbone to the blended California Clarets. Some makers are able to produce a much lighter style of wine which is marketed under the grape name; these wines have a raspberry-like aroma. Many experimental techniques are employed and this is one of the more unusual aspects of winemaking in California.

The vineyards of California are divided into AVAs (American Viticultural Areas). The largest designated area is a 'state' which, when shown on the label, denotes that 100 percent of the grapes come from that State. Next is a 'county', which denotes that 75 percent of the grapes come from that county. Some multi-county regions also exist. Finally, the Single Vineyard Estate label promises that 95 percent of the grapes come from that Estate. If the wine is to be exported to Europe, then these percentages are higher.

Wine Regions

The North Coast of California lies more than 100 miles north of San Francisco. The fog that drifts in from the coastal gaps causes a range of climatic conditions. For example, the Petaluma Gap provides a cooling system for the vast Sonoma vineyards. One of the largest wine-producing areas is Mendocino, with sub-regions of Anderson Valley, Redwood Valley and Potter Valley. Sparkling wines and, increasingly, Syrah and Zinfandel wines are growing in fame. Fetzer is a large producer from the Redwood Valley, while the Louis Roederer Champagne house produces excellent sparkling wines from the Anderson Valley. Northern Sonoma includes districts called Dry Creek Valley, Alexander Valley and Russian River Valley.

To the south of Mendocino in the Sonoma Valley are some of the largest producers. Gallo of Sonoma is established in Dry Creek Valley and produces a number of single-estate wines. Wineries include: Kendall-Jackson, Kenwood, Marimar Torres, Ravenswood and J Rochioli.

The Napa Valley and Carneros Napa Valley is established as a quality wine region, and is the original home of fine wine estates. The region stretches from just across the San Francisco Bay to 30 miles north. The cooling effect of the fog around the Bay is different to the climate found in the northern area of Napa. The cooler Carneros region in the south favours Chardonnay and Pinot Noir and is an area where the fruit is used to make sparkling wine. Calistoga, St Helena, Rutherford, Oakville, Stags' Leap district and Atlas Peak are some of the other AVA regions within the Napa Valley. Wineries include: Robert Mondavi, Opus One, Screaming Eagle and Stag's Leap Wine Cellars.

Central Coast The region lies to the south of San Francisco and stretches down to the town of Santa Barbara, just north of Los Angeles. The AVA regions include Santa Cruz, Monterey County, San Luis Obispo County and Santa Barbara County. Within each county there are up-and-coming AVAs.

The Sierra Foothills. The gold rush of 1849 brought many people to this region. Some people found gold, others established vineyards. Amador County's Shenandoah Valley plays host to old bush Zinfandel, and other Italian varieties also are grown – Barbera is favoured for red wines.

The Central Valley This is a vast region with winemakers E & J Gallo, one of the largest wine companies in the world, a resident. In this warm and dry area irrigation is essential and high-yielding grapes are produced. All major grapes are grown, and made into basic-quality wines. Wineries include: Blossom Hill.

Other Wine Regions

The Pacific North West This includes Washington, Oregon and Idaho. Situated further north than San Francisco the weather is cooler but with longer hours of daylight during the growing season. Oregon vines are grown in the Willamette Valley, Umpqua Valley and Rogue Valley, a region where more wineries are opening up, producing top-quality wines. Maison Joseph Drouhin of Burgundy set up a winery in Dundee, Oregon, which is now producing top-quality Pinot Noir and Chardonnay. Pinot Gris and Riesling are also being produced there. In Washington State, some vineyards are found south of Seattle, with more located in the heavily irrigated Colombia Valley. Three AVA regions are Yakima Valley, Walla Walla and Red Mountain. Chardonnay dominates planting, with Riesling, Semillon and Sauvignon also being planted. Pinot Noir, Merlot, Cabernet Sauvignon and Syrah also enjoy the local climate. Situated just east of Oregon, Idaho produces white wines.

The Eastern Seaboard American hybrid varieties of grape are planted in many of these coastal states. More recently, the better-quality 'Vitis vinifera' varieties are cultivated. New York State is the largest grape-growing state after California and researchers have developed grape varieties suitable for the climates existing around New York's Lake Erie, the Finger Lakes and Long Island.

CANADA

With more flexibility in the rules and regulations controlled by the State Liquor Control Boards, wine drinking in Canada has increased rapidly. Ontario and British Colombia are leading winemaking provinces. The Vintners Quality Alliance (VQA) was established in 1988 to provide a quality control system. Ontario's winemaking regions are the Niagara Peninsula and Pelee Island. Ice wine is a favourite style produced here.

Spirits & Beers

BRANDY

Brandy is a spirit distilled from wine. Spirit from distilled fruits other than grapes is referred to by the name of the fruit coupled with the word 'brandy'. These fruit brandies are classified as *eaux-de-vie*. The word 'brandy' is a generic term and so brandy can be made anywhere. Cognac and armagnac are examples of French brandies but there are a host of other brandies in France and every wine-growing country in the world produces brandy.

COGNAC

Some 70 miles north of Bordeaux in western France lie the Charente and Charente-Maritime departments. Almost in the centre of their combined area is the town of Cognac, which has given its name to the world's finest brandy. With sufficient rainfall and an average annual temperature of about 13°C the Cognac region has the perfect climate for producing high-quality wines.

For centuries trade has been the main activity of this region because of its ports and navigable waterways. In Roman times the people of the Charente mastered the arts of viticulture and extraction of salt from seawater, so that by the Middle Ages the Dutch, Norwegian and English traders were shipping wheat, salt and wine from Charente to the rest of Europe.

The wine itself was highly acidic and light-bodied which meant it did not travel well. Sometime in the mid-sixteenth century the wine was boiled down to strengthen it. There were added advantages to this practice as it saved space on ships and helped avoid taxation, which was then levied on bulk. This *Brandewijn*, a Dutch word meaning 'burnt wine', was regarded as a wine concentrate to be drunk diluted with water.

By the end of the eighteenth century, the superiority of older brandies was recognized because of the quality of the wines in barrel that had made the long sea voyage to the colonies. Unfortunately in 1880 phylloxera completely destroyed the region's vineyards, which allowed whisky producers to take a share of the cognac market. It has taken some decades for cognac brands to regain their share.

The grape-growers are not allowed to distil their wine into spirit unless they have a licence. There are only about 2,000 who are licensed to make brandy, and they must use onlyy their own wine. Most growers sell their wine to one of the 4 co-operatives or to one of the hundreds professional distillers. These firms then sell the distilled spirit to one of the 300 cognac houses which uses the spirit in its blend, matures the cognac and markets it. These cognac houses make the registered brands, many of which are household names in France and abroad.

Very few cognac houses own vineyards and although most do buy wine and distil their own spirit, they also have to purchase spirit to meet their requirements. The essential art in cognac production is the blending process which is the domain of these houses. Although there are about 300 cognac houses, the four or five major houses control the major part of the market. Exports account for 95 percent of cognac sales; the most importnt markets are the USA (mainly three star and VS qualities with a smaller percentage of superior quality), Singapore (mainly superior quality), plus the United Kingdom, Germany, China (mainly superior quality), Finland, Russia, Norway and Japan (mainly superior quality).

THE VINEYARDS

The Cognac Delimited Region was determined by the Decree of 1 May 1909. It extends throughout the Charente-Maritime department, through most parts of the Charente department, and several districts of Deux-Sèvres and Dordogne. It is classified into six regions of descending quality, the determining factors being the soil, climate and light. A high proportion of chalk in the soil produces fine spirits and as the chalk content is reduced, so is the quality of the brandy. The best vineyards are sheltered from the harsh sea winds while being close enough to the coast to escape the extreme temperature variations characteristic of the inland continental climate.

Grande Champagne The French word 'champagne' is derived from the Latin *campania*, meaning 'open countryside' and in this context must not be confused with the region of the same name. The area surrounding the town of Cognac has crumbly chalky soil, which is a major factor in producing spirit with exceptional delicacy and finesse that takes many years to mature.

Petite Champagne There is little difference in the soil of this area but there is a slight variation in the micro-climate. Consequently the spirit is very similar in style to that of Grande Champagne, but it matures more quickly.

Borderies This is quite a small area to the north-west of Cognac with deep clay soil, although the climate is the same as the Champagne areas. Borderies spirit is highly regarded as blending material because of its tendency to firmness.

Fins Bois This large area contains much farming land and forest. The soil is gravelly and the spirit matures early.

Bons Bois The proximity to the sea and clay soil of this region produce a broad-tasting spirit. Only a small percentage of the land in the area is planted with cognac vines and most of the grapes are used in the production of cheap cognac.

Bois Ordinaires Parts of this area border the coast and the soil contains sandstone. Exposure to this maritime influence results in a fairly coarse spirit used in cheaper blends.

PRODUCTION OF COGNAC

The Base Wine

About 95 percent of distilling wine comes from the Ugni Blanc grape although some plantings of Folle Blanche and Columbard grapes are authorized. The wine is allowed to ferment in huge vats for three to five weeks and no additional yeasts, sugar or sulphur dioxide are permitted. This produces a sour high-acid wine with a low alcohol content. The maximum date on which to begin distillation for white wines destined for cognac production is March 31 of the year following the harvest. This is because a secondary fermentation, which occurs naturally around that time, would reduce the acid content. Although nine litres of base wine are required for every one litre of cognac, only about half of the wine actually produced in the Charente is distilled.

The Still   A square brick furnace acts as a base for a small copper still known as the Charentais, the capacity of which does not exceed 30 hectolitres. A curve of copper tubing known as the *swan throat* connects the still to a cooler with a copper condensing coil encased in a cold water tank. The still is often equipped with an energy-saving wine preheater. This optional device preheats the wine that is to be distilled in the next cycle.

Cognac distillation is performed in a two-stage process.
Stage One   Unfiltered wine is poured into the boiler and brought to the boil. Alcohol vapours are freed and collected in the still-head. They then enter the swan-neck and flow into the coil. Upon contact with the coolant, they condense, forming the *brouillis*. This slightly cloudy liquid is returned to the boiler for a second distillation, what is known as *la bonne chauffe*. The distiller must then carry out the delicate operation known as 'cutting' or *la coupe*: the first vapours that arrive, called 'the heads', have the highest alcohol content, and are separated from the rest. Then comes 'the heart', a clear spirit that will produce cognac. Finally, the distiller gets rid of 'the tails' when the alcohol meter registers a 60 percent alcohol by volume (ABV) rate.
Stage Two   The 'heads' and 'tails' are redistilled with the next batch of wine. The success of the distilling cycle, which lasts about 24 hours, lies in constant surveillance and in the extensive experience of the distiller, who may also intervene in the distillation techniques, thus conferring to cognac features of his or her personality.

Ageing   The infant cognacs are matured in Limousin or Tronçais oak casks. These are made from staves that have been weathered for four years to remove excess tannin from the wood. In many cognac houses new casks are used for new brandy as the raw spirit can stand the impact of strong tannin and draws colour from the new wood. After a year the spirit is racked into a slightly older cask and, to stop it absorbing too much wood character, is eventually transferred to an older larger cask. The paler, light-bodied cognacs will have been matured only in old casks which produce a more delicate spirit.
Casks must be topped up and sampled to ensure that a drinkable product is

developing and small amounts of cane sugar or caramel may be added. As the brandy is absorbed by the wood of the cask, oxygen is absorbed by the spirit through the pores of the wood. The brandy becomes a beautiful amber colour, from contact with the wood, and assumes a perfumed vanilla bouquet.

There is, however, some loss from this process, known affectionately as the Angel's share. In fact the French Excise authorities allow for a loss of 5 percent pure alcohol per year, but the loss usually averages 2–3 percent. The loss can be affected by dampness or dryness for if the warehouses (*chais)* are kept too damp, the brandy will lose strength, but if they are kept too dry it will evaporate too quickly. This is the reason for the great care taken in looking after the brandy. Huge amounts of capital are involved, for the older a brandy gets, the greater the financial risk. The oldest and most precious cognacs are kept in a special part of the chais known as the *paradis*. Each house holds its reserve in cask until it is between 50 and 70 years old when it is transferred to glass demijohns, because further ageing might make the spirit too woody. It is then rested quietly until it is needed for blending into the finest quality cognac.

Blending The cellar master (*maître de chai*) is responsible for producing a consistent style of cognac that can be immediately identified as the product of a particular house. He or she is constantly sampling the different casks to check on colour, bouquet and flavour and to determine which casks should be blended together. Any one brand contains many brandies of varying ages and types, and blending is done one stage at a time with long rest periods in between to allow the brandies to marry together.

Bottling Distilled water is used to reduce the cognac to the required strength; it is then filtered, rested and bottled, the corks having been dipped in cognac.

STYLES OF COGNAC
Three Star By French law the youngest brandy in a cognac need be only 18 months old although many countries to which it is exported, including Britain, require that it be a minimum of three years old. The stars or the term VS indicate a firm's standard blend.

VSOP Very Superior Old Pale. Cognac bearing this term is at least four and a half years old, although many houses include much older spirit in the blend.

Vintage In 1963 the cognac houses were prohibited from marketing vintage cognac, i.e. the brandy of a single year. Until 1973 a few vintage cognacs were matured in Britain but entry into the EU meant this was discontinued there also. Recently, some houses have declared vintages under strict regulations.

Early Landed This is a very young cognac that has been shipped specifically to Britain and matured in cask in a British bond. In the damp climate the cognac develops a different flavour and is paler because the spirit takes on less colour from the wood.

Late Bottled This is cognac that has remained in cask for a much longer period and the date of bottling will be shown on the label. Many of the cognacs that have matured in British bonds are late bottled.

Luxury Cognacs Most houses produce a quality cognac that is a blend of old fine brandies. These cognacs carry prestigious names such as Vieille Réserve, Grand Réserve, Napoleon, XO, Extra, Cordon Bleu, Cordon Argent, Paradis and Antique. Many of them are only available in limited quantity.

Fine Champagne This term may be used for cognac blended from brandies produced in the Grande and Petite Champagne areas but must contain a minimum of 50 percent Grande Champagne brandy.

ARMAGNAC

The Armagnac region has long been known for its fine brandy; the first written reference to it was in 1411, about two centuries before any mention of cognac. Although the grape varieties are the same, there is little similarity between the two spirits in methods of production, maturation or final product. There remains a mood of experimentation in Armagnac: they freely use more fragrant grape varieties, along with a variety of distillation methods. It is slightly more rustic in style than ccognac, softer and rounder, with a fuller flavour.

For brandy production, Armagnac is divided into three sub-regions:
Bas-Armagnac The area to the west of Auch has a predominantly sandy soil and the finest brandies are produced from here.
Ténarèze The central area has clay soil which results in early maturing brandies.
Haut-Armagnac The south-eastern area, which has the highest proportion of chalky soil, produces the lowest quality brandy.

The wine is distilled while on the lees so that more flavour passes into the spirit. This is heightened by distilling at a much lower strength, about 53 percent ABV, which allows retention of more flavouring elements, creating a pungent spirit. Armagnac is distilled only once, in a form of continuous copper still developed locally during the nineteenth century, which bubbles the spirit vapour through the base wine before it passes into the condenser.

The infant spirit is matured in Monlezun oak. The high concentration of sap and tannin in this black oak adds flavour and colour to the armagnac, which ages much faster than it would in lighter oak. Good armagnac is a deep nutty brown, with golden lights and a dark heart; it is very very dry on the finish.

If a label bears the name of any of the three regions, then the brandy must come only from that region. The word 'armagnac' indicates a blend; a three-year-old brandy will be Three Star; VO and VSOP indicate at least four years wood maturation; Extra, Napoleon and XO brandies have spent at least five years in wood casks. The phrase *hors d'age* is used for brandies over 25 years old. The label of a blend may carry a date, which must be that of the youngest brandy in the blend, although vintage armagnacs are available. Most armagnac is marketed in a flat-faced bottle known as a *basquaise*.

GRAPE BRANDY

France In France a grape brandy is called *une fine*, and it is gaining an increasing share of the world market. There are few restrictions on brandy production in France and consequently most of the commercial grape brandies are of indefinite origin. Surplus wine is often sent to the French government monopoly for distillation. The brandy is then sold to a firm for blending and bottling. Many of the grape brandies are packaged so that they bear a strong resemblance to good cognacs and most use the same terms such as VSOP and Napoleon, but this is simply a marketing exercise.

Germany The Rhineland is the centre of the brandy industry. After 1918 German brandy was not allowed to use the word cognac, so it is now officially known as *weinbrand*. Distillers are permitted to purchase wine from anywhere in Europe, which is then pot stilled and aged in Limousin oak.

Greece Known locally as *koniak*, Greek brandy is distilled around Piraeus. The spirit is aged for three years and the temperature is allowed to rise in the maturing rooms. There is a particular nose and flavour to a Greek brandy that comes from the species of grapes used for the base wine. Most of the wineries in Cyprus also produce a brandy.

Italy Italian law insists that brandies are matured for three years and both pot still and continuous still brandies are produced for domestic and export markets. Italian brandy has a good clean flavour with a touch of sweetness.

Spain The Jerez district is the major brandy-producing area and most of the sherry shippers market a brandy. Spanish brandy was used as raw material for Dutch gins and liqueurs from the eighteenth century. Today much of the dark sweet brandy produced in Spain is exported to South America.

Australia The local demand is chiefly for mixing brandy. The base wine is made from white grapes that do not show marked varietal characteristics and only the fermented juice of fresh grapes is allowed as a base, so that purity levels are very high. Most of the brandy comes from the irrigated riverland of South Australia.

South Africa This is a spirit-oriented country with about half of its wine harvest being distilled for brandy. It is made by pot still and matured for a minimum of three years although finer brandies are about five years old.

USA Brandy was first made on the Spanish missions in California about 200 years ago and today this state is the major brandy producer. It may be made in either a pot still or continuous still and the California Brandy Advisory Board insists the spirit be wood aged – often in American oak – for a minimum of two years. The base wine has a strong grape flavour, and sweetening, flavouring and colouring additives may be used subject to strict control, so that the end product is usually fruitier and lighter than its European equivalent.

GIN

Today gin is a flavoured spirit obtained by the distillation and rectification of grain, usually malted barley, rye or maize, but this was not always the case.

The spirit originated in Holland over 300 years ago when a doctor successfully combined the juniper berry and alcohol to produce a cheap remedy for kidney complaints. The word 'gin' is a corruption of the French word for juniper – *genièvre*. English soldiers returning from the religious wars of Tudor times took with them a liking for the drink which gave them 'Dutch courage' in times of stress. From this time it became the Englishman's spirit and was politely referred to as Hollands.

In the eighteenth century gin was a cheap solace for London's poor, but there was no control over production and the concoctions could contain aniseed, turpentine and even sulphuric acid, for those were the days of the notorious 'Gin Lane'. The invention of the continuous still in 1831 meant that a better quality spirit could be made. Gradually it became respectable to drink gin, although it was still known as 'Mother's Ruin' because of the juniper berry's supposed ability to induce abortion.

In the USA, too, gin had to weather a period of notoriety before it gained respectability. Prohibition in the 1920s saw vast quantities of 'bath tub' gin produced; with the lifting of Prohibition, the sales of London Dry gin escalated, mainly due to the demand for that famous cocktail, the Dry Martini.

The global gin market is dominated by London Dry styles; however, the new generation gins, such as Bombay Sapphire, have brought a new taste to gin. With at least 10 botanicals including almond oil, lemon peel, liquorice, and orris root, the botanicals are not boiled in the spirit, but the spirit itself is vapourized and passed through the botanicals. The result is a complex and refreshing gin. Other gins, such as Hendrick's, contain the usual botanicals and perhaps a surprising ingredient – rose petals or cucumber.

LONDON DRY GIN

In the production of London Dry gin the first distillation is by continuous still, so as to eliminate the fusel oil and other impurities. This produces a high-quality neutral spirit that forms the base for gin. The second step is to distil a flavouring into the neutral spirit and the resulting distillate is known as gin. Each firm has its own secret recipe for flavouring the gin, but all distillers use juniper berries and coriander seeds. Other ingredients include angelica root, orris root, casia bark, liquorice, orange and lemon peel, fennel, calamus root, cardamom seeds and almond. The collection of berries, spices, roots and bark used as flavouring is known as the *botanicals*. Traditionally these are just added to the neutral spirit in a pot still and heated so that the vapours rise up the

neck of the still into the condenser, which cools them, and they precipitate into the receiver as gin. The botanicals may be suspended in a cage in the neck of the still so that the vapours pass through them and absorb the flavour. Some firms use what is referred to within the trade as the 'two-shot method' of making gin. A much higher proportion of botanicals is added to the neutral spirit so that after distillation the gin has a very high concentration of flavour. This is then mixed with cold neutral spirit to reduce the flavour to drinking strength.

The art of the gin distiller is to determine which part of the distillate is suitable for the gin. The first part of the vapour – the heads – is unsuitable, but when the flavouring has built up to the required strength, the spirit is run into a gin receiver. The distillate is constantly nosed and sampled until a change in the character of the output can be noted and it is no longer suitable for gin. London Dry gin does not have to be made in London to be so called, although it is recognized that the best gins are made in London.

Plymouth Gin This is made only in Plymouth by one distiller. It is wholly unsweetened and is the traditional gin of the British Navy; it is also the correct ingredient for a Pink Gin.

Dutch Gin This gin is also known as Hollands or Genever. The name Genever has nothing to do with the Swiss city or lake of that name but is again a corruption of the French word 'genièvre'. The spirit is made in Holland, mostly in the cities of Amsterdam and Schiedam and the two main styles are *oude genever* and *jonge genever* – old and young gin. Genever is made from a neutral alcohol referred to as malt wine because the malted barley is fermented for a few days before being distilled. The malt wine and botanicals are distilled once to produce oude genever. However, malt wine is expensive and many distillers stretch it by blending it with grain spirit then distilling in a continuous still. Jonge genever is produced in larger quantities and contains even less malt wine. Distillation at a low proof gives Dutch gin a distinctive grain flavour and for this reason is usually taken neat.

Sloe Gin Made by steeping sloes in gin and is more accepted as a liqueur.

Cold Compounded Gin Much of the gin available in many parts of the world is made by an entirely different method from distilled gin and is simply a juniper-flavoured essence that has been added to alcohol and stirred to distribute the flavour. This gin essence can be produced in a chemical laboratory so there is no need to use a still at all. The base spirit is often a low grade of alcohol so the manufacture of cold mix gin is a simple and cheap procedure.

Previous page
Hendrick's Cucumber Collins is made with a unique cucumber gin, with a cucumber wedge for extra flavour.

Opposite
Va-Va-Voom is Kremlyovska vodka, fruit juices, honey and mint flavours all in one highball.

RUM

Sugar cane was introduced into the West Indies by the explorer Christopher Columbus and its cultivation spread rapidly through the Caribbean. By the seventeenth century cane was being distilled to produce a cheap spirit that served as a stimulant, disinfectant and medicinal aid. The name of rum was probably originally used to describe the product of the British West Indies. A raw spirit was produced in the British West Indies as early as 1647 and was chiefly the drink of the slaves of the plantations at that time. This 'rumbullion', or 'Kill-Devil' as it was known, was developed into the drink we know today. It was consumed in vast quantities by the American settlers and, in the early days of Australia's history, rum was so highly valued that it was used as currency. The Royal Navy issued it to warm those at sea, combat scurvy and act as an anaesthetic. One Admiral, nicknamed Old Grog, decided that the heavy consumption of rum was affecting his crew's working capacity and he had the rum watered down; even today 'grog' indicates a mixture of spirit and water.

Many French households keep rum in the kitchen as a culinary aid and its ability to heighten the flavour of fruit drinks makes it the traditional base of punch. The best-known rum drinks are the Daiquiri, Caipirinha, Cuba Libre and Planter's Punch.

PRODUCTION

To make the spirit, the sugar cane is stripped of its leaves and crushed, and the juice produced from this process collected in vacuum pans, where the water of the juice is evaporated, to leave behind a syrup which eventually granulates. When this is sufficiently granulated it is placed in huge drums which revolve rapidly, extracting a thick sticky substance known as molasses from the sugar, which it leaves behind. The molasses is again reboiled producing a lower grade of sugar, and the extract of this second processing is used for the distillation of all types of rum.

It is first mixed with water and fermenting agents, which depend on the area of production. Some areas use the yeasts produced from previous production. This wash, as it is known, is fermented out and distilled, producing rum. Rum differs according to the strain of the yeast used in the wash, as well as to the method of distillation and the type and amount of caramel used in colouring. Rum needs maturation in the same way as whisky or brandy. Rum that is under three years of age cannot be sold in the UK.

Puerto Rican Rum Generally these are dry light-bodied rums. The molasses is fermented in gigantic vats together with some of the mash from a previous fermentation. After four days the wash contains 7 percent alcohol and goes into a column still, consisting of six connecting columns. The first is the purifying column which cleans the wash, the second is the analysing column where the alcohol is vaporized from the wash. The vapour passes into the rectifying column but the residue goes to the aldehyde column for reprocessing. The liquid passing over from the rectifying column is the rum, but two more columns are available for the production of neutral spirit.

Premium brands, such as Bacardi, triple distil at a higher proof and filter the spirit five times in order to eliminate impurities. This is the base of the famous Cuba Libre and Bacardi cocktails.

If the rum is matured for only a year in uncharred oak casks, it is light-bodied and fairly neutral in flavour and is known as white (light) rum. Three years in charred barrels and the addition of caramel results in gold rum. Some rum is aged for over six years, acquiring a dry mellowness. Often referred to as *vieux* or *liqueur* rum, it bears comparison with matured brandy or deluxe whisky.

The Virgin Islands and Cuba also produce light-bodied rum.

Jamaican Rum   Traditional Jamaican rum is full-bodied with a pungent aroma and assertive flavour. The molasses is allowed to ferment naturally. This can take up to three weeks but allows the development of more flavouring elements which eventually add dimension to the spirit. The wash is double distilled in a pot still and only the middle fraction is taken off as an infant rum. It is aged in oak for at least five years but the very dark colour comes from the added caramel. Much of it is aged and blended in the UK, which is the largest customer for Jamaican rum.

Martinique Rum   This is distilled from the concentrated juice of the sugar cane, rather than from molasses. It is produced by pot still and takes on colour from oak maturation. Haitian rum is produced in a similar manner.

Demeraran Rum   The Demerara River flows through Guyana and the individual flavour of the dark-coloured local rum results from the soil character. Some Demeraran rum is marketed with a high alcoholic content and is the traditional rum for grog. If a rum is labelled 'Demeraran style' it usually indicates a dark-coloured rum with less pungency than Jamaican rum.

Batavia Arrack   This is produced in Indonesia. Little red rice cakes are put into the molasses which ferments naturally from wild yeasts. After some ageing in Java, the arrack is shipped to Holland where it is further aged for up to six years before blending and bottling.

Aguardente de Cana   This sugar-cane spirit is the South American equivalent of rum. It is known as cachaça in Brazil, where its annual consumption figures surpass the combined world sales of white, dark and golden rums.

Australian Rum   The Bundaberg Distilling Company based in Bundaberg in Queensland began producing rum in 1888, and in 2004 it was voted Australia's number one spirit. The newest release is softer and gentler than the original rum.

Flavoured Rums   Tropical fruits are macerated in white rum to create fruit-flavoured rums. They are then distilled, resulting in a rum liqueur. The most popular flavours are banana, pineapple and coconut.

TEQUILA

Tequila is Mexico's national drink and fast becoming a global favourite. Over 200 million litres are produced annually; about half is exported to the USA. The spirit is named after a small town in the state of Jalisco – only spirit made in Jalisco and four surrounding areas may be called tequila. There are over 350 brands in Mexico alone, with the best being 100 percent blue agave. Forty percent of the tequila market is held by global brand Jose Cuervo, which recently celebrated its 200th anniversary by releasing Reserva de la Familia as a limited edition.

The younger a tequila is, the more fiery it can taste; the older tequilas are smoother and richer. Known as the base for Margarita and Tequila Sunrise cocktails, the modern trend is to imbibe tequila as a long and refreshing party drink, for instance, over ice with ginger ale and a slice of lime. The tequila shot, taken with salt and a wedge of lemon or lime , is a popular party drink.

PRODUCTION

Tequila is made from the blue-green *Agave tequilana weber*, known as maguey or blue mezcal in Mexico, or as century plant in the USA.

It grows slowly, taking eight to 10 years to reach maturity. The spiky leaves are removed and the heart – called the *pina* because of its strong resemblance to a pineapple – and weighing between 23 and 115 kilos is roughly chopped and steam-cooked in ovens, or autoclaves, for seven hours. After cooling, the *pinas* are washed, shredded and pressed between rollers to extract all the juice. Sugar and yeast are added to this juice, which is then fermented for two or three days in tanks, before double distillation in a pot still. The tequila is allowed to mature for a minimum of three years in huge 40,000-litre vats before bottling.

Mezcal

Mezcal comes from the agave plants in Oaxaca, Southern Mexico. Tequila and mezcal are produced and classified in similar ways, but there is a difference: in mezcal production, the pina are baked and roasted over charcoal in ovens in the ground for three days. This method produces a smoked flavour not found in tequila. And the bloated worm in the bottle? Some claim it is the mark of the drink's authenticity, while others say it is simply a gimmick.

STYLES OF TEQUILA

White or Silver This tequila has been allowed to mature in vats that are lined with wax and therefore remains colourless.
Gold or Anejo (aged) This tequila is matured in white oak vats, which give it a golden hue and mellow taste.

VODKA

Vodka, like gin, is distilled from a base of grain and is highly rectified, but no flavourings of any kind are added. Indeed, the finest vodkas such as Stolichnaya's Elit and newer boutique brands such as Sputnik and Ketel One, are filtered through materials such as activated charcoal and even fine quartz sand to ensure absolute purity. This would be an accurate description of what the western world today calls vodka; history, however, tells us a different story.

The origins of vodka – the word means literally 'little water' – lie in twelfth-century Russia and Poland, where 'vodka' was the generic name for any spirit drink whether it was distilled from grape, grain or potato. These potions were often highly flavoured and aromatic. In Russia, the Czar banned the production of vodka at the beginning of World War I, but a flourishing black-market trade continued and to control this a state monopoly was established in 1925.

Emigrés who fled from the Russian Revolution began to distil unflavoured vodkas in their new homelands, but vodka did not become a fashionable drink in the western world until the late 1940s. The fashion started in the USA with such cocktail combinations as the Moscow Mule, Bloody Mary and Screwdriver. By 1975 vodka sales in the USA had the major share of the spirit market and it was the first spirit to outsell bourbon in its own homeland. Vodka now accounts for more than 26 percent of all spirits sales in the USA.

The advantage of a basic vodka made for the USA and western European countries is its versatility: it is colourless and has no flavour. This makes it such a good mixer with everything. It is a great base for cocktails, adding strength but not altering the taste. It is also odourless, with digestive properties.

However, some of the finer vodkas produced in eastern Europe are created with distinctive flavours, which make them interesting to drink, chilled, on their own.

STYLES OF VODKA
Neutral Vodka This is distilled from potatoes, molasses or grain (rye and wheat). Barley is used in Finland and maize in the USA. They are then rectified, diluted to the required strength and filtered through activated charcoal. The source of the water and the choice of grain can have an effect on the quality – Polish vodka, for instance, is always made from rye.
Green This is made by steeping Zubrowka grass in Polish vodka, and has a delicate aromatic bouquet. The bottle frequently contains a stem of the grass.
Other Flavourings Lemon, currant, pepper, peach, strawberry, raspberry, vanilla, basil, rose and horseradish are some of the new vodka flavours.

Serving Vodka
Traditionally, serve straight from the freezer in shot glasses, with caviar.

WHISKY

SCOTCH WHISKY

The earliest record of spirit being distilled in the British Isles is the barley-based 'Pot Ale' of the Irish religious establishments. It is likely that the art of distillation reached Ireland from Spain and it certainly travelled with the Irish monks when they settled in western Scotland. The Scots quickly developed a taste for the product and literature abounds with references to *uisge beatha*, the Gaelic for 'water of life'; *uisge* is pronounced 'whisky'.

Spirits were first taxed in 1643 and so began the long-running battle between the whisky-makers and the Excise men. Up to the early nineteenth century illicit stills were operating on a massive scale. Then in 1831 an Irish distiller, Aeneas Coffey, registered the patent for a new design of still. This was the continuous still, which revolutionized the whisky-making process.

Prohibition in the USA stopped the production of rye and bourbon, creating a new demand for Scotch. One British firm produced a blend specifically for the American public, who clamoured for its soft light style which reminded them of rye. It was sold across the blockade by Captain McCoy, who guaranteed that this product was 'the real McCoy' and not a 'cut' spirit. Strangely enough, although there was a huge market for blends, single malts were not generally appreciated until after World War II.

Today, whiskies are marketed in two styles: blended and single malt. Blended whiskies are made by mixing malt and grain whiskies together to create a spirit. Single malt whisky is a premium whisky product, made only from malted barley at a single distillery.

Many countries have tried to emulate the success of Scotland in producing this fine spirit, but Scotch whisky has a unique quality that defies imitation. This can be attributed in part to Scotland's soft spring water that begins as melting snow and flows through granite and peat, which act as natural filters so that the water is of unquestionable purity but still contains the valuable minerals that add character to the whisky. The Scottish climate also allows the spirit to age slowly in cask without too high a rate of evaporation, producing mature whisky with a complexity of flavours.

PRODUCTION OF MALT WHISKY

Conversion Barley is malted by soaking in water for about 48 hours; it is then spread out on a concrete floor where the warmth and moisture cause it to germinate. The barley secretes the enzyme diastase; this makes the barley starch soluble and capable of producing sugars, which can then be converted to alcohol. Germination is stopped by drying the green malt in a kiln over a peat fire. The smoke adds character and flavour.

Extraction The crushed dried malt is put into a mash tun with boiling water and churned violently, reactivating the enzyme and extracting the sugar. The resulting liquid is known as the wort.

Fermentation The wort goes into deep wooden or steel vessels and cultured yeast is added. This attacks the sugar, and after about three days of violent action, converts it to crude alcohol of low strength known as the wash.

Distillation The liquid is put in the wash still and gently heated to a point where the alcohol vaporizes, rises up the still through the condenser which is kept water-cooled, and precipitates as low wines of 30–40 percent alcohol.

The procedure is repeated in the smaller spirit still. Firstly the low alcohol foreshots pass over, then when the spirit has built to around 12 percent alcohol, the stillman, who closely observes progress through the glass spirit safe, throws the tap to channel off the potable spirit. This is the critical stage as it determines how much of the congenerics are allowed to pass into the spirit, contributing to the flavour. The undesirable last runnings – the *feints* – still contain alcohol, so both the feints and the foreshots are channelled into the wash still for further distillation. The shape of the still, the height of the head of the still and the angle of the pipe connecting the head to the condenser all affect the character of the whisky.

Maturation The spirit is reduced to 68.5 percent ABV and piped into sherry casks or American oak casks. The minimum legal period of maturation is three years, but a period of five years is advisable. Highland malts are at their best at between 15 and 20 years old, after which there is a danger of a slimy texture developing from prolonged contact with the wood.

Blending The blender's skill lies in his abilities to combine whiskies from different distilleries as well as the combination of malt and grain whiskies. The whiskies may be added to the blend because of colour, bouquet or flavour but the blender rarely tastes them; he makes his selection by colour comparison and nosing of the spirits. There may be as many as 70 whiskies in one blend. The new whisky is mixed then rested for a few months. Caramel is added to give a tawny tinge to the colour, soft water is added to reduce the alcoholic content, then the whisky is filtered and bottled.

MALT WHISKY REGIONS

Highland Malts Light-bodied but full-flavoured malts are produced north of the line drawn from Greenock to Dundee and many of the single malts come from this region. The distilleries around the River Spey in the Glenlivet area produce superior malts and the Dufftown basin distilleries produce smooth and peaty malt whiskies.

Lowland Malts These are produced south of the Highland line and the majority of them are used for blending with Highland malts.

Campbeltown Malts The Mull of Kintyre is the original home of whisky. However, it produces a heavy smoky spirit that is not good in blends.

Islay The whiskies from the Isle of Islay are individual, being sharp and pungent. Most blends have Islay whisky in them to provide depth of flavour.

PRODUCTION OF GRAIN WHISKY

The cereal, usually maize, is ground then cooked in a converter under steam pressure to burst the starch cells. It then goes into the wash tun with a little green malt and hot water. The origin of the water is immaterial and after fermentation the low wines have a lower alcoholic content than that produced for pot distillation.

The Coffey still employs the principle of distillation by steam and is a continuous process. It consists of two columns: an analyser, which separates the constituent parts, and a rectifier, which raises the strength of the spirit. Steam enters the base of the analyser, and when both columns are filled with steam, the cold wash is fed into the top of the rectifier and progresses through it inside a pipe. The body of the rectifier is filled with heated vapour, which warms the wash so that it is almost at boiling point by the time it reaches the analyser. There the hot liquid wash meets the hot steam that has been injected under pressure, so that the alcohol vaporizes, mixes with the steam and is channeled back into the base of the rectifier. Inside the rectifier the vapour passes through a series of perforated plates. The tails – feints – are piped off into a cooler, the oil is separated out of them and the remainder is fed back into the analyser. About two-thirds of the way up the vapour hits a cold spiral plate and precip-itates. It is immediately mixed with water to dilute it below flash point. The vapour that continues out of the top of the still is known as the heads or foreshots and is immediately re-distilled.

This process removes many of the congenerics of the original alcohol, making grain whisky milder in flavour and aroma than malt whisky.

STYLES OF WHISKY

Blended Whisky There are over 2,000 registered brands of blended whiskies and the best of them contain a good proportion of malt to give flavour to the neutral grain whisky.

Single Malts A single malt is the unblended product of one distillery and although the majority of their output goes for blending with grain whisky to make the well-known proprietary brands seen all over the world, more and more distilleries are now marketing their product as single malt. There has been a surge of interest in malt whiskies and, with the continuing interest in high-quality products among consumers, this trend is expected to continue.

Vatted Malts These are a blend of malt whiskies from different distilleries. Until the 1860s any blend consisted of malts but the advent of grain whisky meant vatted malts were rarely marketed.

IRISH WHISKEY

The process for making Irish whiskey differs from that used to make Scotch. The barley is dried and ground with a small proportion of green malt and other cereal, then mashed with boiling water in a kieve or mash tun that resembles a giant strainer. This mashing is repeated four times, producing the worts which are allowed to ferment. Once fermented the liquid is known as the wash and is distilled in enormous copper pot stills. A first distillation produces low wines, a second distillation produces feints, which are then distilled a third time resulting in whiskey. It is matured in sherry casks for at least five years while the minimum age for whiskey used in a deluxe blend is 12 years. Poteen is an illicitly distilled Irish whiskey made from potatoes.

CANADIAN WHISKY

Although Canadian whisky is usually called 'rye', the main grain used is corn with some wheat and rye. The abundance of grain and soft fresh water provide the vital ingredients for excellent whisky. Production is in a continuous still.

The law requires the spirit to be matured in oak for a minimum of three years and sometimes charred barrels or bourbon casks are used for ageing. Canadian whiskies range between fresh and dry to rich and succulent, and are the finest spirit of their type in the world.

USA WHISKEY

The early Americans consumed large quantities of Cuban and West Indian rum until supplies were cut off by the British blockade during the American War of Independence. Many of the famous brands of whiskey, made from corn, rye and sour mash, date from the late eighteenth century. Jack Daniel's and Maker's Mark are brand leaders.

Bourbon   Bourbon has been traced back to Bourbon County, Kentucky. In 1789 a Baptist minister, the Reverend Elijah Craig, set up a still beside a limestone creek in the desolate Bluegrass Country and distilled corn to produce his 'Kentucky Bourbon Whiskey'.

Today, American regulations define bourbon whiskey as that produced from a mash of not less than 51 percent corn grain. It must be aged for a minimum of two years in new charred oak barrels that must not be re-used to make whiskey. Distillers hold that the natural wood caramel produced by charring gives the golden lights and particular flavour of bourbon.

Straight Bourbon is the product of one distillery and *Blended Straight Bourbon* is a blend from several distilleries. Blended Bourbon indicates a mixture of bourbon and other spirits, usually grain spirits or light whiskey. Bottled in *Bond Straight Bourbon* indicates that it has been matured in bond – and consequently tax free – for a minimum of four years and this extra ageing often produces a finer quality spirit. A whiskey can only be labelled 'Kentucky Bourbon' if it is distilled and matured in Kentucky for at least one year.

Sour Mash After the wort has been fermented and the low alcohol wash, also known as beer, has been drained off, the spent mash is left behind. Some of this is added to the next vessel of mash to be fermented, ensuring a continuity of flavour and style. This process is used in the making of some bourbons and Tennessee Whiskey.

Rye The word rye can be used only if the spirit is distilled from a mash of not less than 51 percent rye. Most rye whiskey comes from Pennsylvania and Maryland, although there is wide variation in taste and quality between the numerous brands. There are some straight ryes and blended straight ryes but most are blended ryes indicating the inclusion of other whiskey or neutral spirit.

Light Whiskey A mixture of grains is distilled at a much higher proof than for other types of whiskey, thus producing a purer spirit, which has a much lighter flavour and character. It is stored in used or uncharred oak until required for blending purposes. This is a recent development in whiskey styles and a few straight light whiskeys are available, although most of it goes into blended whiskey.

Corn Whiskey Spirit distilled from a minimum of 80 percent corn mash is known as corn whiskey. It is frequently immature when marketed, which has contributed to its poor reputation.

JAPANESE WHISKY

Japan has been making whisky since the late 1800s. Distillers use pot stills for full-bodied malt whisky and continuous stills for lighter-bodied whisky for blending purposes. The top quality whiskies do contain some imported Scotch malt whisky to heighten the flavour. Most blended Japanese whisky is made from a combination of millet, corn and rice. It is aged in used charred oak before blending and maturation and has its own particular flavour and character.

OTHER SPIRITS

Aquavit

All Northern European countries produce some type of aquavit. The word derives from *aqua vitae,* the Latin for 'water of life'. This spirit is also known as schnapps. The Danes have been distilling it for over 400 years and the Danish spirit is regarded as the finest aquavit. Grain or potato is distilled to produce a neutral spirit which is then redistilled with flavourings. Caraway is the main flavouring and citrus peel, cardamom or anise can also be added. Aquavit is traditionally served chilled, and usually with food.

Arrack

Most Eastern countries produce an arrack, which is a spirit that may be distilled from various bases such as grapes, milk, rice or cane. Toddy is the spirit distilled from the fermented sap of palm trees and raki is the favourite Turkish drink. It is an anise-flavoured spirit that turns milky when mixed with water. Batavia arrack is a rum. Most arrack is quite fiery and is rarely matured.

Grappa

This is the Italian spirit distilled from the residue of skins, pulp and stalks after the juice has been run off. It can be quite fiery but a quality, mature grappa is full of flavour. *Invechiata* refers to aged grappa and *stravecchia* indicates extra maturation.

Marc

After grapes have been pressed to remove the juice suitable for winemaking, the cake that is left contains the grapeskins, pips and often the stalks. In France, the spirit distilled from this fermented pulpy residue is known as marc. It is highly pungent because of the flavouring elements that derive from the tannic pips and skins and so must be matured for many years. Marc de Bourgogne is quite well known both in France and internationally, and Marc de Champagne is one of the lightest types of marc currently available.

Brandy made in Burgundy from wine lees or wine is known as Fine de Bourgogne.

Okolehao

This is the local spirit of Hawaii where it is known as Oke. The roots of the ti plant are fermented and the mash is then distilled in a column still. It is filtered through charcoal and sold unaged. There is a Crystal Clear and a Golden Oke, and the spirit is used as a base for many of the local cocktails.

Ouzo

This aniseed-flavoured spirit is the local drink of Greece and Cyprus. Quality ouzo is made by double distilling the basic spirit then adding aniseed and other herbs for a redistillation. There are many styles of ouzo as most wineries produce their own. When water is added to ouzo it turns pale and milky, and good-quality ouzo becomes very milky. In Greece, it is always served with some kind of food.

Pisco

In South America a spirit is distilled from the residue of muscat grapes and matured in clay jars. It is called after the town of Pisco in Peru. This spirit is the base of the cocktail Pisco Sour, which is extremely popular in Chile and Peru.

Sake

A rice-based liquor that has been produced in Japan for over a thousand years, saké is actually a beer with a high alcoholic content because it is refermented to 17° GL, and cask matured for about a year. It has a delicate sweet flavour but a dry finish. It is traditionally served hot in a small porcelain pot with tiny cups.

Swedish Punsch

This is a blend of Batavia arrack (rum), aquavit and syrup. These ingredients are stirred together for a few months, wine is added and the blend is cask matured for a few more months. It can be drunk hot or cold or used in mixed drinks.

BEERS

About 6,000 years ago the ancient Egyptians were adept at brewing beer and virtually every civilization since has produced an alcoholic beverage from fermented cereal. Germanic tribes were brewing in the first century AD and in Roman Britain ale remained the national beverage despite the introduction of wine by the invaders. Farmers, lords and monks all brewed their own beer, which was consumed in preference to the contaminated water supplies. The introduction of hops to fifteenth-century Britain meant that brewers were able to stop their beer going sour, but it took the 'ale' drinkers over a century to adapt to the lighter, more bitter drink. The art of brewing was carried by the first settlers to the American colonies where most households also brewed their own beer until the rise of the commercial brewers.

English beer is no longer the remembered warm liquid of past decades because as the country's drinkers became more sophisticated through opportunities to travel and taste other beers, they demanded the same at home. The Campaign for Real Ale has also been behind the revitalized taste of ales throughout the UK since 1971, much to the delight of ale drinkers.

Today, the world's best-selling beer style is lager, a light gold style that originated from the town of Pilsen in Bohemia, Czech Republic. The brand Pilsner Urquell, produced since the mid-nineteenth century, is the original pilsner beer, and the most-imitated light beer.

Beer is now considered a serious drink by both young and old, male and female, and there are hundreds of styles to choose from. You can also buy beers brewed in Mexico, Australia, Germany, Belgium, the USA, the UK and Japan as well as from the Czech Republic – virtually every country will have its own style of beer.

Generally, global brands may dominate the marketplace but, in the true independent way, the micro-breweries keep the true spirit of beer bubbling.

PRODUCTION

The first step in beer production is *malting*. Barley wheat is soaked in water to stimulate germination, which converts the starch content into sugars. The germinated grain, green malt, is then dried and roasted in a kiln to stop further germination and add flavour to the final beer. The *brewing* process involves grinding the dried malt into a rough grist and mashing it with hot water to form the wort, which is filtered before the addition of hops to give bitterness to the beer; sometimes fruit and spices are added. The wort and dried hops go into a copper brew kettle, and are boiled for one to two and a half hours, according to the style of beer being made. The hopped wort then runs into a hop back vessel. The spent hops settle on the screen base and the hot wort filters through them. It is then cooled and run into the fermenting vats where *fermentation* will take place in one of two ways. Today yeasts are selected and cultured in a laboratory to ensure brewers get the most flavour from them.

The strains of yeast used to make lagers sink to the bottom of the brew and ferment very slowly, for up to three weeks, or until the brewer decides. After the fermentation period, the lager is carbonated to give it a sparkle, filtered and filled into kegs, bottles or cans.

Traditional beers are made by top fermentation method. 'Ale yeasts' form a surface on the liquid that results in ale. The liquid ferments for about a week at a much higher temperature than lager does; sugar is then added and the cask is sealed. The brew continues to ferment and the carbon dioxide that is released is trapped and absorbed in the liquid. Sometimes a handful of hops is dropped into the cask before sealing; this produces a 'bitter' beer. It is then left to settle before being consumed. Some draught beer, and all bottled and canned beer, is *pasteurized* by subjecting it to steam which sterilizes the beer and lengthens its shelf life but removes much of the flavour.

STYLES OF BEERS

Ales range from barley wine, blonde, brown, dark, and double stout to Pale Ale, Strong Ale, Bière de Garde, Saison and Witbier. English ales range from Bitter, India Pale Ale and English Porter to Stout, Strong Bitter and Sweet Stout. German ale styles include Dunkel Weizen, Kölsch and Weizenbock. These ales range in colour from pale gold to deep amber, and even chocolate brown, with flavours strong in malt and mild in hop, with fruity hints.

Lager styles range from the German Bock, Doppelbock, Dortmunder and Munich Dunkel Lager to Czech Pilsner, Japanese Rice lager, American Amber and American Double Pilsner. These are pale, golden beers with crisp hop aromas, with light malt and a dry hop bitter edge.

Aperitifs, Digestives & Cigars

INTRODUCTION

The principle of a drink before dinner is so widespread that some South American countries refer to that time as the 'vermouth hour', the Dutch call it the 'bitter hour', the Americans 'the cocktail hour' and in France it is the 'hour of l'Aperitif. The word 'aperitif' is derived from the Latin aperire, to open – the inference being that an aperitif will stimulate the gastric juices and so sharpen the appetite in readiness for the evening meal. Each country has its own favourite beverage for this purpose, although what is consumed in one part of the world as an aperitif will raise many an eyebrow in another.

Vermouths and bitters are widely regarded aperitifs as their tangy after-taste primes the appetite. In parts of France, however, port or a kir may be offered before a meal; in Britain a chilled fino sherry is the time-honoured aperitif and Scandinavians will take schnapps. Spirit is still consumed before dinner in most parts of the USA, and the Spanish are partial to the local brandy with water. Chilled Sercial madeira is very palatable while the classic aperitif, accepted everywhere, is fine champagne.

A digestive is something that aids digestion and as such usually refers to an after-dinner drink. Most liqueurs fall into this category, and aniseed drinks are accepted as digestive aids although in many countries they are drunk before a meal. Europeans particularly enjoy a post-prandial eau-de-vie; port and madeira are often passed around after dinner and cognac is held in high esteem as a digestive.

EAUX-DE-VIE

These are true fruit brandies made by distilling the fermented mash of a fruit. They have a higher alcoholic content than most liqueurs and are dry to the taste. Many European countries distil eaux-de-vie but the most famous are from the Alsace region of France. The French also refer to them as *alcools blancs* – white alcohols – as they are aged in glass and therefore colourless. Eaux-de-vie are expensive because of the amount of fruit needed to produce them and they are best served chilled in chilled glasses with enough room to allow the liquid to be swirled, so releasing the bouquet.

Applejack
The New England brandy distilled from the fermented mash of cider apples. The best is made in pot stills and the minimum maturation period is two years in wood. It may be bottled as a straight brandy or combined with neutral spirits to be sold as a blended applejack.

Calvados
A brandy made from a mash of cider apples. Only apple brandy produced in the defined areas of the provinces of Brittany, Normandy and Maine is entitled to the name 'Calvados'. In the heart of this large defined area is the Pays d'Auge, and apple brandy from there can bear the appellation *Calvados du Pays d'Auge*. The fermented mash of apples is double distilled in a pot still and then matured in oak casks for up to 25 years, picking up colour and flavour from the wood. Some apple brandy is made in continuous stills and when cider is distilled the spirit is known as *eau-de-vie de cidre*.

Poire Williams
Eau-de-vie de poire distilled from the pear known as Williams or Bartlett. It is sometimes marketed in a pear-shaped bottle with a ripe pear inside. The Swiss product may be wood aged and in Germany it is known as Birnenwasser.

Stone Fruit Brandies
Stone fruits fermented with their kernels and then double distilled. The bitter almond tang comes from the essential oils contained in the crushed kernels. The brandies are bottled immediately, or stored in glass, to preserve the fragrance. The best-known are:
   Barack Palinka Hungarian apricot brandy
   Coing quince brandy
   Kirsch cherry brandy
   Kirschwasser German or Swiss cherry brandy

Mirabelle brandy from the small gold Mirabelle plum
Prune plum brandy
Prunelle sloe brandy
Quetsch brandy from the black Switzen plum
Slivovitz plum brandy from the Balkan countries

Soft Fruit Brandies

A distilled mixture of soft fruit macerated in alcohol. Wild berries produce the most delicate eaux-de-vie, although it takes as many as 30 kilos of fruit to produce one bottle of brandy. The best-known are:

Brombeergeist German or Swiss blackberry brandy
Erdbeergeist German or Swiss strawberry brandy
Fraises strawberry brandy
Fraises de Bois wild strawberry brandy
Framboise raspberry brandy
Himbeergeist German or Swiss raspberry brandy
Hoax Alsace holly berry brandy
Mûre blackberry brandy
Myrtille bilberry brandy

LIQUEURS

All liqueurs consist of a base spirit blended with a flavouring agent and sweetener. Herbs are the traditional flavouring, and it is probable that liqueurs were developed from potions made from herbs steeped in alcohol to extract their medicinal properties.

In medieval Europe the resulting liquids were occasionally applied to wounds, but were more often taken internally. Some were sweetened to make them more palatable. People who could afford these liquors treasured them as protection against infection and plague, but many apothecaries fell foul of religious laws because of the claims they made for their potions.

Until the nineteenth century many households had their own blend, made from garden herbs and local spirit. Particular areas became famous for certain styles of liqueurs: the elixir of the monks at Fécamp in the fourteenth century was known as a preventive against malaria; the dark red liqueur made from Dijon blackcurrants was reputed to ward off physical diseases; and the bitter wormwood liquor of Marseilles dulled the senses of those in distress until 1915 when the government halted production.

The Spirit Base
To produce a fine liqueur the alcohol used must be as pure as possible. Constituents of alcohol such as aldehydes contribute to the aroma of wine but are undesirable in a liqueur base. The manner of distillation and the degree of rectification will determine the purity of the spirit. Whisky, rum, grape brandy, cognac, fruit spirit and rice spirit are all used although most liqueurs have a neutral or grain spirit base.

The Flavouring Agent
Some liqueurs are made with one flavour predominating whilst others have over 70 constituents. The most usual agents are:

herbs (herbal oils are extremely concentrated and used in minute amounts) such as:

basil – *preservative and tonic*	hyssop – *stimulant*
peppermint and melissa – *digestive*	rosemary – *clears the head*
sage – *tonic and lowers fever*	thistle – *encourages perspiration*
thyme – *antiseptic and stimulant*	wormwood – *depressant.*

flowers such as camomile, lavender, lily, orange blossom, rose, saffron

fruits such as citrus peel, edible fruits, raisins

barks such as angostura, cinchona, cinnamon, myrrh, sandalwood, sassafras

roots such as angelica, celery, gentian, ginger, henna, liquorice, orris root, turmeric

seeds such as aniseed, apricot stones, almonds, caraway, clove, cocoa, coffee, coriander, dill, juniper berries, musk, peppers, star anis, vanilla

Sweetener
Liqueurs are usually sweetened with a sugar syrup after the blending has been completed, but honey is used in some. The traditional classification of French liqueurs relates to the alcohol-sugar ratio. The higher the sugar content, the finer the liqueur as sugar gives the liqueur body and finesse.

PRODUCTION
Extraction
The flavouring agent must be extracted from the natural substance – the essential oil can then be used as an ingredient in the blending process. There are four methods used to extract the oil, depending on the solubility and chemical stability of the ingredient:

Pressure in which mechanical presses are used to extract the oil from citrus peel.

Maceration where the flavouring agents are soaked in cold spirit, then pulverized to gain maximum flavour. The mixture is filtered and the resulting liquid may be concentrated or used in distillation. This method is employed for natural products that do not react favourably to heat.

Infusion which is maceration in warm spirit maintained at a constant temperature for several days. More flavour can be extracted, much more rapidly, by infusion than any other method.

Percolation when the spirit is continuously bubbled through the flavouring agent. Alternatively, the spirit is boiled and the vapours pass up through the flavouring agent, condense and return to the boiling spirit.

Distillation
The natural products are steeped in the alcohol until it is well impregnated with flavour, then it is distilled – often under vacuum – to protect the delicate essences. As in all distillation, it is the middle fraction which is most useful, being a colourless dry distillate of high alcohol strength. This liquid is further purified by rectification (re-distillation) to remove impurities which would change the flavour.

Compounding

Once the ingredients have been assembled, it is the function of the compounder to blend them in strict sequence to produce a desired flavour. Most liqueurs are made to secret recipes, many of which are centuries old.

Maturing

As with other blended alcohols, liqueurs must be given time to allow the ingredients to marry together. The finest liqueurs are matured in oak casks, which aid in mellowing the liquid.

Fining

Vegetable matter is still suspended in the liquid and must be removed. The procedure is similar to fining wine.

Bottling

The liqueur is topped up with spirit to bring it to the correct alcoholic strength. Sometimes sugar syrup is also added to adjust sweetness and many liqueurs are coloured with harmless vegetable dyes. All liqueurs are given a final filtration to ensure starbright clarity before bottling.

GLOSSARY OF LIQUEURS

Absinthe A very dry bitter drink with high alcoholic content. Ingredients include aniseed, liquorice, fennel, hyssop, coriander and wormwood. Dr Ordinaire, the Frenchman who invented it, sold the recipe to the Pernod family in 1797 and the liquor was subsequently marketed as Pernod. The French government legislated against the use of the depressant wormwood (*Artemisia absinthium*) in 1915 so that the ingredient was dropped from the Pernod recipe. Star anis, a plant native to China, then became the base of Pernod 45. It was fashionable for women to drip the bitter liqueur on to a lump of sugar which was cupped in a small long-handled spoon with drain holes.

Advocaat A Dutch liqueur made from egg yolks and grape brandy. The alcoholic strength is not high and it is generally used in mixed drinks especially at Christmas time. Imitations made from cornflour and raw spirit are marketed in some countries.

Amaretto An Italian liqueur with an almond-apricot base. Amaretto was first made in Saronno near Lake Como in the sixteenth century.

Amarula A South African cream liqueur made with the fruit of the African Marula tree (*Sclerocarrya birrea*). Amarula, first marketed in September 1989, has the taste of caramel.

Amer Picon An orange bitter cordial created by a Frenchman named Gaetan Picon in 1837. Its formulation consists of cinchona bark, oranges, and gentian.

Amourette A French liqueur, violet in colour.

Anesone A potent anise-liquorice liqueur produced in Italy and USA.

Angelica A sweet yellow Basque drink similar to Chartreuse.

Anis del Mono An aniseed liqueur from Barcelona, available as sweet and dry.

Anisetta Stillata An Italian aniseed liqueur from Pescara.

Anisette There are a number of sweetened aniseed liqueurs. Marie Brizard produced her anisette in Bordeaux around the middle of the eighteenth century.

Aperol A sweet, dark orange Italian aperitif made from selected spirits, rhubarb, chinchona, genziana and other herbs.

Apple Gin A colourless liqueur compounded at Leith, Scotland.

Apricot Liqueurs These are made by macerating apricots in brandy that is then sweetened. A true apricot brandy is an eau-de-vie but apricot liqueurs can be called Apricot Brandy as long as they have the required amount of fruit.

Archers A clear, peach-flavoured, low-strength liqueur.

Atholl Brose A Scottish drink based on Highland malt whisky, uncooked oatmeal, honey and cream.

Aurum A pale gold Italian liqueur, aromatic with a delicate orange flavour.

Baerenfang A German liqueur which is predominantly honey flavoured with lime and mullein flowers.

Bahia A Brazilian blend of coffee and grain spirit.

Baska A French coffee liqueur from Angers.

Bénédictine Possibly the oldest liqueur in the world. It is distilled at Fécamp in Normandy, and its origin has been traced to the Bénédictine monks of Fécamp as far back as 1510. The liqueur is golden, aromatized and sweet. The company markets an official 'B & B' which is brandy and Bénédictine.

Bescen A Dutch blackcurrant liqueur.

Blackberry Liqueur A liqueur made from blackberries macerated in sweetened brandy, which is often topped up with eaux-de-vie to add finesse.

Bocksbeeren The Eastern European name for blackcurrant liqueur.

Brontë An English liqueur from Yorkshire. French grape brandy is blended with honey and herbs, then bottled in a squat pottery jug.

Cacao Mit Nuss A colourless German liqueur made from chocolate and hazelnuts.

Capricornia An Australian liqueur based on tropical fruit. It takes its name from the Tropic of Capricorn.

Cayo Verde A lightweight American liqueur based on key limes.

Cédratine A sweet Corsican liqueur with good digestive properties.

Cerasella A red Italian liqueur with fine cherry flavour.

Chambord Made from black raspberries infused with cognac, red raspberries, currants and blackberry extracts, oranges, lemons and spices, this was the favourite of King Louis XIV.

Chartreuse A liqueur which contains over 130 herbs and spices, manufactured at the Grande Chartreuse monastery near Grenoble in France by Carthusian monks from 1607 until 1901, when they were expelled from France. The monks set up a distillery in Tarragona, Spain and the liqueur was produced there until production resumed in France in 1931. After 1901 the French government sold the trademark; however, in 1932 the monks regained the use of the name. The Green Chartreuse is 96° proof whilst the sweeter Yellow Chartreuse is 75° proof.

Cheri-Suisse A Swiss cherry chocolate liqueur.

Cherry Blossom Liqueur A delicate pink liqueur with a strong fragrance of Japanese cherry blossoms.

Cherry Brandy Liqueurs Most of these are labelled as cherry brandies but are produced by maceration of the fruit in spirit, sometimes with the addition of herbs. Some examples are Cherry Marnier, Peter Heering, de Kuyper, Marie Brizard and Lejay Lagoute, Guignolet and Grants Morella.

Cherry Nalivka A low-strength cherry liqueur of Baltic origin.

Cherry Whisky Cherry-flavoured whisky presents some blending problems because of the acid levels of both ingredients. The most well-known is Chesky, a French liqueur.

C.L.O.C. A Danish caraway liqueur, clear and weaker than Dutch Kümmel.

Citronen–Eis A yellow German liqueur made from the juice and essential oil of lemon. The word '*Eis*' indicates that it is meant to be drunk over ice.

Coconut Liqueurs White rum, flavoured with essences from macerated coconuts. These are widely available under such brand names as Malibu and Cocoribe.

Cointreau One of the best-known French triple sec curaçaos, sold in a distinctive square bottle under the name of Cointreau liqueur; it is colourless and has an orange flavour. The alcoholic strength of the liqueur is the same throughout the world; the liqueur itself is manufactured at Angers in the district of Anjou.

Cordial Campari A dessert liqueur of a light yellow colour, obtained from distillation of raspberries.

Cordial Médoc A dark red French liqueur. Something in the nature of a distilled claret flavoured with herbs.

Cordial Reby A liqueur with a cognac base, brown in colour.

Cream Liqueurs Cream, spirit and flavourings can now be combined successfully to produce thick, rich-textured liqueurs. The biggest-selling liqueur in the world is Baileys Irish Cream; the Scottish brand is made in the Shetlands from Blackwoods Shetland Vodka, natural vanilla, and pure Scottish cream from the local Shetland herd. Dooley's uses toffee and vodka.

Crème d'Amandes A sweet almond liqueur.

Crème de Banane A pungent liqueur made from a maceration of bananas in spirit. It was a particular pre-war favourite.

Crème de Cacao A very sweet liqueur with a strong cocoa vanilla flavour. The name Chouao, which usually figures on crème de cacao labels, is that of a district in Venezuela reputed to produce the best cocoa beans in the world.

Crème de Cassis In Dijon, crème de cassis has been produced by maceration for centuries. The high vitamin C content of the blackcurrants means it is still regarded as a health-giving digestive.

Crème de Ciel A Dutch liqueur, after the style of curaçao, light blue in colour.

Crème de Fraises A sweet French liqueur flavoured with strawberries. Strawberry red in colour.

Crème de Fraises des Bois A French liqueur made from wild strawberries.

Crème de Framboise A sweet French liqueur flavoured with raspberries, a speciality of the Dordogne Valley, France.

Crème de Mandarine The general term used for tangerine liqueurs.

Crème de Menthe A popular liqueur with digestive properties. It is made of grain spirit flavoured with peppermint and sweetened. When it leaves the still it is absolutely colourless, and some crème de menthe is sold in pure white form. As a rule, however, it is coloured green.

Crème de Mokka A French liqueur, light brown in colour with a coffee flavour.

Crème de Noisettes A sweet hazelnut liqueur.

Crème de Noix This sweet walnut-based liqueur is a local speciality in Périgord, France.

Crème de Noyeau A pink or white French liqueur made from the extracted oils of peach and apricot kernels. It has an almond flavour.

Crème de Pecco A Dutch liqueur with a tea flavour. Semi-sweet, colourless.

Crème de Prunelles A sweet liqueur plum-green in colour.

Crème de Roses A pink liqueur, flavoured with rose petals, vanilla and citrus oils.

Crème de Vanille A smooth, rich French liqueur made from vanilla beans.

Crème Yvette The best known of the crème de violettes. It is an old American liqueur, highly alcoholic, with the flavour, colour and perfume of Parma violets.

Cuarenta-y-Tres A sweet yellow liqueur from Cartagena, Spain

Curaçao A sweet digestive liqueur made from grape spirit, sugar and orange peel. The Dutch first used the bitter oranges from the island of Curaçao near Venezuela. The name is now applied to all orange liqueurs.

Drambuie The oldest of the whisky liqueurs. Scottish legend says originally the Mackinnon family had the recipe from Bonnie Prince Charlie, although it was not made commercially until 1906. Its base is Scotch whisky and heather honey. The name Drambuie is from the Gaelic *An Dram buidheach* meaning 'the drink that satisfies'.

Elixir d'Anvers A green-yellow liqueur with a bitter-sweet flavour. Made in Antwerp, it is extremely popular with the Belgian people.

Elixir di China A sweet Italian anise liqueur.

Enzian Calisay A sweet, pale gold liqueur based on Spanish herbs.

Escharchado A Portuguese aniseed liqueur containing sugar crystals.

Falernum An almond-flavoured liqueur from Barbados.

Flifar A Cypriot curaçao usually bottled in stone jugs.

Fior d'Alpi An Italian liqueur flavoured with alpine flowers and herbs. It is highly sweetened so that sugar crystals will collect on the branch inside the tall fluted bottle. Isolabella, Edelweiss and Mille Fiori are of this style.

Forbidden Fruit A highly alcoholic American liqueur. Extract of grapefruit and orange compounded with honey to give a bitter-sweet taste.

Frigola A thyme-flavoured liqueur from the Balearic Isles.

Galliano A golden yellow liqueur made from over 25 herbs and spices, including vanilla, star anise and mint. It is produced in Milan, Italy, and packaged in a tall, fluted bottle that hasn't changed since 1896.

Gallweys An Irish liqueur based on whisky, honey, herbs and coffee.

Ginepy A white or green Italian liqueur with a predominantly anise flavour.

Glayva This is a Scottish liqueur made with whisky, herb and spices.

Glen Mist A dry Scottish liqueur with a whisky base. The spirit is compounded with herbs, spices and honey then matured in whisky casks.

Godet An opaque white chocolate liqueur made by blending white chocolate with aged brandy.

Godiva A chocolate liqueur made by the Belgium chocolate maker, Godiva. The original liqueur is made using dark chocolate blended with a spirit base.

Goldschlager A clear schnapps with gold leaf flakes. It has spicy, cinnamon aromas and is sweet on the palate.

Goldwasser Danzig Goldwasser is a white aniseed and caraway liqueur with gold flakes in the liquid. Produced in Danzig from 1598 by the Der Lachs.

Gorny Doubnyak A bitter Russian liqueur compounded from ginger, galingale, angelica, clove, acorns and oak shavings.

Grand Cumberland A golden sweet Australian liqueur with a passionfruit flavour and a hint of citrus on the finish.

Grande Liqueur A French liqueur made in two colours, green and yellow, with a Chartreuse-type flavour.

Grand Marnier A French curaçao invented in 1880 with a cognac base; of the two versions, Cordon Jaune is of a lower alcoholic content than Cordon Rouge.

Greensleeves A green English liqueur made from peppermint and brandy.

Guignolet A French cherry liqueur.

Gyokuro Rikyu A low-alcohol Japanese liqueur based on green tea and grape brandy.

Half-Om-Half A Dutch liqueur which is half curaçao and half orange bitters.
Irish Mist An Irish liqueur based on aged whiskies, herbal extracts and Irish heather honey. Its largest market is the USA.

Irish Velvet An Irish liqueur of Irish whiskey, strong black coffee and sugar.

Izzara A Basque angelica and honey liqueur similar to Chartreuse with an armagnac base. The green version has a higher alcohol content than the yellow.

Jerzynowka A Polish liqueur made from maceration of blackberries.

Kahlua A Mexican coffee liqueur.

Kaiserbirnlikor An Austrian lemon liqueur.

Karpi A wild cranberry liqueur from Finland.

Karthauser A German version of Chartreuse.

Kirsberry A Danish cherry liqueur.

Kirschwasser (Kirsch) This clear brandy, made from double distillation of the fermented juice of a small black cherry, is colourless and not sweet.

Kitron A Greek liqueur from the leaves of lemon trees distilled with grape brandy and sweetened.

Krambambuli A German liqueur flavoured with angelica and violet extract.

Krupnick A Polish honey liqueur.

Kümmel One of the most popular of all liqueurs with definite digestive properties. Made in Holland since 1575, Kummel has in its base some highly distilled or almost neutral spirit, sometimes distilled from grain, sometimes from potatoes. It is flavoured with caraway seeds which give it digestive qualities. It is always water-white. Normally served over ice.

Lakka A Finnish liqueur with a bitter-sweet tang from cloudberries grown only in the Arctic. Also known as Suomuurain.

Lapponia A Finnish liqueur made from Arctic liggonberries.

La Tintaine A French anise liqueur.
Licor 43 A light gold herbal liqueur from Murcia, Spain.

Liqueur d'Angélique A French liqueur produced from angelica and cognac.

Liqueur d'Or A sweet French liqueur with flakes of gold.

Lochan Ora A honeyed Scotch whisky liqueur.

Macvin A liqueur from the Jura region of France where newly fermented red wine is mixed with marc, cinnamon and coriander.

Mandarine Napoléon A Belgian liqueur distilled from Andalusian tangerine peel macerated in eaux-de-vie then compounded with cognac.

Mandarinetto A tangerine liqueur produced in Italy.

Maraschino A white Italian liqueur produced from distillation of sour Marasca cherries including the crushed kernels. Sometimes a small amount of Kirsch is added to give extra finesse.

Marnique An Australian quince liqueur similar to Grand Marnier.

Masticha A Greek liqueur made on the island of Chios from aniseed and gum mastic on a brandy base.

Mazarin A light-brown French liqueur with a flavour similar to Bénédictine.

Melette Anisette produced in Ascoli Pinceno, Italy.

Mentuccia An Italian liqueur with a mint base which makes it a good digestive; there are maybe 100 herbs in the liqueur. Also known as Centerbe or Silvestro.

Mersin A Turkish triple-sec curaçao.

Mesimarja An aromatic Finnish liqueur made from Arctic brambles.

Mokka mit Sahne A German liqueur produced from coffee and cream.

Monte Aguila A bitter Jamaican liqueur based on pimento.

Mozart An Austrian chocolate liqueur produced since 1981 and named after Wolgang Amadeus Mozart, it is a blend of fruit distillates with finest chocolate.
Mus A Turkish banana liqueur.

Nassau Orange A pale gold Dutch liqueur with the flavour of bitter oranges. Also known as Pimpeltjens Liqueur, it was served in 1652 at a banquet to mark the landing of the Dutch at what is now Cape Town, South Africa.

Nocino An Italian liqueur made by infusing nut husks in spirit. It imparts a delicate aroma to ice-cream.

Ocha A Japanese tea liqueur.

Old Krupnik A Polish liqueur, made of natural wild bee's honey and exotic spices, it has a sweet taste and spicy bouquet, with a strong, warming effect.

Oxygenée An aniseed-flavoured absinthe substitute.

Pasha A Turkish coffee liqueur.

Paradisi A Dutch grapefruit liqueur.

Parfait Amour A sweet pink or violet liqueur with a citrus base; it contains spices and flower petal extract.

Passoa A Brazilian liqueur with the flavour of passionfruit underlying others.

Pastis A liquorice-based liqueur from Marseilles. The taste is not as pronounced as anis and it turns white when added to water. Some of its characteristics resemble those of absinthe but it contains no wormwood.

Pimento Dram A dark red liqueur made by steeping green and ripe pimento berries in rum.

Pineau des Charentes A liqueur from the Charentes region of France produced from fresh grape juice and one-year-old cognac, blended then matured in oak.

Pomeranzen A German curaçao-type liqueur in green and gold made on a base of unripe Pomeranzen oranges.

Ponche A brown Spanish liqueur based on sherry.

Rabinowka A pink liqueur, dry or sweet, flavoured with rowanberry.

Raki An aniseed Turkish liqueur drunk with ice and water.

Raspail A yellow French liqueur compounded with herbs such as angelica, calamus and myrrh. It is known for its digestive properties.

Ratafia Any sweetened liqueur on a spirit of wine base. The flavouring agents are usually almonds or the kernels of peaches or cherries.

Reishu This is a Japanese melon liqueur.

Riemerschmid A German fig liqueur.

Rock and Rye An American liqueur made from fruit flavouring, rock sugar candy and rye whiskey. The sugar crystallizes inside the bottle.

Royal Cherry Chocolate A rich English liqueur with a cherry and chocolate base.

Royal Ginger Chocolate An English liqueur compounded from root ginger and cocoa beans.

Royal Mint Chocolate A recipe of English origin which is produced in France. It is based on milk chocolate and peppermint and has digestive properties.

Royal Orange Chocolate An English liqueur based on oil of orange, cocoa beans and pure milk.

Sabra An orange chocolate-flavoured liqueur from Israel.

Sacco A peppermint liqueur produced in Turin.

St Hallvard A bright yellow Norwegian liqueur on a potato spirit base.

Sambuca A highly alcoholic Italian liqueur made from an infusion of witch elderbush and liquorice. It is traditionally served ignited with three coffee beans floating in the glass. Opal Nero is one of the well-known brands.

San Michele A tangerine-based Danish liqueur.

Sapan d'Or A greenish liqueur not unlike Bénédictine.

Silverwasser (Danzig) A colourless sweet liqueur with flakes of silver, flavoured with aniseed and orange.

Previous page
Pilsner Urquell is the original light beer from the small town of Pilsner in Czechoslovakia; its style is often copied, but the pretenders never capture quite the same rewarding taste.

Opposite
Monkey Shoulder triple malt whisky is used in this intriguing cocktail appropriately named Howling Monkey, for it also features a dash of absinthe, mint, amaretto and Peychaud bitters.

Sloe Gin A deep-red liqueur made by steeping sloe berries (wild plum) in gin, then maturing the liquor in wood. The traditional English name for it was Stirrup Cup.

Solbaerrom A fruity Danish liqueur.

Southern Comfort An American liqueur, 87.7° proof with an orange-peach flavour. There is some dispute as to whether it is a liqueur or a spirit.

Strega A yellow Italian liqueur compounded from over 70 herbs and barks.

Tangao A tangerine brandy liqueur.

Tangerinette A French liqueur, red in colour with the flavour of tangerines.

Tapio A dry water-white Finnish liqueur based on juniper berries.

Thitarine A sweet North African liqueur compounded from figs, herbs and liquorice.

Tia Maria A Jamaican liqueur based on rum flavoured with Blue Mountain coffee extract and spices.

Trappistine A pale yellow-green liqueur made with herbs and armagnac from the Abbayé de la Grâce de Dieu, Doubs, France.

Triple Sec A description of sweet white curaçao used for a number of brands of curaçao.

Van der Hum An aromatic liqueur made in South Africa, its chief flavour comes from the *naartjie* or tangerine.

Vandermint A Dutch chocolate and mint liqueur.

Verveine du Vélay A bitter French liqueur based on the herb vervain and available in green or yellow.

Vieille Cure A brown French liqueur of high strength with an aromatic flavour from its 50 herbs macerated in cognac and armagnac.

Wisniowka A sweet Polish liqueur made from cherries and vodka.

MADEIRA

This fine fortified wine comes from the island of Madeira in the Atlantic Ocean. In the eighteenth century, ships trading between Britain and her colonies stopped at Madeira for provisions and some of the local wine was included, often as ballast. The wine was slowly heated during the sea voyage, developing a mellow burned flavour that became popular. The wine is very long lived and, although essentially sweet, the finish of good madeira is very dry and never cloying.

VITICULTURE AND VINIFICATION

The vines are trained on overhead pergolas to protect the grapes from the scorching sun. After pressing, the juice is transported as quickly as possible to Funchal, the capital of the island and centre of manufacture. It is here that the juice is fermented. The fermented juice, known as *vinho claro*, is then fortified with grape brandy. After resting, the cask of wine, known as a *pipe*, is put into the *estufa*, a large central-heated store. The pipes of madeira are very gradually heated to a maximum of 50°C, held at this temperature for up to three months, then very slowly cooled to normal temperature. This process, called *estufagem*, develops the same caramel-like flavour of wine that the long sea voyages used to produce. The madeira is now indifferent to heat and cold and is able to stand long exposure to air, for example in an opened bottle.

STYLES OF MADEIRA

There are four types, named after the grapes from which they are produced:

Sercial A dry wine with a slight almond flavour, needs time to mature. The dry finish makes it an excellent aperitif served chilled.

Verdelho A golden wine with a smoky flavour, soft and nutty, it benefits from a few months bottle age. This is an elegant madeira, the classic to serve with soup.

Bual Elegant and smoky, spicy, with dried fruit flavours.

Malmsey A dark, rich wine with soft, full flavour. The sharp, tangy finish balances the sweetness and many consider it one of the world's finest wines.

Blended madeira is also available. Less expensive blends seek to mimic the flavour of the style of one of the noble madeiras. Rainwater Madeira, though indicating no single grape variety on the label, is made to taste like a softer type of Verdelho.

PORT

Port is the name given to the fortified wine produced around the Douro River valley from a point near Barca d'Alva on the border of Spain to within 80km of Oporto. The river is at the base of a narrow valley, between 457m and 609m deep, the sides of which are layered rock. The vineyards have been hacked into the mountain side and walled terraces have been built like contour lines to prevent the earth from disappearing down into the river bed. The vineyards, some 83,000, are all classified through the *Cadastro* (register) of the Region. This is held by the *Casa do Douro* (Association of the Wine Growers) in Régua.

Until the eighteenth century the upper Douro valley produced coarse feeble wine. Elderberry juice was frequently used to improve the colour and various methods of stabilization were tried, one of which was the addition of grape brandy to a cask during fermentation. The winemakers began adapting their red table wine to the English palate by adding brandy to create a sweeter drink, and by the second half of the eighteenth century vintage port was shipped to Britain. English merchants established offices in Oporto and purchased vineyards so that many of the port shippers now have British names, such as Taylor's, Graham's, Churchill and Sandeman. It is from the port of Oporto and Oporto alone that this wine is shipped to the rest of the world, but Oporto gives only its name to the wine for it is in the town of Vila Nova de Gaia, across the river from Oporto, that it is aged for years. Most port was shipped in bulk and even vintage port was bottled in Britain until recently.

VITICULTURE

In the deep river gorges of the upper Douro and its tributaries the winter air currents are icy and thick fog often develops. When summer comes the storms build up and their effects are felt over the entire region. The sun heats the stones and the valleys become ovens of up to 50°C without a breath of air. Vines are planted from water level to a height of 300m, above which the grape would not ripen satisfactorily. When the vine shoots turn green and the grape bunches begin to lengthen, it is a perilous time for the vinegrower who must watch for the morning frost and beware of the storms. Then comes the summer with its dryness and burning winds. If the grapes can survive all this, then the harvest takes place in September. At the ideal moment for each estate, known as a *quinta*, the women harvest the ripe grape bunches with scissors and baskets. The baskets are emptied into hods at the end of each row of vines and collected by *barracheiros*, stalwarts who can carry a 75 kilo load on their shoulders. The barracheiros are irreplaceable, for no other method of transporting the grapes down the steep slopes has been found.

VINIFICATION

The practice of treading the grapes has nearly become obsolete because of the lack of seasonal labour and the grapes now go into a gigantic centrifugal crusher. The juice is pumped into a concrete or stainless steel vat known as a *cuba* where fermentation takes place. The *auto-vinificator* is being used increasingly to aid fermentation. The cuba is enclosed and fitted with a system of valves which use the pressure built up by the carbon dioxide given off during fermentation to spray the must over the cap of skins, so extracting maximum colour in the minimum time. The new wine is then placed into *tonneaus* with one-year-old grape brandy. The timing of the addition of the brandy is critical, as it determines the sweetness of the wine for the rest of its life. The wine rests in the cellars of the quintas until the spring when it is transported by road tanker to the port lodges in Vila Nova de Gaia for blending and maturation. Traditionally a flat-bottomed boat known as a *barcos rabelos* was used for transportation to the port, but there are now dams across the river.

Depending upon its early characteristic the new wine will be put into one of the two great port families: the blends or the rarer and more highly prized vintages. In the production of blends the wine is left in cask for two years, after which it is tasted and appraised. Other wines are then added, either to strengthen the port or enhance its bouquet and colour. This blending process is based on a successful formula which can be followed and maintained so that a trade product can be consistently marketed. The blends are put into enormous wooden casks in order to prevent oxidization and too rapid an evaporation. As it takes on greater age the wine is enlivened and enriched with the careful addition of younger wine. It reaches fullness after about 30 years but one can drink ports of 60 years or more which are still perfect.

STYLES OF PORT

Vintage Port In a very good year, a shipper will produce a vintage port. This is still a blend, but only of wines of the same year. To preserve the fruit, the wine must be bottled before all impurities have had time to settle out in cask, so a sediment will form in a bottle of vintage port. A white splash on the glass indicates the topside of the bottle during its early maturation in the lodge and so the crust will have formed on the opposite side. This crust will form again after the wine has been moved if it is left to rest for a few weeks. The port must be decanted off the crust before being served.

The Institute of Port (*Instituto do Vinho do Porto*) requires vintage port be bottled in Portugal and carry the white seal over the neck that states *Garantia do Vinho do Porto* – the wine was grown, aged and bottled in Portugal. A *quinta* may declare a particular year due to the quality found in their best wine as a 'vintage'. This may be done in a period of 18 months after harvesting the crop. It is then bottled six months later and a minimum maturity period of 15 years is then allowed. All vintage ports need to be decanted prior to being drunk.

A vintage year is declared about every three to five years. Only 14 vintages were declared from 1901 to 1999. Generally declared vintages have been 1945, 1947, 1948, 1950, 1955, 1960, 1963, 1966; five shippers declared 1967, 1970, 1975, 1977; 1980, 1982, 1983 and 1985; some shippers 1987; and some shippers declared 1991, 1994, 1995 1997, 2000, 2003.

Single Quinta As the name implies this port is from a single vineyard and can often be a vintage port.

LBV This is a 'Late Bottled Vintage' single year port that has been matured in wood for not less than four years before being bottled. The label must indicate the year of bottling and its vintage.

Vintage Character This title is misleading in that the port is similar to that of a fine Ruby Port and not that of a Vintage.

Crusted This port is a blending of wines from different years. Kept in casks for four years, and then three years in the bottle, prior to being sold.

Fine Old Tawny This is pale amber in colour and less full-bodied. It is a blended wine from different years and its label will indicate its age as an average year of its content. It is bottled and racked for 10 to 20 years or more, and assumes a smooth silky texture and a mellow nutty flavour.

Vintage-dated Tawny These attractively priced ports are as a Fine Old Tawny but also considered a Vintage. They can spend 20 or 50 years in a cask.

Tawny Less sweet in flavour and composed of blending from different aged wines and could even be a mixture of red and white. Do not improve with ageing.

Fine Old Ruby Blended from different years and kept in the cask for about four years before being ready to drink. They have a fruity-spicy flavour and are classified as inferior to Tawny.

Ruby A fruity style and deep red in colour, they are blended from wines of different years and take no more than one to three years to mature.

White This is either dry or sweet in flavour. Normally chilled before serving and acts as an attractive aperitif in the same manner as a Spanish sherry.

SHERRY

The word 'sherry' is the anglicized version of Jerez, the name of the town at the centre of the trade. By the sixteenth century there was a thriving British community in Jerez because of the number of merchants who operated their sherry shipping businesses from there and many of the firms still have British names. In 1967 a British court decreed that only wine from the Jerez District of Spain was entitled to be called sherry and all other wines of a similar style must clearly state their country of origin with the word sherry.

VITICULTURE AND UNIFICATION

Soil in the Jerez area is graded on the proportion of chalk contained in it. *Albariza* soil is about 50 percent chalk and so is very absorbent. The dried hard surface reflects the heat and holds in the moisture, thus producing superior sherry grapes; *barros* soil is clay with 10 percent chalk and the wines are coarser and heavier; *arenas* soil is sandy with ten per cent chalk, resulting in much lower quality grapes. The Palomino de Jerez grape is widely planted in the *albariza* soil and the Pedro Ximinez (PX) and Moscatel grapes used in making sweet dessert sherries are grown elsewhere.

The traditional method of producing sherry has been modified by the introduction of modern machinery. Once harvested, grapes used to be placed on *esparto* mats to dry in the sun leaving a concentration of sugar. Now they are placed on sheets covered with tents of polythene sheeting which draw the moisture from the grapes. The harvest goes to efficient central wineries capable of handling immense volumes of fruit. The must is pumped into traditional wood butts open to the air or stainless steel fermenting tanks. Palomino must is fermented right out, but PX and Moscatel musts have wine spirit added to stop fermentation and retain the sugar content.

It is at this stage that a scum called *flor* (flower) develops on top of the wine. In most wine other than sherry, this would be considered a disaster and the wine would soon turn to vinegar. It is the result of a natural yeast peculiar to Jerez and man has no say in whether the flor will develop or not. If it does, then the wine will be a fino; if it does not, the wine will become an oloroso, and if only a slight flor develops it will be an amontillado. A very close watch is kept on the wine and the olorosos receive a larger amount of fortification which prevents any late flor from developing. Eventually the flor drops through the wine to the bottom of the cask and after racking, fining and maturing the new sherry is put into the solera system.

In the lodges sherries are blended through the solera system to maintain the desired quality and style of each shipper's product. The system can best be understood by imagining an inverted pyramid of wine barrels known as butts.

The word 'solera' refers to the butts nearest the ground, which contain fine old wine. On top of these is a row of butts of slightly younger wine and the butts continue in tiers with each tier, known as a *criadera*, containing progressively younger wine; the new wine goes into the last criadera. Each criadera is numbered and the solera butts may be backed up by six to twelve criaderas. When old wine is withdrawn from a solera butt, it is replaced with younger wine from the criadera above. The younger wine then takes on the quality of the old wine, and after a few months the wine in the solera butt is indistinguishable from what it was before. This systematic replacement from the criadera above is known as the solera system. It is impossible to produce a vintage sherry by this method, but a wine may bear the date the solera began. A brand of sherry can be a mixture of several soleras. After the blending, coloured wine may be added before fining and refrigeration. The sherry is then bottled or shipped in bulk.

While olorosos are drunk at room temperature, the lighter amontillados and finos are best served chilled.

STYLES OF SHERRY

Fino A very pale light dry wine with a delicate aroma and clear refreshing taste.

Amontillado An aged fino with an amber colour and dry nutty flavour.

Manzanilla A fino that has been aged at Sanlucar de Barrameda. It is pale, dry and very crisp with a faintly bitter aftertaste.

Oloroso A dark gold wine with plenty of body and a distinctly nutty flavour. Pure olorosos are dry but most are sweetened for export markets.

Cream, Brown and Amoroso Oloroso sherries with a high proportion of sweet wine added for export markets.

Palo Cortado
A rare oloroso, not produced every year, with the body and colour of an oloroso but the nose and dryness of an amontillado.

Montilla
The region of Montilla has the same albariza soil and produces a style of wine very similar to sherry. Fermentation takes place in traditional large earthenware jars or modern cement-lined vats. Wines have a naturally high alcohol content.

British 'Sherry'
Much of the cheaper wine sold in Britain is made from dehydrated grape juice from Greece or Cyprus. Water and yeasts are added to the concentrate, which then ferments until it is ready to be fortified and sweetened.

VERMOUTH

Vermouth is an aromatized wine. Its name is derived from the German *wermut* (wormwood). This herb was added to wine as early as AD 78 for medicinal purposes, but there were further advantages in that it could mask the flavour of sour wine and act as a preservative. The best vermouths were produced on both the French and Italian sides of the Alps, for it was in the foothills of the mountains that many of the herbs and flowers that are used for flavourings were originally found. The French traditionally produced the lighter, drier vermouths and the Italians the sweeter, heavier ones. Vermouths of all types are now produced in both areas, but some people still use the terms 'French' for a dry vermouth and 'Italian' for a sweet one. Dry vermouths should be drunk within two weeks, the sweet versions within a month of the bottle being opened.

PRODUCTION

Vermouth production is a complicated process and each producer jealously guards his exact recipe; the production sequence, however, is generally standard. The wine base is usually white wine, never of a fine or distinctive quality, for so many transformations will occur that this would be an unnecessary expense. The base is sweetened by an addition of *mistelle* – unfermented grape juice and brandy – followed by the flavoured alcohol. The flavour is extracted from the aromatic ingredients by maceration, infusion or distillation or even a combination of these methods, depending on the maker's requirements.

The ingredients can include hyssop, quinine, coriander, juniper, cloves, camomile, orange peel, calamus roots, gentian roots, oregano, cinnamon, sandalwood, sage, orris, mace and even violet and rose petals.

After thorough blending, alcohol and sugar are added to achieve the correct strength and sweetness. Caramel is added for red vermouth. Both types are then aged for up to six months to allow the flavours to marry, and refrigerated to precipitate any tartrate crystals. The vermouth is then filtered to ensure it is crystal clear and pasteurized to stabilize the flavours.

French Vermouth It takes almost four years to make a French vermouth and the centre of the industry is Marseilles. Here the base wine is stored in thick oak casks and spends some time outside to allow exposure to the sea air. Consequently, these vermouths – sweet or dry – have a distinctly spicy aroma.

Chambéry A fine example of dry vermouth is made in the foothills of the Alps at Savoie. It was granted Appellation d'Origine Contrôlée status in 1932. Herbs found only in the Chambéry region are used as flavouring and pure sugar, rather than mistelle, is used as the sweetening agent.

Italian Vermouth Turin is the centre of the Italian vermouth industry, although most of the wine comes from southern Italy. It takes about two years to produce a vermouth and all styles have much broader flavour than the French counterparts.

Other Vermouths Virtually every country that produces wine also makes vermouth, most of which is consumed locally. The South American countries have a big market for vermouth, especially Argentina, and it is taken almost entirely as an aperitif – over ice, or with soda and a dash of bitters.

STYLES OF VERMOUTH
Red Caramel and sugar are added to make a sweet red vermouth.

Bianco A vermouth of medium sweetness is usually a golden colour.

Dry The colour varies from water-white to light gold.

Rosé Vermouth made with a base of rosé wine flavoured with herbs and spices has a bitter-sweet flavour.

Fruit-Flavoured This style is becoming more popular and some very fine examples include orange and strawberry flavours.

OTHER AROMATIZED WINES
There are a number of well-known proprietary brands that are aromatized wines produced in a manner similar to vermouth. Many of them contain quinine and gentian to heighten the bitter flavour. These are especially popular in France, where they are served as aperitifs, but their fairly low alcoholic content makes them suitable for drinking at any time. The most widely available are Ambassadeur, Amer Picon, Dubonnet, Lillet, Primavera, St Raphael and Suze.

BITTERS
Essences extracted from plants, bark, roots and stems are compounded with alcohol to form a tincture known as bitters. Some bitters are supposed to have a medicinal character, such as acting as a stomach tonic or as a malaria preventative. In the USA the law distinguishes between ordinary commercial bitters and medicinal bitters, which may be sold by grocers, drug and department stores.

Bitters have been rediscovered as ingredients in cocktail recipes. In Finland they are even served frozen. When used with other spirits and mixers, a bitter can provide a balance of flavours. Traditionally, bitters are used as 'pick-me-ups' or taken with soda and include brands such as Fernet Branca, Ferro China and Campari from Italy, Toni-Kola from France, and Underberg from Germany. Bitters used as flavourings are Angostura from Trinidad, Peychaud from New Orleans; peach and orange are the most popular fruit-flavoured bitters.

CIGARS

A well-stocked bar will always carry a good selection of cigars of all types, because the smaller panatella, cheroot and whiff styles are always popular with pre-prandial cocktail drinkers.

The smaller cigars are usually machine-made and the inner filler may be from a different part of the world than the outer wrapper. The leaf from which a cigar is made may be grown in places as far apart as Java, Borneo, Sumatra in the East Indies, the USA, India, Japan, Central and South Africa, and many others. There is a very fine leaf from the West Indies, as well as from Jamaica and Cuba.

THE HAVANA CIGAR

Although fine cigar leaf is grown, and cigars are made, in many parts of the world, indisputably the best cigars in the world come from Cuba and are called after its capital city, Havana. It is the climate, geology and skill of the people of Cuba that together produce the leaves of sun-cured tobacco from the red earth of this Caribbean island.

Tobacco is grown all over Cuba, the finest from the areas of Vuelta Abajo, Partidos, Remedios and Oriente. All four produce a fine quality cigar leaf, but the best of all comes from the Vuelta Abajo, which provides the all-important wrapper leaf. The Vuelta Abajo is a natural hot-house just as the whole island of Cuba is a natural humidor.

In this unique climate and soil the Cuban tobacco plants grow to about 182cm in height with leaves of up to 45cm in length. The leaves are cut between February and March, strung over bamboo poles and hung out to dry in huge barns. They are then stacked in great heaps to dry in the sun. It is now that the mysterious fermentation begins to take place within the leaves as they turn to a rich golden brown. The cured leaves are tied in bundles of five, known as hands, put into bales and stored in warehouses to mature for 18 months to two years when they are judged to be ready for the cigar maker.

A cigar is made of three constituent parts – the *filler*, the *binder* and the *wrapper*. The filler, as the name implies, forms the interior of the cigar and to a large extent determines its flavour. To make a cigar, two to four leaves of filler tobacco are laid end to end and rolled into the binder, a leaf with good tensile strength chosen from the lower half of the plant. Great skill is required to ensure that the filler is evenly distributed so that the cigar will draw properly.

The next step is the wrapper. A whole leaf of the finest quality is chosen for this, the outside of the cigar. It must be smooth, not too prominently veined and of a good colour. Above all, it must give a noble flavour and aroma because the wrapper is a vital ingredient in the taste of a cigar. Once this important leaf has been selected, the stalk is stripped from it by hand; the top point is nipped out between thumb and fingernail and the stalk wound around the fingers to remove it completely. The half-shaped leaves are sliced into two wrappers each with hook-shaped tops facing opposite directions. This is why if you examine a number of individual cigars carefully you will find that some of them are wrapped left-handed, others right-handed. All the cigars in a quality box of cigars should be wrapped in the same direction.

Finally, the cylinder of tobacco in its binder leaf is laid at an angle across the cut strip of wrapper. The wrapper is then wrapped carefully around the binder, overlapping at each turn until at the end of the hook it is stuck down with a pinhead of vegetable gum, forming the rounded closed head of the cigar which is then guillotined at the other end to the correct length.

The well-known names with which the brands are prefixed, such as Petit Corona, Corona and Corona Grande, describe the size and not the make. Corona, for example, simply means a cigar that is about 14cm in length, straight-sided with a rounded end.

The leaf used for wrappers varies considerably in natural colouring and when cigars are packed they are sorted into colour groups and these are marked on the boxes as follows:

Claro or CCC blonde light golden brown

Colorado–Claro or CC darker tawny colour

Colorado or C ripe dark brown

Maduro or M mature rich, very dark

A colour known as *candella* is popular in the United States and this is of a greenish-yellow tint, but it has been artificially produced and is seldom found in the rest of the world.

There are pressed and unpressed cigars. The pressed cigar is made with the tobacco in the filler packed more loosely so that when the cigars are put in boxes, the pressure of the shut lid will compact the cigar into the correct smoking density, making it almost square. Unpressed cigars are made at the time of manufacture as compact as they should be for perfect smoking.

Whether cigars are pressed or unpressed is largely a matter of the tradition of individual factories. Havana cigars are usually packed in oblong, colourfully labelled cedarwood boxes, some of which have become collectors' items during the past decade or so. However, for the specialist there are also bundles of 50 tied with ribbon in square plain cedar boxes – these are known as 'cabinet' selection. The idea is that cigars packed in such a way will interact with each other so that their flavour improves as they mature.

For those who like their cigars green, that is to say fresh, moist and unmatured, there are the cigars from the humidor glass jars which preserve this condition. Another way of packing a cigar is in an individual aluminium tube. This is a popular and safe way of carrying a cigar in a pocket to prevent it being damaged. It is also an advisable package for people who have to keep their cigars near odours which might affect the flavour, or by the sea where salt air can damage the cigar.

SELECTING A CIGAR

There are many elaborate rituals indulged in when selecting a cigar. One is holding the cigar up to the ear and twirling it between finger and thumb. This is known rather scathingly as 'listening to the band', and reveals absolutely nothing for a faint crackle can be heard even in a cigar that is immature. Sniffing is another popular practice that does no harm but that does no good either. If you sniff a cigar you will find it will smell, not surprisingly, of tobacco. Another pointless ritual is that of warming the length of the cigar before lighting it. This was originally done to burn off a rather disagreeable gum used for sticking down the wrappers of certain cigars made 100 or more years ago. The pinhead of gum used these days is odourless and tasteless.

For some it is part of the cigar-smoking ritual to remove the band. If you feel you must remove it, do so by pressing the cigar gently below the band and easing it off with delicate care. But the experts believe that the band should only be removed when the cigar has reached its 'cruising' temperature, when about one-fifth of it has been smoked, and the band should come off easily as the cigar will have shrunk slightly.

Before you can light a cigar you have to open the closed end to allow the smoke through. Biting it off is a favourite practice with fictional house detectives but it is not to be recommended as there are more elegant and efficient ways of achieving the same result. Piercing the closed end with a match or spike is also not to be recommended. The opening thus created is too small and draws the smoke and oils down on to the tongue in a hot concentration which can be very disagreeable.

Make your cut with a V-shaped or flat cutter which makes a good-sized but not too large clean-edged opening through which it is possible to draw cigar smoke at its fragrant best. After cutting, the cigar should be tapped lightly on the finger to remove particles of loose tobacco. Light a cigar with a wooden match, a spill of wood or a gas lighter, but not with sulphur or wax matches or a petrol lighter because they affect the flavour. Light it gently, holding the flame some little distance from the cigar. Rotate the cigar in the flame to make sure that the end surface glows and lights evenly.

Fine Havanas can live in the right conditions for up to 15 years. The most satisfactory way to maintain the condition of a cigar is to keep it in a humidor, a cabinet with a tight-fitting lid in which there is a moisture pad. This will regulate the humidity by moistening dry air and, if the pad is kept dry, absorbing excess moisture in wet weather.

Should it be impossible to obtain a humidor, then cigars are best left in their original cedar-wood boxes, well away from any extremes of heat and cold and away from any strong-smelling substances. If cigars are stored in bulk, they should be kept in a cupboard used only for that purpose and kept at a constant temperature of 15°–18°C.

From the time they are packed, cigars may take up to several years to mature and during this time they may sweat slightly, depositing a fine grey powder on their surface – a natural and unharmful process – and it should be removed with a soft, camel-hair brush.

Cigars that have been allowed to become dry should never be moistened and those that, through excessive damp, have began to smell musty will have been spoilt irreparably and can only be thrown away. There is no remedy for a failure of this kind.

To give the care and attention that prevents such disasters is to understand the delicate nature of cigars and the immense pleasure they offer to those who treat them well.

Cognac producers have developed fine cognacs that are compatible to the taste and aroma of fine cigars, thus enhancing the flavours of both luxuries. Cognac brands, such as those produced by cognac houses Hine and Frapin, advise people to be careful not to have a strong cigar and a smooth cognac or vice versa because the idea is for both of them to complement each other, not kill each other's flavours. As a general rule, a young cognac goes with a smooth cigar, something that does not have a great personality just yet. Antique cognac, for example, goes very well with the Monte Cristo Number Three. When you want to match Triomphe and very old cognac try more robust styles of cigars, like Punch, Churchill and Lusitania because these are big-bodied cigars.

GLOSSARY

Acetic Term used to describe wine that has turned sour because bacteria has converted the ethyl alcohol into acetic acid.

Agave (century plant) Source of cocui, tequila pulque and mescal.

Agraf, Agraffe (Fr) Clamp that holds the pressure of the second fermentation in a champagne bottle.

Alcohol Ethyl alcohol (C^2H^5OH) is a colourless liquid with a faint but pleasant smell. The ethyl alcohol level is measured to determine the alcoholic content of a beverage.

Methyl alcohol A toxic substance produced by the breakdown of pectin in the skins of the fruit. A minute amount is permissible in wine as it adds to the bouquet but it must be distilled off when making a high grade spirit to render it odourless.

Amaro 'Bitter' in Italian. It is a generic term applied to the hundreds of proprietary brands of bitter digestive drinks sold in Italy.

Apoplexy Vine disease.

Appellation Contrôlée (AC) Limited production of wine districts and protection of names under French Law.

Astringent A mouth-puckering sensation. The degree of astringency depends on the amount of tannin in a beverage.

Bacchus Wine god, also American hybrid grape.

Balthazar Bottle size (16 bottles) 12.80 litres.

Barrique (Fr) barrel or hogshead.

Baumé The measurement of sugar in wine. 10 baumé equals 18 grams of sugar.

Beeswing The light film that occasionally clings to the glass. It occurs in port.

Bond The store, vault or cellar in which wine and spirits are kept under Customs and Excise supervision before duty has been paid. The purchaser is liable for the payment of the duty thereon before he can take delivery of his purchase and clear it from bond.

Bottle stink A stale smell can come from wine for a few minutes after the cork has been pulled. This will dissipate if the wine is left for a few minutes or is decanted. Bottle stink must not be confused with corked wine.

Bouquet The fragrant impression left after nosing a beverage.

Broyage Crushing of grapes.

Bung Stopper for wine or beer cask.

Caramel Burnt sugar for colouring.

Carbonated Impregnated with carbonic acid gas (CO^2).

Carbon dioxide CO_2 is a product of fermentation. For still wine it is allowed to escape into the air. If fermentation takes place in a closed container such as a tank or a bottle, the gas is trapped and the liquid absorbs it to produce a sparkling wine. When only a little CO_2 is absorbed into the wine it will give a faint prickling sensation on the tongue. The wine is then said to be *spritzig, frizzante* or *petillant*. The presence of CO_2 accelerates the absorption of alcohol into the bloodstream.

Chambrer To place a wine in a room where it will gradually acquire the temperature of the room.

Chaptalisation The practice of adding sugar to the grape must. This occurs in Germany, Burgundy and other cold areas where the natural grape sugar level is not enough to produce sufficient alcohol. It must be strictly controlled to maintain high standards of winemaking.

Collage Fining of wine.

Congenerics The flavouring and aromatic elements that are retained in a spirit after distillation. The more highly distilled the spirit, the less congenerics there are in the beverage.

Co-operative A cellar belonging jointly to a number of small producers.

Corkage A fee paid to a restaurant when bringing one's own wine and having it served in the restaurant. This does not apply in Australian and New Zealand BYO (Bring Your Own) restaurants.

Corked wine Wine permanently tainted by a mouldy cork.

Cru Growth.

Crystals Tartrate crystals can appear in red and white wine. Tartaric acid is the principal acid in wine and it gradually precipitates as tartrate crystals as the wine matures. Sometimes they can be seen clinging to the bottom of the cork. The presence of tartrates is a sign of quality. However, most uninformed people object to their presence and modern winemaking practice is to refrigerate white wines to hasten this precipitation so that the bottled wine will remain free of them.

Decanting Wine benefits from being poured into a special glass container. This separates the liquid from any deposits that may be in the bottle. It also exposes the wine to the atmosphere which allows it to open out its bouquet and flavour.

Demijohn A bulging, narrow-necked glass container holding from three to 10 gallons, used mostly for the storing of Madeira wine, and also for spirits. It is usually cased in wicker with wicker handles or lugs.

Demi-Sec Half dry. It is applied to champagne and also to other sparkling wines. Sometimes it can apply to certain rosé wines.

Deposit The sediment that many red and some white wines throw while in bottle. In white wines this is tasteless and harmless, but red wine deposit contains tannin and can be very bitter and unpleasant. It should be left in the bottle when decanting.

Distillation The process whereby a liquid base is heated so that it vapourizes. The vapour is cooled and condenses as another liquid which has a higher alcoholic content. This is so because alcohol has a much lower boiling point than water so it vapourizes first.

Dosage The final addition of sugar in the champagne-making process.

Fermentation The process whereby yeasts break down the sugars in a substance and convert them to ethyl alcohol and carbon dioxide. By-products of this conversion are glycerine, volatile acids and higher alcohols such as fusel oils. Fermentation ceases when all the sugar has been converted, which results in a dry wine. The process can be halted by the addition of brandy, which raises the alcohol content above the level at which yeasts are able to work. This retains most of the natural grape sugar in the liquid, which is known as a fortified wine.

Filtration Most wine is filtered prior to bottling. It is pumped through a succession of asbestos and porous porcelain plates, which remove any solids. Care must be taken to ensure the wine is not contaminated during this important process.

Fining The traditional method of clearing a wine is to mix a clay such as bentonite through the liquid. Any solid particles in the wine cling to the clay which eventually falls to the bottom of the container. However this process takes about eight days and many wineries now prefer to filter the wine or clarify it in a centrifuge.

Fortified Wine is fortified by the addition of grape spirit. This raises the alcohol content and stops fermentation so that some sugar is retained in the beverage. It also acts as a preservative. Examples of fortified wines are port, sherry, madeira and marsala.

Frappé A liqueur that is frappé is served over crushed ice. Any other beverage such as wine means very cold.

Frosting A glass is frosted by wetting the rim with a wedge of lemon and dipping it in caster sugar or salt.

Generic A general name applied to a group of wines, which does not relate to their origin.

Hectare One hectare equals 2.47l acres.

Hogshead Cask containing about 256 litres (56 gallons) or half a pipe. This measurement may vary depending on content.

		GALLONS	
	LITRES	US	IMP
Burgundy and Bordeaux	225	59.5	49.5
Beer and cider	246	64.8	54.1
Sherry	246	64.8	54.1
Whisky	250	66	55
Port	259	68.4	57
Brandy	273	72	60

Jeroboam Bottle size (four bottles) is equal to 3.20 litres.

Jigger American bar measure of 40ml (4cl) or 1.5oz (Imp.)

Lees The sediment deposited by wine during maturation.

Maderisation Wine that has been exposed to air (usually because of a faulty cork) will develop a brown hue. This will adversely affect the flavour of wines that are meant to be fresh and crisp. However white wine that has been aged in oak will be slightly maderised and this contributes to its soft round flavour.

Magnum Bottle size (two bottles) is equal to 1.60 litres.

Mash Prepared ingredients before fermentation.

Mead An alcoholic beverage made from fermented honey.

Methuselah Bottle size (eight bottles) is equal to 6.40 litres.

Mousec French term for sparkling.

Must Grape juice before fermentation.

Nebuchadnezzar Bottle size (20 bottles) is equal to 16 litres.

Nip A quarter bottle.

Noggin English measure equal to a traditional quarter pint.

Oxidised Wine that has been over-exposed to air will turn brown and have a burnt caramel smell.

Pipe The standard cask for port in the British Isles; its gauge is 523 litres (traditionally 115 gallons), averaging 56 dozens (672) when bottled.

Posset A drink of hot milk mixed with ale or wine and flavoured with honey and spices.

Punt The hollow in the base of a wine bottle. The French term is *pointe*.

Pupitre Rack with oval holes in which champagne bottles are placed for turning.

Racking Wine is transferred from one container to another. This removes it from its lees and possible contact with bacteria. Red wine may be racked several times during its initial ageing period.

Rectification (redistillation) of spirit.

Rehoboam Bottle size (six bottles) 4.80 litres.

Salmanazar Bottle size (12 bottles) 9.60 litres.

Sediment Fine wine is a living product and chemical changes continue as it matures in bottle. Thus the tannins and colourants gradually precipitate out and this is why old red wine is usually a tawny colour. The deposit can vary from a fine film to a heavy crust.

Shrub A term used to describe a drink with a spirit base that contained orange or lemon juice.

Soft wines In the USA, wines that have a very low alcohol content are referred to as 'soft' wines.

Sulphur Sulphur dioxide is added to wine as a disinfectant. Sometimes it can be detected in recently bottled wine, but the smell should dissipate after a few minutes contact with the air.

Syrups High quality fruit syrups are essential ingredients in many mixed drinks. They are sweet non-alcoholic essences that give colour and/or flavour to the drink. The most readily available are grenadine (pomegranate), cassis (blackcurrant), fraise (strawberry), framboise (raspberry) and orgeat (almond). Falernum is a milky-coloured syrup flavoured with lime, almond and ginger. Sugar syrup is the sweetener used most frequently in cocktails as it mixes readily. A simple sugar syrup is made by dissolving 2 cups of sugar in 1 cup water then simmering for 10 mins. This keeps indefinitely if refrigerated. A commercial preparation marketed as gomme syrup is an acceptable alternative.

Tannin Tannin is contained in the skins, stalks and pips of grapes. It is readily absorbed into the juice once the grapes are crushed. A red wine needs a high tannin content to age for a long period.

Ullage The ullage is the amount of space between the wine and the cork. A large ullage may result from incomplete filling or may indicate that the bottle has leaked at some stage. Very old wine often has a large ullage. The term is also used for a barrel of beer that has been tapped.

Vinification The process of making wine.

Viticulture The science of grape growing.

VSEP (Very Superior Extra Pale) cognac.

VSO (Very Superior Old) cognac.

VSOP (Very Superior Old Pale) Armagnac and cognac.

VVSOP (Very Very Superior Old Pale) cognac.

Weeper A bottle showing signs of a leaky cork.

XO Designation of grade of cognac.

TABLES OF MEASUREMENT

IMPERIAL MEASURES	
160 fluid ounces	1 gallon
5 fluid ounces	1 gill
20 fluid ounces	1 pint
4 gills	1 pint
2 pints	1 quart
4 quarts	1 gallon

METRIC MEASURES	
10 millilitres	1 centilitre
10 centilitres	1 decilitre
10 decilitres	1 litre
10 litres	1 decalitre
10 decalitres	1 hectolitre
10 hectolitres	1 kilolitre

CONVERSION TABLES

In the following table the key figure is printed in the centre column. This can be read as either the metric or Imperial measure, thus:

1 gallon = 4.546 litres or 1 litre = 0.220 gallons.

Gallons		Litres
0.220	1	4.546
0.440	2	9.087
0.660	3	13.631
0.880	4	18.174
1.101	5	22.718
1.321	6	27.262
1.541	7	31.805
1.761	8	36.349
1.981	9	40.892

Pints		Litres
1.761	1	0.568
3.521	2	1.136
5.282	3	1.704
7.043	4	2.272
8.804	5	2.840
10.564	6	3.408
12.325	7	3.976
14.068	8	4.544
15.846	9	5.112

Fluid Ounces		Millilitres
0.035	1	28.416
0.07	2	56.832
0.106	3	85.248
0.14	4	113.664
0.176	5	142.080
0.211	6	170.496
0.246	7	198.912
0.282	8	227.328
0.317	9	255.744

Fluid Ounces	Gallons	Cls.	Litres
1	.00625	2.84	.0284
2	.0125	5.68	.0568
4	.025	11.36	.1136
5 [1 gill]	.0312	14.20	.1420
6	.0375	17.04	.1704
8	.050	22.72	.2272
10 [1/2 pint]	.0625	28.41	.2841
12	.075	34.09	.3409
14	.0875	39.76	.3976
16	.1	45.43	.4543
18	.1125	51.11	.5111
20 [1 pint]	.125	56.82	.5682
22	.1375	62.48	.6248
24	.15	68.19	.6819
26	.1625	73.83	.7383
28	.175	79.51	.7951
30	.1875	85.23	.8523
32	.2	90.87	.9087
34	.2125	96.55	.9655
36	.225	102.20	1.022
38	.2375	107.96	1.079
40 [1 quart]	.25	113.64	1.136

1 hectolitre = 100 litres = 22 gallons

To convert:
GALLONS TO LITRES
multiply by 4.546

To convert:
LITRES TO GALLONS
multiply by 0.22

Ounces	No. of measures per standard bottle
5	5
2.5	10
1.67	15
1.25	20
1.00	25
0.835	30
0.715	35
0.625	40
0.556	45
0.500	50

The standard spirit bottle contains 75cl [centiliters], *except brandy, which contains 68cl [centiliters].*

There is a difference between the British and American gallon. The British Imperial gallon is equal to 1.20 American gallons. The British Imperial gallon contains 160 fluid ounces and the American gallon contains 128 American fluid ounces. Whilst the American gallon is smaller than the British gallon, the American fluid ounce is a larger measure than the British fluid ounce.

1 American fluid ounce = .960 British fluid ounces.

1 British fluid ounce = 1.0416 American fluid ounces.

To convert American fluid ounces to British fluid ounces multiply by 1.0416.
To convert British fluid ounces to American fluid ounces divide by 1.0416.

Hydrometer

An instrument for determining the specific gravity of liquids. Attributed to Archimedes, but not much used until re-invented by Robert Boyle.

It takes the form of a narrow sealed instrument of cylindrical section and consists of three parts – counterpoise at the bottom, a bulb containing air, and the scale at the top. It can be made of glass, poised with lead shot or mercury, or of gilt brass.

Sikes' hydrometer has an arbitrary scale and has to be used with a thermometer and book of tables.

The Gay-Lussac's Alcoholometer is for testing alcoholic solutions, and its scale reads percentage per volume, 0° to 100°.

SPIRIT STRENGTHS

Traditionally, there have been three main scales used in measuring alcoholic strength.

1 **The Sikes scale** as used in Britain and the Commonwealth;
2 **The Gay-Lussac (GL) Scale** as used in France and most of Europe;
3 **The American scale** as used in the USA.

This has led to many misunderstandings in the past and has given producers some labelling problems. Since the new EU regulations dated January 1, 1983, alcoholic strength in Europe (and Britain) has been expressed in percentage of alcohol by volume as on the Gay-Lussac scale.

During the lifetime of this book, however, labels will still be found with the old Sikes measurement and, as the American scale still exists, it is hoped that the following explanations, examples and scale will be of some assistance.

To understand the three scales used, one must first accept that for all three scales water (no alcohol) is rated as 0 and that absolute (pure) alcohol is the top of each scale.

On the Sikes scale absolute alcohol is given as 175. On the Gay-Lussac scale it is 100 and on the American scale, 200. Therefore it will be seen that 70° proof Sikes = 40° GL or 40% alcohol by volume = 80° US proof.

To convert GL to US proof one merely has to multiply by 2 and vice versa, but the formula for converting to and from Sikes is slightly more complicated.

To convert from Sikes to GL divide by 1.75 and from GL to Sikes multiply by 1.75.

For example:

[i] 70° Sikes   = 40° GL   = 80° US
     70 + 1.75   = 40 x 2   = 80

[ii] 100° US   = 50° GL   = 87.5° Sikes
      100 ÷ 2   = 50 x 1.75   = 87.5

COMPARATIVE SCALES FOR ALCOHOLIC STRENGTHS

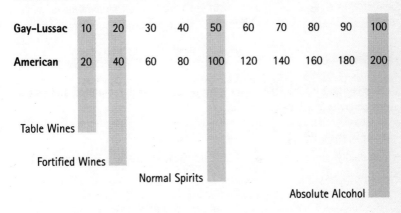

Gay–Lussac	10	20	30	40	50	60	70	80	90	100
American	20	40	60	80	100	120	140	160	180	200

Table Wines

Fortified Wines

Normal Spirits

Absolute Alcohol

INDEX OF SPIRIT BASES

GENERAL INDEX

ACKNOWLEDGMENTS

The United Kingdom Bartenders' Guild would like to thank everyone who worked to make this new edition a success, including administrator Jim Slavin, Armand Fasola, Regis Lemaitre and Luca Cordiglieri.

Thanks also to each of the sponsors who made this book possible: Bacardi, Bombay Sapphire, Campari, Chivas Regal, Stolichnaya Elit, Hendrick's gin, Jose Cuervo , Ketel One, Kremlyovska, Martell, Mattoni, Monkey Shoulder, Pilsner Urquel, Sputnik Vodka, and Sagatiba.

The BookMaker would like to thank Salvatore Calabrese, President of the UKBG, and Carey Smith and Natalie Hunt at Ebury Publishing, Random House for supporting the new edition.

Our thanks also go to the staff at Salvatore at FIFTY for their assistance with making the cocktails for the photography shoot, and to Hannah Cooper for her tireless help. The UKBG thanks David Morgan for his update of the wine chapter, and Lynn Bryan for the editorial work on this new edition.

Thanks to William Yeoward for the loan of the brilliant crystal glasses used in the Monkey Shoulder triple Malt, Bombay Sapphire and Bacardi photographs. Other glasses used in images are from The BookMaker's personal collection.